THE
ANTI-
BULLYING
HANDBOOK

I dedicate this book, with love, to my children, Jacob, Hannah, and Amy.

THE ANTI-BULLYING HANDBOOK

Keith
Sullivan

OXFORD
UNIVERSITY PRESS

OXFORD

UNIVERSITY PRESS

540 Great South Road, Greenlane, Auckland, New Zealand

Oxford University Press is a department of the University of Oxford.
It furthers the University's objective of excellence in research, scholarship,
and education by publishing worldwide in

Oxford New York

Athens Auckland Bangkok Bogotá Buenos Aires Cape Town Chennai
Dar es Salaam Delhi Florence Hong Kong Istanbul Karachi Kolkata
Kuala Lumpur Madrid Melbourne Mexico City Mumbai Nairobi Paris
Port Moresby São Paulo Shanghai Singapore Taipei Tokyo Toronto Warsaw

with associated companies in

Berlin Ibadan

OXFORD is a trade mark of Oxford University Press
in the UK and in certain other countries

ISBN 0 19 558388 4

Edited by Anna Rogers
Indexed by Ginny Sullivan
Cartoons by Jacob Sullivan
Text and cover designed by Polar Design Pty Ltd
Cover photograph from Stock Photos
Typeset by Polar Design Pty Ltd
Printed through Bookpac Production Services, Singapore

Foreword

Bullying affects a proportion of children and young people in all primary and secondary schools. It is an issue of growing concern to practitioners, parents, and researchers in many countries. Children who are the targets of this peer-led aggression risk being physically hurt, rejected and socially excluded, or being the butt of rumours, name-calling, and put-downs. Over time, the effect on young people's mental health can be devastating. Children who are the victims of such aggression are significantly more likely to be depressed, to have low self-esteem, and to report feelings of loneliness.

For these reasons, this is a timely book. The author, Keith Sullivan, is already well known for his anti-bullying work. He brings to the task of tackling the problem a wealth of practical experience, knowledge, and research. He recognises that bullying affects individuals, school classes, families, the school ethos, and the wider community. So he urges us all to take responsibility for owning the problem and for viewing bullying in its social context.

To help achieve this goal, he offers practical guidance for teachers to help them understand more about the complexities of children's interpersonal relationships within the peer group, to create safer classrooms, and to mediate in children's disputes. He also reiterates the need for schools to develop and maintain effective policies to counteract bullying. There is a clear-cut role here for administrators and managers within school systems. These professionals face the difficult task of balancing policies that are acceptable to different members of the school community with clear sanctions against antisocial behaviour. Professionals in the wider community will find guidance in this book about the role they can play in designing and implementing interventions. We learn how they can collaborate with school staff to work directly with perpetrators and victims (for example, through the Pikas method), how they can harness the prosocial energies of the peer group (for example, through Circle of Friends), or how they can work in the community with families. We learn, too, about cooperative interdisciplinary innovations distinctive to New Zealand (for example, *Kia Kaha*).

Parents' perspectives are also considered. They will find some of the answers to urgent questions about how they should respond when they suspect that their child is involved in bullying in some way.

A growing body of evidence shows that the problem of bullying can be tackled and that the incidence goes down when policies are applied and sustained, and where a range of interventions is consistently implemented. Children and young people are more likely to tell someone—adult or peer—that they are being bullied in schools where these active policies and practices are in place. It is important, therefore, that parents, teachers, and other adults involved in the care and education of young people should be as knowledgeable as possible about the conditions which facilitate or inhibit bullying behaviour.

This book will greatly assist in the process.

Helen Cowie, Roehampton Institute, London
Peter K. Smith, Goldsmiths College,
University of London

Contents

Diagrams

Preface

School bullying has been identified as a major problem in many countries around the world. Everybody I know has a story they can tell about it.

It is imperative that bullying is stopped within our schools. It can create a hell on earth for someone who is victimised, and can seriously threaten that person's opportunities in life. And, equally important, the social climate of a school is a model of the world outside. It is where people develop a large part of their morality, their understanding of how the world works, and their sense of responsibility towards the society they live in.

Over the last six years, I have been examining school bullying in order to answer such questions as: 'What is the nature of bullying?' 'Why do people do it?' and 'How can it be prevented?' In order to develop a far-reaching and deep understanding of bullying, I decided to devote my last study leave from Victoria University of Wellington to this purpose. I was very fortunate to be elected to the 1995-96 Charter Fellowship in Human Rights at Wolfson College, University of Oxford, England. Oxford fellowships are very sought after and internationally competitive, and the area of human rights has many worthy causes. So it was significant that bullying was acknowledged in this way as an important human rights issue.

The fellowship gave me access to the excellent resources of the Bodleian Library and a base from which to visit the key scholars and the excellent anti-bullying initiatives that have been developed in England, Scotland, and Wales. Also in 1996, I was a visiting scholar at the University of South Australia in Adelaide, which provided me with the opportunity to go through a similar process there. On my return to New Zealand, the police asked me to evaluate their anti-bullying initiative, *Kia Kaha*, which I did as part of a study of New Zealand anti-bullying research and schemes. In my examination of the scholarship and initiatives in these settings, and more generally in relation to American, Canadian, and other international anti-bullying work, I was able to form a clear picture of the range of behaviour that is covered by the term 'bullying', and an appreciation of the many strategies that have been developed to deal with it.

When I provided a keynote address and worked in problem-solving groups with some Australian teachers a few years ago, I kept hearing the cry, 'Tell me what I can do tomorrow in the classroom and the playground to prevent and deal effectively with bullying'. I have also found, repeatedly, that although bullying is a problem which occurs at school or on the way to and from school, its effects are much more far-reaching. Not only teachers but also parents, school administrators, counsellors, psychologists, and therapists need to know about bullying.

It is for all these people that this book has been written.

Keith Sullivan
Wellington

Acknowledgments

This book is, both directly and indirectly, the result of work carried out over the past six years. It has been a long and interesting journey and I have made many useful and influential contacts along the way. An important initial event for me was an exceptionally well-organised international conference on peer relations at the University of South Australia in Adelaide in January 1994. There I had the opportunity to meet the key bullying researchers from around the world and to have my interest truly whetted. I would like to thank the organisers of this conference, Professor Ken Rigby and Associate Professor Phillip Slee.

I would also like to thank the President and Fellows of Wolfson College, University of Oxford, who elected me to the 1995-96 Charter Fellowship in Human Rights which enabled me to explore bullying initiatives in the UK. I am grateful to members of the Department of Educational Studies of the University of Oxford who welcomed me there as a Visiting Scholar and Tutor, particularly Professor Richard Pring, Dr David Phillips, and the departmental librarian, Judy Reading.

In the UK I visited the following anti-bullying experts, and I would like to express my gratitude to all of them for the commitment they showed to their subject matter and for the time they gave me (in the order in which I visited them): George Robinson and Barbara Maines, from the University of the West of England and the Bristol City Council, who developed the *No Blame Approach*; Delwyn Tattum at the Anti-bullying Unit, Cardiff College of Further Education; Angela Glaser of Kidscape, London; Professor Peter K. Smith of Goldsmiths College, University of London, formerly of the University of Sheffield (the Sheffield Project); Mike Sullivan, Sandy Clark, and Gwen Wallace of the Tayside Anti-bullying and Truancy Initiative, Dundee; Kevin Brown, Psychologist, of Penicuik, near Edinburgh; Andrew Mellor, of the University of Edinburgh, formerly the Anti-bullying Development Officer for Scotland; Val Besag, Psychologist, Gateshead County Council, Gateshead; Sonia Sharp, formerly of the Sheffield Project, Senior Psychologist, Lincolnshire County Council, Lincoln;

and Professor Helen Cowie, Head of Department, Psychology and Counselling, Roehampton Institute, London.

Thanks to Professor Ken Rigby, I was invited as a visiting scholar to the University of South Australia in May 1996. My time there was valuable and I would like to thank Ken and his wife Jean, and the following people, for making my time in Adelaide so worthwhile: Barbara Leckie (University of South Australia), Associate Professor Phillip Slee and Dr Larry Owens (Flinders University), Rob Loielo (South Australia Department of Education), Bill Bates (Adelaide Police Department), and Kate Prescott (Australian Guidance and Counselling Association). In New Zealand I would like to thank Gill Palmer, Owen Sanders, and Maurice Cheer of the New Zealand Police for inviting me to evaluate *Kia Kaha*; Yvonne Duncan for her open and helpful access to Cool Schools; and to those at the Special Education Services who gave me access to the Eliminating Violence materials (particularly James Brodie and Sylvie Wilkinson).

I wish to thank the Internal Grants Committee of the Faculty of Humanities and Social Sciences of Victoria University of Wellington for providing me with funding both to carry out the research and to prepare the document for publication. I am grateful to the university for giving me my sabbatical; to my head of school, Professor Cedric Hall, for his support; and to the School of Education librarian, Margaret Anderson, for her unfailing help. I am also grateful to Dennis Moore and Vivienne Adair of Auckland University; and Elizabeth Putnam, Grievance Officer, and Don Brown and Charlotte Thomson of the School of Education, Victoria University. I would like to acknowledge Professors Roger and David Johnson of the Center for Cooperative Learning, University of Minnesota.

Mark Cleary, Principal of Colenso High School, Napier, has done much to bring bullying to the fore in New Zealand as an important educational issue, and I am grateful to him for his unstinting and generous support of my endeavours over the past four years. My thanks also to the following teachers for sharing ideas and information: Noelene Anderson and Paul Denford; and to Kathryn Billing for her insightful conversation about school bullying.

My martial arts colleagues who have supported me in my karate learning have also helped to influence this book: Shihan Robert McCallum, Sensei Chris Gower, Sempai Matthew Cameron, and Sempai Paul Michalek. I wish to acknowledge the seminal knowledge I gained from Paddy Paltridge on psychodrama and the work of auxiliaries. And to thank four very talented people in particular for their contributions in making this book the attractive and well-presented final document it is: Sharon Bowling who created the diagrams, Jacob Sullivan who conceived and drew the cartoons, and Anna Rogers and Ginny Sullivan who edited the book.

To Linda Cassells and Peter Rose, publishers, of Oxford University Press, many thanks for recognising the merits of the project, and the sensitive handling of it through its various stages.

I would like to acknowledge the use of excerpts from the following publications, and to thank the authors and publishers for giving their permission for me to use these extracts:

Adair, V. 1999, 'No Bullies at this School: Creating Safe Schools', *ChildreNZ Issues, Journal of the Children's Issues Centre*, Vol. 3, No. 1, p. 35.

Besag, V. 1989, *Bullies and Victims in Schools: A Guide to Understanding and Management*, Open University Press, Milton Keynes/Oxford University Press, Bristol, p. 117.

Camdean School, Fifeshire, Scotland, for the use of its anti-bullying policy.

Colenso High School, Napier, New Zealand, for the use of its anti-bullying policy.

Duncan, A. 1994, 'Resolving Group Bullying in Schools. Anatol Pikas' Shared Concern Method in Tayside's Experience 1993-94', Unpub. Paper, Tayside Regional Council, Dundee, pp. 8, 21.

Duncan, Y. & M. Stanners 1999, *Cool Schools Peer Mediation Programme: Training Manual* (3rd edition), Foundation for Peace Studies Aotearoa/New Zealand, Auckland, pp. 4-5, 11.

Lind, J. & G. Maxwell 1996, *Children's Experiences of Violence at School*, Office of the Commissioner for Children, Wellington, p. 5.

McLean, A.C. 1994, *Bullyproofing Our School: Promoting Positive Relationships. Book 7*, Strathclyde Regional Council, Glasgow, pp. 17-19, OHTs 1C (for Figures 7.2, and AIIIa, b, & c).

Salmivalli, C. et al. 1998, 'Aggression in the Social Relations of School-aged Boys and Girls', in P.T. Slee & K. Rigby (eds), *Children's Peer Relations*, Routledge, London & New York, p. 72, Figure 4.4 (for Figure 7.3).

Slee, P. 1997, *The P.E.A.C.E. Pack: Reducing Bullying in Our Schools* (2nd edition), School of Education, Flinders University, Adelaide, pp. 4, 5.

Smith, P.K. 'England and Wales', in P.K. Smith et al. (eds), *The Nature of School Bullying: A Cross-National Perspective*, Routledge, London & New York, p. 82.

part 1

What is Bullying and What We Know About It

'I believe that schools and other
institutions, where they stand in the
place of parents of young people, do
have a positive duty to be vigilant, to put
in place programmes to guard against bullying,
whether it is physical or emotional, and to deal firmly
with it and stamp it out if it occurs.'

Coroner's report on the death of Matt Ruddenklau,
Dominion, 30 August 1997

1 Introduction

In 1997, a coroner's report on the suicide of fifteen-year-old Matt Ruddenklau found that 'Bullying and victimisation were a significant factor in [the Invercargill] ... boy's life in the months leading up to his suicide' (*Dominion*, 30 August 1997). Matt was reported to have been a victim of bullying at both Otago Boys' High School in Dunedin and Invercargill's James Hargest High School. Although carefully worded, the coroner's report makes it clear that the bullying of Matt by his peers was instrumental in his suicide. Similar reports can be cited from newspapers around the world, and the important research that initiated anti-bullying work internationally by Professor Dan Olweus of the University of Bergen was a response to the bullying-related suicides of three boys in the north of Norway in 1982.

Suicide as a result of bullying is tragic and final. It is a startling and hard-hitting indictment on the schools and societies in which it occurs. But there are many more cases of bullying that do not reach this utterly hopeless and irretrievable point but still must be dealt with.

Newspaper reports tend to focus on the tragedies, and on the type of bullying epitomised in *Tom Brown's School Days*, where large rough boys beat up smaller and cleverer boys who somehow do not fit the mould. Although these cases are the most dramatic and have the most visible impacts, bullying is much more than this. It can be psychological. It can include acts of exclusion and isolation, humiliation, name-calling, spreading false rumours, and teasing. It can involve the extortion of money and the theft of possessions. It can be done by and against girls. Although cuts and bruises are the external signs of aggressive bullying, research shows that the internal hurts from psychological bullying can be just as painful. Recent research also shows that reported cases of bullying are only the tip of the iceberg: the bulk is below the surface and hard to detect.

School bullying is a major problem in many countries. Lind and Maxwell's (1996) study of first- and second-form pupils in the North Island of New Zealand asked its respondents to identify the three worst things they had ever experienced. The death of a somebody close to them was the most often mentioned, but being bullied by other children came second (p. 5).

Although the greatest worry parents may have for the safety of their children is in relation to their getting to and from school, and random attacks of the stranger-danger type, Lind and Maxwell state that '... 90% of the incidents of emotional abuse and most of the physical violence between children occur at schools ...' (p. 5).

The Purpose of This Book

This book has been written to provide a useful resource to combat school bullying. Its specific intentions are:

To summarise what we know about bullying

Over recent years scholars from around the world have generated much useful information about the characteristics of bullying. Although each country has its own culture and its own bullying events, there are underlying similarities which together illuminate the syndrome of bullying behaviour.

To provide a guide for schools for the development, implementation, and evaluation of effective anti-bullying philosophies, policies, and programs

In order to combat bullying, schools need to tackle it in a unified and concerted effort. Guidelines for the creation and clarification of school policy and practice are outlined. This book is intended to be a useful resource for all schools, from those just starting to consider setting up an anti-bullying initiative, to those with well-established programs which wish to consider what other anti-bullying strategies and innovations are now available.

To recommend anti-bullying programs that deal effectively with bullying

Choosing from the growing amount of materials on bullying is a difficult task. I have selected the most useful approaches and programs, and created some new ones, so that schools can choose which approaches are best for them.

To support a culture of problem-solving that uses the scholarship and research information available but also taps into the knowledge and experience of those involved (including teaching and administrative staff, students, and the wider community) in developing and implementing anti-bullying programs

Although it is clear that anti-bullying programs are useful tools, it is also clear that any school contains knowledge that is fundamental to problem-solving. This consists of the years of experience and knowledge of the school's teachers and administrative and ancillary staff, and the experience and potential for involvement of the peer group in the creation of solutions.

What is the Viewpoint of This Book?

I have chosen to write this book from a constructivist perspective. Many studies of bullying, while providing important information, also tend to generalise about the components of the bullying dynamic, to make judgments about the individuals involved, and to deal more with the components than with the whole system. There is a tendency to make causal links between individuals and events, and to lock people into roles. This is commonly called the deficit perspective. The constructivist approach seeks to provide positive alternatives for those taking part in or subjected to antisocial behaviour.

This humanistic perspective recognises that bullying is a serious problem, and it aims to work hard to find solutions that improve everybody's chances, both bully and bullied. In the first instance, it seeks solutions for individuals in the short term, but also argues that such approaches will benefit our society as a whole in the long term.

Who Has This Book Been Written For?

In the literature on effective anti-bullying strategies, one issue stands out as being most important—the adoption of a whole school approach, that is, developing an anti-bullying program that is taken up and implemented wholeheartedly by the entire school community.

Those involved are, within the school, the students, the teaching staff, and the administrative staff; and, outside the school, parents, and social and community agencies.

If all these people understand the dynamics of bullying, and know that something can be done about it, then there is a chance that it can be halted. Once a school decides to deal with bullying, as many people as possible must be included so that they can develop a sense of 'ownership' of the processes and programs that are adopted. I will address specifically the concerns of these groups and of those who prepare teachers for their profession.

The Teaching Staff

The teachers' main job is effective classroom management and teaching of a group of children with whom they spend all day (in the case of primary school teachers), or across a range of classes and at various levels (in the case of secondary school teachers). Many teachers are ill-equipped to deal with relationship problems and specific antisocial behaviour like bullying, simply because they have not been trained to do so, and because teaching is so demanding.

Nonetheless, teachers want to handle bullying effectively, and these are some of the questions they may wish to ask about it:

- What counts as bullying? How do I detect it? What can I do about it?
- If I see what looks like bullying, when do I become involved? When should I let the children sort it out themselves? How do I know when things have gone too far?

- What resources are there to help me solve bullying problems effectively?
- Is it my job to handle bullying or should I go to somebody else?
- Who can I turn to for support when I do not seem to be handling things very well?
- How can I create a classroom that is safe for all of the children in my care?

Deputy principals in New Zealand schools are usually responsible for issues of crisis and discipline; the guidance staff have a pastoral role. The questions they may ask would probably be complementary.

The deputy principal may ask:

- What do I need to do to make sure bullying is handled effectively?
- How will an anti-bullying strategy fit into our overall program for dealing with disciplinary problems, such as disruptive behaviour, truancy, and drugs at school?
- What programs are available for dealing with bullying? How do I know what the best options are for our school?

The counsellor may ask:

- What resources are available to inform me about the nature and dynamics of bullying?
- What anti-bullying strategies and programs are available for dealing with bullying? How do I know which ones work best?
- If I am the person who will implement an anti-bullying policy, how can I best be prepared for this?
- With whom can I discuss how best to deal with the problem of bullying from within the school community and/or the social services community?

The School Administrators

Over and above their concerns to have a school that runs well and achieves in a variety of ways, the principal/head teacher, other administrators, and governors of the school have a moral and legal responsibility to make their school a safe place. If a school has a reputation for being unsafe, parents may choose another school. Bullying is bad for any school. The concerns of administrators are therefore philosophical, legal, and practical.

Administrators may ask the following questions:

- What can I do to develop and support policies and programs that will eliminate or reduce bullying in my school?
- What can I do to promote this school as a safe school?
- Providing an effective and proactive anti-bullying scheme is an excellent idea but can give the impression we have a major bullying problem. How can we adopt such schemes to show we are proactive and forward-looking rather than a 'bullying school'?
- What is our role as administrators in such developments—to provide support and structures, to implement or help implement the developments, to provide ongoing evaluations?
- What can best be done within the constraints of limited resources and competing demands?

The Parents

Parents create the family environment of victims, bullies, and onlookers to bullying. Their involvement in the adoption and implementation of any anti-bullying scheme is crucial.

Parents may ask the following questions:
- Is my child involved in bullying in any way?
- What can I do to help?
- How do I know if my child is being bullied?
- How can I follow things up with the school? Who do I go to? What are the school's procedures?
- What should I do if I know bullying is taking place but I feel that the school is not doing enough about it?
- Who else can I go to for help?

Social and Community Agencies

Individuals in social and community agencies, such as counsellors, educational psychologists, police personnel, social workers, and therapists, often work with the after-effects of bullying, school failure, and violent and disruptive behaviour. This may occur in the community; on other occasions, these people are brought into the school to share their expertise.

The questions they may ask are:
- What can I find out about bullying in the school?
- How is it reflected in the family and society at large?
- How can I contribute my skills to help develop a school anti-bullying initiative that, if it is well implemented, will have beneficial effects in the community?

Teachers' College/University Lecturers

Teachers' college and university lecturers who are helping to prepare future teachers also need to know about the bullying dynamic so that they can pass this knowledge on to their students. Teacher trainers may ask the following questions:
- What knowledge can I give my students so that they have a good understanding of peer group dynamics and how they work in relation to bullying?
- How can I help my students to develop skills to deal effectively with bullying?
- How can I best fit this understanding of bullying into the overall framework of classroom work?

The Structure of the Book

Part One introduces the topic. A definition of bullying and a summary of what we know about it are provided (Chapter 2).

Part Two deals with planning, philosophy, and policy. Chapter 3, 'How to Create an Anti-Bullying Initiative', clearly states why schools need to be proactive in developing an anti-bullying initiative and provides a step-by-step plan for doing this. 'Clarifying a School Philosophy' (Chapter 4) argues that schools must be clear about their philosophical foundations before they can develop policies that have any chance of success. This includes looking inwards to determine the underlying values and beliefs of the school and what this means for the resultant policies and programs; and looking outwards to examine which anti-bullying strategies and programs are consistent with the school's philosophy. Chapter 5, 'Planning and Information Gathering', describes two useful tools for gathering information about the school in general and about the extent of bullying in the school. First, a SWOTSS analysis process is outlined and illustrated with a case study. Second, a questionnaire has been designed to allow schools to gather and quantify information on bullying. Chapter 6, 'A School Policy on Bullying', discusses how to develop and establish an anti-bullying policy. It covers consultation, discussion, writing a policy document, implementation and monitoring, and maintenance. A template for writing a school policy is provided (and two examples of actual school policies appear in the appendices).

Part Three provides a variety of preventative strategies to help make schools safe places. Chapter 7, 'Strategies for Teachers', discusses methods teachers can use to understand and tend to the social relationships in their classes. The chapter covers reflective practice, Circle Time, cooperative learning, and sociometry. Chapter 8, 'Interactive Strategies in the Classroom', examines two ways teachers and students can explore the nature of bullying: by working as a group to develop a deep understanding of bullying and solutions for it ('On the Bus') and through role play. Chapter 9, 'The School Environment', provides suggestions for making the school a safer place aesthetically, environmentally, and in terms of the use of space.

Part Four offers information on the interventions, ranging from those that are preventative and informal, to those that are prepackaged programs. Chapter 10, 'Peer Strategies: Befriending', describes two one-to-one peer support approaches. First, peer partnering is designed as a befriending process for individuals who may need some support in the school for a limited period of time, and for groups of students such as new third formers in a secondary school. Second, peer mentoring is a similar program that generally continues for a longer period and provides friendship, general support, and help with dealing with a bullying problem (it can be used for either bullies or victims of bullying). Chapter 11, 'Peer Strategies: Counselling and Mediation', discusses two approaches to conflict resolution: peer counselling, and peer mediation. The first part examines how peer counselling works and provides a model for schools to develop their own scheme. Peer mediation focuses specifically on the Foundation for Peace Studies Aotearoa/New Zealand's *Cool Schools* program in which children are trained to mediate disputes that occur in their schools.

Chapter 12 provides an overview of the *No Blame Approach*. This feelings-based program is designed to enlist those who bully (and others from the peer group) to find solutions to bullying rather than attributing blame. Chapter 13,

'A Circle of Friends', describes a program that endeavours to create a supportive group around a child who is experiencing difficulties (and may be considered a bully or victim), so that the child's behaviour is understood by his or her peers as sad and troubled rather than naughty, and so that an environment can be created to support the child to act in a more prosocial way.

Chapter 14 examines the *P.E.A.C.E. Pack*, an excellent Australian anti-bullying program that provides a clear overview of bullying and a series of strategies for dealing with it (a complementary video is also discussed). Chapter 15 describes the New Zealand Police's initiative, *Kia Kaha*, which has been extensively used in and well received by New Zealand schools. A description of *Stop Bullying*, a very accessible video designed for parents, is also provided.

Chapter 16 describes the much lauded Method of Shared Concern developed by Professor Anatol Pikas of Uppsala University, Sweden. Similar to the *No Blame Approach*, the program intends to break the mob characteristics of group bullying and to encourage the perpetrators to take responsibility for solving the problem. Two useful case studies of its use in Dundee, Scotland, are provided.

Chapter 17 gives a selection of follow-up strategies that can be used by those who are victims of bullying or who bully. These include assertiveness training, anger management, and self-defence and martial arts training. The conclusion brings the threads of the book together.

The appendices contain two examples of school anti-bullying policies, descriptions of other anti-bullying programs that are available, diagrams for sociometry, some suggested ice-breakers, and a guide to useful Internet sites. Each chapter has its own list of readings or resources, listed at the end of the book, and there is a select bibliography and an index.

2 What We Know About Bullying

This chapter provides the reader with a summary of the information that has been gathered about bullying, and answers the most important questions about bullying.

There are eight headings: What is bullying? Are schools safe? Are there gender and age differences in bullying patterns? Those who bully, The victims of bullying, The third parties to bullying, What are the dynamics of bullying? and Can school bullying be stopped? A series of topics is covered under each heading.

1. What is Bullying?

In order to deal effectively with bullying, it is important, first of all, to know what it is. This means also knowing what it is not. Behaviour interpreted as bullying may be something else—an error, or play, or criminal offending.

How is Bullying Defined?

Bullying is a conscious and wilful act of aggression and/or manipulation by one or more people against another person or people. Bullying can last for a short period or go on for years, and is an abuse of power by those who carry it out. It is sometimes premeditated, and sometimes opportunistic, sometimes directed mainly towards one victim, and sometimes occurs serially and randomly.

Bullying is a cowardly act because it is done to cause hurt without fear of recrimination. The victimised person is unlikely to retaliate effectively, if at all, or to tell anyone about it. Bullying relies on those who are marginally involved, often referred to as observers, onlookers, or watchers, doing nothing to stop the bullying or becoming actively involved in supporting it.

Bullying contains the following elements:
- harm is intended;
- there is an imbalance of power;
- it is often organised and systematic;

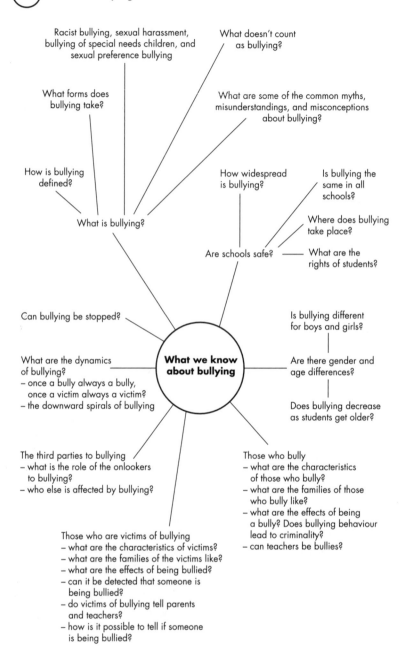

Racist bullying, sexual harassment, bullying of special needs children, and sexual preference bullying

What doesn't count as bullying?

What forms does bullying take?

What are some of the common myths, misunderstandings, and misconceptions about bullying?

How is bullying defined?

How widespread is bullying?

Is bullying the same in all schools?

Where does bullying take place?

What is bullying?

Are schools safe? —— What are the rights of students?

Can bullying be stopped?

What we know about bullying

Is bullying different for boys and girls?

What are the dynamics of bullying?
– once a bully always a bully, once a victim always a victim?
– the downward spirals of bullying

Are there gender and age differences?

Does bullying decrease as students get older?

The third parties to bullying
– what is the role of the onlookers to bullying?
– who else is affected by bullying?

Those who bully
– what are the characteristics of those who bully?
– what are the families of those who bully like?
– what are the effects of being a bully? Does bullying behaviour lead to criminality?
– can teachers be bullies?

Those who are victims of bullying
– what are the characteristics of victims?
– what are the families of the victims like?
– what are the effects of being bullied?
– can it be detected that someone is being bullied?
– do victims of bullying tell parents and teachers?
– how is it possible to tell if someone is being bullied?

2.1 What We Know About Bullying

- it is repetitive, occurring over a period of time, or it is a random but serial activity carried out by someone who is feared for this behaviour;
- hurt experienced by a victim of bullying can be external (physical) and/or internal (psychological).

What Forms Does Bullying Take?

Bullying can take a number of forms. Physical bullying often causes visible hurt such as cuts and bruises. It is tangible and easy to identify. Extreme physical bullying has resulted in murder. Bullying, both physical and non-physical, has made some children so desperate that they have attempted or succeeded in committing suicide. All bullying causes psychological damage.

The different forms of bullying are as follows:

- Physical bullying, which includes biting, hair-pulling, hitting, kicking, locking in a room, pinching, punching, pushing, scratching, spitting, or any other form of physical attack. It also includes damaging a person's property.
- Non-physical bullying, which can be verbal and non-verbal.

Verbal bullying includes abusive telephone calls, extorting money or material possessions, intimidation or threats of violence, name-calling, racist remarks or teasing, sexually suggestive or abusive language, spiteful teasing or making cruel remarks, and spreading false and malicious rumours.

Non-verbal bullying can be direct or indirect. Direct non-verbal bullying often accompanies physical or verbal bullying. Indirect bullying is manipulative, sneaky, and subtle. Direct non-verbal bullying includes mean faces and rude gestures. Indirect non-verbal bullying includes manipulating relationships and ruining friendships; purposely and often systematically excluding, ignoring, and isolating someone; and sending (often anonymous) poisonous notes.

Bullying can be any one of the above or a combination of them.

> **Comment:** Everyone who carries out research has a slightly different definition and description of bullying. Although a distinction can be made between physical and psychological bullying, I would argue that both physical and non-physical bullying have a psychological dimension. I have chosen not to use the descriptor emotional bullying because I equate emotional with psychological bullying.

Racist Bullying, Sexual Harassment, Bullying of Special Needs Children, and Sexual Preference Bullying

Some children are picked out to be bullied because of particular identifiable characteristics that set them apart.

Racist bullying

Racist bullying occurs in all countries and is usually aimed at minority groups. At Burnage High School in Manchester, England, in 1986, Ahmed Ullah, a 13-year-old Asian boy, was murdered in the playground by a white teenager who had a history of bullying and disruptive behaviour. For many ethnic minority children, racist intimidation and bullying is the gauntlet that they have to run in the classroom, the playground, and the world at large on a daily basis. Incidents like the murder of Ahmed Ullah stand as a symbol of this danger.

Racist bullying is where racism and bullying meet. It is an abuse of power involving physical or psychological bullying, or both, to demean or cause harm.

The most common form of racist bullying is racist name-calling, which is widely experienced by ethnic minority children. In a survey of over 6000 British school children, Whitney and Smith (1993) found that, of those being bullied, 14.8 per cent in junior/middle schools and 9.4 per cent in secondary schools reported being called derogatory names about their colour or race. In New Zealand, Moore et al. (1997) report a very high incidence of racist name-calling, with between 31 and 47 per cent of students in their study reporting having been called names because of race or colour. (See Sullivan, 1999, for further information.)

Sexual harassment

Sexual harassment is unwanted sexual attention. It makes the recipients feel uncomfortable, demeaned, or humiliated. Sexual harassment is usually directed against girls but can also be directed against boys. It includes obscene gestures or communication, remarks about a person's body, sexual demands, suggestive statements or remarks, and taunting or teasing. Any form of bullying could have a sexual dimension to it. In this case, bullying equates with harassment.

Unwanted sexual touching is sometimes referred to as bullying or harassment. This can be part of an act of bullying but, in itself, is more than bullying. Unwanted sexual touching is an assault and can be a criminal offence.

Bullying of special needs children

A study by Whitney et al. (1994) in conjunction with the Sheffield project showed that, when matched with mainstream children of the same age, ethnicity, gender, and year, special needs children were two or three times more at risk of being bullied and more likely to bully. Three reasons for this were identified: their learning difficulty or other disabilities made them a target, they tended to be less well integrated into their class, and some children with behavioural problems acted out in aggressive ways and, as a result, were susceptible to becoming provocative victims.

Sexual preference bullying

Some students are bullied because of their sexual orientation. In most Western countries, homosexual relationships are legal and accepted within society as a whole, but the culture within many mainstream institutions, including some schools, is often homophobic. Within such schools, those who have declared themselves as lesbian or gay, or are perceived as being inclined towards these sexual orientations, can become the victims of bullying in its various forms.

In the UK, Rivers (1995, 1996) surveyed 140 gay or lesbian secondary school students. He found that 80 per cent had been teased because of their sexual orientation and more than half had been physically assaulted or ridiculed by other students or by teachers.

What Does Not Count As Bullying?

It is also important to be clear about what is *not* bullying. Some incidents that at first appear to be bullying, upon closer examination, are not.

Criminal behaviour

Bullying is antisocial but it is not criminal behaviour. Some very aggressive acts have all the hallmarks of bullying (it is physical, has happened before, and constitutes an abuse of power), but go beyond the bounds of school bullying and the jurisdiction of the school. These are criminal offences and should be handled by the police or juvenile authorities, depending on the age of the offenders. The following are examples of criminal behaviour:

- seriously assaulting someone or attacking them with a weapon or an object such as a broken bottle, knife, or razor;
- serious theft;
- seriously threatening to cause grievous bodily harm or to kill;
- sexually abusing someone (including unwanted sexual touching).

Sub-bullying and non-bullying behaviour

Children often play exuberant physical and verbal games that may appear rough to adults. These activities include play-fights, rough and tumble play, and playful teasing. Children, especially boys, sometimes end up in full-scale, one-off physical conflicts when a play-fight or verbal sparring has got out of hand. Although these may be considered disciplinary matters, they are not instances of bullying. Similarly, teasing is often only playful and is not concerted, collective, and repetitive.

Teachers need to be able to tell the difference between bullying, sub-bullying, and non-bullying behaviour. The differences between these behaviours can soon be picked up through careful observation.

What are Some of the Common Myths, Misrepresentations, and Misunderstandings About Bullying?

There are a number of commonly held myths (long-standing societal 'truths'), misrepresentations (when someone argues in favour of something they know is not the truth), and misunderstandings (when people genuinely believe something to be the case when it actually is not) about bullying that need to be dispelled.

Can be mistaken for but is not bullying	← ———— Bullying ———— →	Criminal activity
	PHYSICAL	
– playful teasing	– biting	– assault with a weapon
– a one-off fight	– hair pulling	
– rough and tumble or playfighting with no intention of causing damage	– hitting – kicking – locking in a room – pinching – punching – pushing – scratching – spitting – any other form of physical attack – damaging a person's property	– grievous bodily harm – seriously threatening to cause harm or kill – serious theft – sexual abuse
	NON-PHYSICAL	
	Verbal – abusive language – abusive telephone calls – extorting money or possessions – intimidation/threats of violence – name calling – racist remarks/teasing – sexually suggestive language – spiteful teasing (cruel remarks) – spreading false/malicious rumours	
	Non-verbal Direct: – mean faces/rude gestures Indirect: – manipulating/ruining friendships – systematically excluding, ignoring and isolating – sending (often anonymous) poisonous notes	
	• can be any one of the above or a combination of them	
	• bullying is usually repetitive	
This should be handled by the school where appropriate but not treated as bullying	This should be handled by the school	This should be handled by the police or other appropriate authorities

2.2 What Is and What Is Not Bullying

We don't have bullying in our school

This is a common myth. Bullying is seen as something that happens only in 'other' schools, usually those in 'rough' areas.

Bullying occurs in all schools and to a greater degree than most people realise. Acknowledging that it occurs is the first step towards preventing it.

> **Comment:** A short while ago, a newspaper article reported that a popular, highly regarded school located in a New Zealand city had a bullying problem. This article was the result of an Education Review Office report which stated that the school had adopted an anti-bullying program. Rather than seeing this as a responsible and preventative measure, the newspaper article implied that this was a 'bad school', a 'bullying school'. The principal had to do a lot of work to counter the bad publicity the school received as a result.

You have to learn to stand up for yourself in life: being bullied is character-forming

This is probably the most dangerous myth because it suggests that victims of bullying are to blame for the bullying because they do not stand up for themselves.

Part of the process of bullying is the almost imperceptible isolating or discrediting of those who are bullied. Their self-esteem is gradually lowered until they feel worthless, and this sense is conveyed to others both through their own worsening perception of themselves and the relentless negativity that is expressed towards them.

Bullies have power over their victims. The process of exclusion and humiliation that is inherent in bullying almost guarantees that the victim will not be able to stand up to the bully(ies). Any efforts to do so become part of the fuel that inflames the bullies. The situation is characterised by menace and an imbalance of power. It invites further humiliation for the victim and, in the case of physical bullying, an escalation of violence.

Bullying is abusive and humiliating behaviour. It is neither character-forming nor good for anyone in any way. Those who stand up to bullying are just as likely to be hit down. If they succeed in avoiding this, then the bullies may turn their attention to somebody weaker. As they get older, victims sometimes bully newer and younger children. In this setting, a culture of bullying is constantly renewed. Those who state that bullying is normal and acceptable are either deluded or bullies themselves.

It was just a bit of fun. No harm was done. Can't you take a joke! Boys will be boys!

These are all representations of a similar theme, that it is OK to bully, that it is part of life, and that it is natural for boys to act 'tough'. These are all misrepresentations of the truth. Bullying is not fun, it is not harmless, and it is not acceptable. Schools must develop policies and programs that reinforce this message and create safer environments.

When accused, a bully with a sense of personal power and good self-esteem will have no difficulty in blinding a teacher to the truth. Adults can be swayed by the argument of a person with charm (or intimidated if the menace is turned against them). And, because of the fear of reprisal, the perpetrator will be sure that his or her victims and witnesses will not speak up.

They were asking for it. They got what they deserved

This is a misrepresentation. A common response, when people are caught bullying, is that the victims were asking for it, that they did something provocative, and got what they deserved. Bullying is not about justice, however, it is about victimisation.

Sometimes, a child is annoying and provokes other students. Olweus (1993, p. 33) calls such children 'provocative victims'. Provocative and annoying behaviour needs to be looked at carefully and treated gently within the school, perhaps with the help of counselling and other interventions (see Chapter 13, 'A Circle of Friends').

Teachers know how to handle bullying. It's their job!

This is a misunderstanding. Whereas bullying in schools is often acknowledged as an important issue, for most teachers it is only one of many things they have to deal with, and in most cases they have no training for doing so. Most bullying, purposely, occurs out of their sight, and the fact that most children do not report the problem makes it doubly difficult for teachers to handle. Being a teacher does not automatically make anyone an expert.

Bullies are thick kids from dysfunctional families picking on academic, nerdy kids with glasses

This is a myth. Although recent articles in the New Zealand media about school bullying have all been about older, stronger, and mean-spirited boys (usually a group of them) beating up, robbing, and generally humiliating younger, weaker, and often cleverer boys, and this type of bullying does occur, there are many other forms of bullying that are just as devastating. Bullies come in all shapes and sizes, as do victims, and some people can become victimised only by being in the wrong place at the wrong time. Schools and their communities must develop a better understanding of bullying so that they can deal effectively with all its forms.

2. Are Schools Safe?
How Widespread is Bullying?

Recent international research indicates that school bullying is widespread.

New Zealand and Australia

In a recent study of school bullying in New Zealand carried out with 2066 secondary schools students from the upper North Island, Adair et al. (1999)

found that 75 per cent of respondents had been bullied, and 44 per cent reported they had bullied others at some time during their schooling.

In *The Impact of Bullying on Children*, a study carried out by Maxwell and Carroll-Lind (1997), similar findings were reported. The authors asked 259 Form 1 and 2 (years seven and eight) students about bullying experiences at school over the previous nine months. In terms of:

Direct experiences of physical violence
- 49 per cent reported having been punched, kicked, beaten, or hit by children
- 23 per cent reported being in a physical fight with children.

Direct experiences of emotional abuse
- 70 per cent reported having tales told, being the subject of catty gossip, or being narked on by children
- 67 per cent reported being threatened, frightened, or called names by children
- 54 per cent reported being ganged up on, left out, or not spoken to by children
- 14 per cent reported being treated unfairly or bullied by adults.

Direct experiences of sexual abuse
- 3 per cent reported unwanted sexual touching
- 40 per cent reported being asked unwanted sexual things.

Witnessing violence or abuse
- 64 per cent watched someone threatened, frightened, or called names by children
- 62 per cent watched someone ganged up on, left out, or not spoken to by children
- 53 per cent watched someone punched, kicked, beaten, or hit by children
- 51 per cent watched a physical fight
- 15 per cent watched others being treated unfairly/bullied by an adult (p. 4).

Rigby and Slee (1999) report that, in Australia, one child in six or seven (20.7 per cent of boys and 15.7 per cent of girls) is bullied at least once a week.

International studies
In their introduction to a recent study of bullying internationally (Smith et al., 1999), Smith and Morita (1999) say that wherever institutionalised schooling has been established, bullying occurs and, broadly speaking and despite cultural differences, many of the features are the same. All of the countries described in this book show a high incidence of bullying.

In a study conducted in Sheffield, England (Whitney and Smith, 1993), 27 per cent of primary school students reported being bullied 'sometimes' or more frequently, and 10 per cent reported being bullied once a week or more. For secondary school students, these figures were 10 per cent and 4 per cent respectively.

Charach et al.'s (1995) study of twenty-two Toronto classrooms (with children aged four to fourteen) found that one-third of students had been involved in bullying situations, with involvement higher among boys in Grades 5 and 6.

Nolin's (1996) American study of 6504 Grade 6 to 12 students showed that half of the students witnessed some form of crime or victimisation and that one in eight reported having been victimised at school.

Is Bullying the Same in All Schools?

The extent of bullying can differ from school to school. For instance, in his large-scale study of bullying in Norway, Olweus (1993) reports that he came across schools where the extent of bullying was four or five times higher than in another school in the same community.

Why does the rate of bullying differ from school to school? Three reasons have emerged from the literature.

- Bullying occurs more frequently in poorer areas. The suggestion here is that, in economically depressed areas, there are higher levels of alcoholism, drug use, theft, unemployment, and vandalism; a higher percentage of one-parent families; and a general breakdown of the cement that holds society together. In the Sheffield study, Whitney and Smith (1993) found there was some truth to this perception but that it accounted for only a small difference in the level of bullying (10 per cent).

- Bullying occurs less in more academically focused schools. In support of this suggestion, in Germany, Lösel and Bliesener (1999) found there was less bullying in the more academic grammar schools than in secondary general schools and special schools. Similarly, in Switzerland, bullying was found to occur least in the highest academic school, the gymnasium (Alsaker and Brunner, 1999). The underlying argument is that, in more academically orientated schools, students are more focused, more successful in their studies, and more prosocial in their attitudes and behaviours (and probably socio-economically better off). Consequently, the incidence of bullying (and other antisocial behaviour) is thought to be lower in these settings. Although there is some evidence to support this hypothesis, it is inconclusive.

- A school's ethos determines the extent of bullying. In relation to the Sheffield study, Whitney and Smith (1993) argue that a good school ethos and effective anti-bullying policies are more important than a school's socio-economic classification in determining the rate of bullying. Smith and Sharp (1994), too, found that those schools with a good ethos (they were serious, thorough, and consistent) were the most successful in making their schools safe from bullying. In his study of ten Scottish schools, Mellor (1999) reached the same conclusion.

In Holland, Mooj's research cited in Junger-Tas (1999) provides evidence that effective management and teaching methods can produce a positive school ethos at the classroom level. He found schools that encourage cooperative teaching methods and small group learning, and employ teachers who offer a high level of both academic and social group supervision, are more likely to have relatively low levels of bullying.

In conclusion, although there is some evidence that socio-economic difference and the academic nature of a school can influence the level of bullying in a school, research evidence suggests that the development and maintenance of a positive school ethos is more important.

Where Does Bullying Take Place?

In order to deal effectively with bullying, it is important to know where it most often occurs.

In Australia, Rigby (1996) suggests the four main places where bullying occurs are (in order of frequency): the playground, the classroom, on the way home from school, and on the way to school. With variations, similar findings are made for: Belgium (Vettenburg, 1999), Canada (Ziegler and Rosenstein-Manner, 1991), England and Wales (Smith, 1999), Germany (Lösel and Bliesener, 1999), Portugal (Almeida, 1999), Spain (Ortega and Mora-Merchan, 1999), and Switzerland (Alsaker and Brunner, 1999).

Lösel and Bliesener (1999, p. 232) give an interesting proportional analysis of violent bullying in Germany: 60.1 per cent occurs in the playground, 17.3 per cent on the way to and from school, 10.4 per cent in the school corridors, and 9.2 per cent in the classroom. The washrooms and toilets are another location for bullying.

What are the Rights of Students?

The United Nations Charter of Rights for Children states that every child has the right to an education and every child has the right to be safe. It is a basic human right in a democratic society to be safe at school and in the classroom. Most countries have legislation and government guidelines to ensure the rights of students in their care. (It is easy to find out what the rules and regulations are from any local university education or law library.) In New Zealand, for example, through the legislation in Section 60 of the Education Act 1989, and as translated into practice through the National Administration Guidelines for the running of schools, the government directs that schools are to provide a safe physical and emotional atmosphere for their pupils. Schools are also required to analyse and find ways to remove any barriers to learning.

Recently, in Britain, the results of bullying have been dealt with through the legal system. Smith (1999, p. 86) cites several recent cases in which people have been prosecuted for bullying activities. A girl was jailed for three months for leading a gang attack on another girl who later committed suicide. Two boys received nine- and twelve-month detention orders respectively for bullying. A twenty-year-old woman received an out-of-court settlement of £30 000 (approximately $NZ100 000) from a London school where she had been victimised for four years.

3. Are There Gender and Age Differences in Bullying Patterns?

Is Bullying Different for Boys and Girls?

Boys bully and are bullied more than girls

In Adair et al.'s study (1999), victims of bullying said that 76 per cent of bullying incidents were perpetrated by boys.

In the Australian context, Rigby and Slee (1995) found that, of boys who were victimised, 69 per cent reported that this was always by a boy, 3.9 per cent always by a girl, and 27.1 per cent sometimes by a boy, sometimes by a girl. For girls who were the victims of bullies, 24.1 per cent reported that this was always by a boy, 24.5 per cent always by a girl, and 51.4 per cent as sometimes by a boy, sometimes by a girl.

Generally, boys tend to bully and be bullied more than girls, especially in the lower secondary school. This is particularly the case with direct physical bullying (see, for instance, Alsaker and Brunner, 1999; Olweus, 1999b).

Boys tend to use more physical bullying and girls more psychological bullying

Smith (1999) and Smith and Sharp (1994) report that, for both primary and secondary schools in the Sheffield project, the bullying experiences of boys and girls were different. Boys were more likely to be physically bullied and threatened than girls, and girls were more likely to experience indirect forms of bullying, such as being purposely left out and having false rumours spread about them. In the USA, Eron et al. (1987) found boy bullies three or four times more likely to assault physically than girl bullies.

There are cases, however, of serious physical bullying among girls in which the victims have been very badly hurt. Boys, too, use psychological bullying, especially as they get older (Björkqvist et al., 1992; Björkqvist, 1994).

Lloyd (1994) refers to girls as 'hidden bullies'. She suggests that, while boys use physical means, girls rely on a range of psychological weapons: isolation from the group, persistent teasing, and spreading malicious rumours. This sort of bullying may be harder to detect.

Boys and girls bully differently and this reflects their friendship patterns

Owens (1996) argues that differences in aggression between boys and girls are linked to differences in friendship patterns. His study shows that boys use more physical and verbal aggression than girls, and that older girls in particular use more verbal aggression and indirect aggression in the form of exclusion and the destruction of friendships. He links this to early socialisation, in which boys tend to play in large hierarchically dominated groups, and girls in smaller, more intimate groups. In girls' relationships there tend to be stronger boundaries between close friends and others, and they are more conflict-prone. Boys' relationships tend to be held together by common interests, and they are loose and relatively conflict-free. Besag (1989) suggests that, in their relationships, 'boys seek power and dominance, whereas girls need a sense of affirmation and affiliation, a feeling of belonging and shared intimacy expressed in exchanging confidences and gossip' (p. 40).

Lagerspertz et al. (1988) argued that the small, intimate nature of girls' groupings increases the opportunities for indirect aggression, that girls become abandoned as a form of punishment. For girls, an understanding of the 'in' group and the 'out' group is very important. My younger daughter recognised this type of bullying when I talked to her about it, and she called it 'bitch power', which is a good descriptor.

Indirect bullying can be as harmful for girls as physical bullying is for boys

Owens (1996) argues that, with the focus on boys' physical aggression, indirect aggression by girls gets overlooked, probably because it is subtle and there is no outward sign of damage (see, also, Sullivan, 1998). It is, however, as harmful for girls as physical bullying is for boys, and more attention needs to be paid to it.

Boys and girls respond differently to being bullied

In an Australian study, Rigby (1998) found that girls tend to respond to bullying with sadness and boys with anger, and that, among severely bullied children, girls are more likely to tell someone than boys are. Rigby argues that this is because, even in very hurtful situations, the strength of the Australian macho culture prevents males from reporting. He also found girls more willing to work with adults to find solutions.

Girls are more willing defenders than boys

Finnish researchers Salmivalli et al. (1998) provide interesting information about the roles of boys and girls in bullying. They found that whereas lots of boys were prepared either to assist with or to reinforce acts of bullying, almost no girls were. Few boys were prepared to become defenders of the victim, but at least five times as many girls were. And five times as many girls were totally uninvolved in or unaware of the bullying.

Does Bullying Decrease As Students Get Older?

Generally, the incidence of bullying decreases as children get older, perhaps because, as children move up through the school system, the cohort of potential bullies decreases and students develop better anti-bullying skills.

Research indicates, however, that the incidence of bullying is highest when children start secondary school, because each new cohort is vulnerable to the predations of older children who know the school culture and have already run the gauntlet of acceptance and initiation into it (Rigby and Slee, 1995; Olweus, 1999b). This is particularly the case for boys. It has also been found that, as children get older, they tend to show less sympathy for their victims, and that in a culture where bullying is part of the status quo they are more likely to be hardened in this role (Rigby, 1996).

Although there may be a statistical pattern of an overall decrease in bullying as children mature, there are also individual reported cases in which bullying becomes more severe over time. When bullying occurs between children of the same age, it is called horizontal bullying. When older children bully those younger than themselves, this is referred to as vertical bullying.

4. Those Who Bully

What are the Characteristics of Those Who Bully?

Stephenson and Smith (1989) identified three types of bullies:
- confident bullies, who are physically strong, enjoy aggression, who feel secure, and are of average popularity;
- anxious bullies, who are weak academically, have poor concentration, and are less popular and less secure (accounting for 18 per cent of the bullies and largely boys); and
- bully/victims, who are bullies in some situations and are bullied in others. Bully/victims are very unpopular.

Many researchers have characterised bullies as aggressive, domineering, having a positive view of violence, impulsive, and lacking empathy with their victims (Fonzi et al., 1999; Lösel and Bliesener, 1999; Olweus, 1999a). Such profiles of bullies tend to focus on the confident bully and deal only with physical bullying done by boys. They do not account for most types of psychological bullying, or for girl bullying. In the case of girls, the bullying tends to use indirect aggression (Owens, 1996, p. 46) and to be covert, focusing on destroying friendships and exclusion. It is therefore more difficult to typify the sorts of children who are bullies but whose modus operandi is not physical aggression.

But, because all forms of bullying are dependent on unequal power relationships, it is accurate to say that most bullies are dominant individuals. In the case of boys, this dominance is often claimed by physical prowess, and in the case of girls through control over and the creation and dissolution of cliques (Owens and MacMullin, 1995, p. 33). Another identified general characteristic is that bullies tend to be older than their victims, which is another type of dominance.

A constructivist argument is that if the dominant behaviour of bullies is channelled into leadership and prosocial acts, the apparent deficits may be reformed into better peer relations and an improvement in attitudes to and performance at school. Generalisations about the characteristics of those who bully do not imply that bullies cannot change or, at the other extreme, that there are not bullies who are as mean as the generalisations say they are.

What are the Families of Bullies Like?

Recent research claims that there are some links between bullying and the family.

Bullying can be passed on from generation to generation. Farrington (1993) states that males who are bullies and are aggressive at school are likely to have sons who will repeat this behaviour. Batsche and Knoff (1994) similarly argue that being a bully is intergenerational and, what is more, that bullies at school are victims at home.

Children who bully often come from dysfunctional homes. Good communication helps adolescents to develop a positive sense of self and higher levels of coping and social skills (Noller and Callan, 1991). Rigby's (1994b) study concludes that, when this communication is lacking, children are more likely to become involved in bullying or turn into victims. He argues that bullies often come from families in which all the relationships are poor and where communication is minimal or non-existent. Rigby (1994a) found that a majority of self-reported male bullies came from dysfunctional families, which were characterised by little sense of belonging, and a lack of love or support.

Bowers et al. (1992) suggest that families with strong hierarchical power structures (where a father controls a child through harsh physical punishment) predispose a child towards aggressive behaviour. Similarly, families that do not provide monitoring and boundaries are likely to produce children with poor relationship skills who know little except haphazard reactions and random antisocial behaviour. This is reflected in how they deal with peer relationships.

Aggressive and manipulative behaviour in a family is transferred to the world at large, and can be expressed as bullying in school. Rigby (1993, 1994a, b) and Bowers et al. (1994) argue that how children act outside their families is closely related to what goes on inside the family. Bullying at school is linked to the poor psychosocial functioning of families, and this is the case for both boys and girls. Rigby (1994a, b) suggests that families can influence peer relations at school in direct and

Which one is really the bully?

indirect ways. A family member may encourage a child to behave aggressively towards others at school or to model aggressive and manipulative behaviour. As suggested by Reinken et al. (1989), children may internalise this model of behaviour and use it as a modus operandi at school and in the world at large.

In general, then, researchers do make links between bullying and the family, but some of the research findings are contradictory, making it hard to draw definitive conclusions. For example, in looking at the families of bullies, Olweus (1980, 1981) concluded that there were only very weak links between aggression levels and amount of education, parental income, social class, or socioeconomic conditions. On the other hand, Lösel et al. (1997b, cited in Lösel and Bliesener, 1999) found that children who bullied came from higher risk, disadvantaged family backgrounds, which included the possible characteristics of alcohol abuse, divorce, parental conflict, and unemployment.

This contradiction underlines the fact that a person may bully for a variety of reasons: because of the family or because of life events, because of the power of an antisocial peer group, because of the social climate of the school or surrounding community, because of personality characteristics, or a combination of these and other factors. It is important, therefore, not to assume that a certain type of family will produce bullies, but to bear the research findings in mind and to use them wisely and with discretion.

What are the Effects of Being a Bully? Does Bullying Behaviour Lead to Crime?

Rigby and Cox (1996) found that adolescents identified as bullies were likely to be involved in other forms of antisocial behaviour such as shoplifting, truancy, writing graffiti, and getting into trouble with the police. Does this mean that bullying will lead to criminal offending?

Several researchers have found a strong relationship between bullying, criminal offending, and recidivism. In a follow-up to his 1980s study in Norway, Olweus (1993) found that around 60 per cent of boys considered as bullies in his Grade 6 to 9 cohorts had at least one criminal conviction by the time they were twenty-four. As many as 35 to 40 per cent of former bullies had three or more convictions by this age, as compared with those who were not bullies. An American study (Eron et al., 1987) found that those who were identified as bullies early at school had a 25 per cent chance of having a criminal record by the age of thirty.

Other researchers found that, while their criminal informants may have been bullies, they were just as likely to have been victims of bullying (Olweus, 1993; Cullingford and Morrison, 1995). This suggests that the issue is a complex one, and simple correlations should not be made between bullying and criminality. All these findings do, however, underline the destructive character of bullying.

Can Teachers be Bullies?

In Maxwell and Carroll-Lind's New Zealand study (1997) of lower secondary school students, 14 per cent reported being treated unfairly or bullied by adults at school. This finding is not uncommon.

Until recently, teachers had authority by virtue of their role. Although corporal punishment at school has been made illegal in many countries, teachers are not barred from being abusive, derisory, or insensitive. It is still possible for them to misuse their positions of power.

Olweus (1999b) suggests that the issue of teachers who bully is a serious one that deserves more attention than it currently receives. He makes the point that a person who bullies students is not going to be good at solving student-on-student bullying problems. He or she could contribute to the problem by treating particularly vulnerable students with disdain or put-downs and by providing negative role modelling for other students to emulate. Olweus further suggests that when students are bullied by teachers they may develop anti-teacher and anti-school attitudes.

5. The Victims of Bullying

What are the Characteristics of Victims?

Stephenson and Smith (1989) and Olweus (1978, 1991) have identified three types of victims:

- Passive victims are characterised as anxious, lacking in self-esteem and self-confidence, physically weak, and unpopular. They do nothing to provoke attacks and do little if anything to defend themselves.
- Provocative victims are characterised as being physically stronger and more active than passive victims. Olweus (1978, 1984) describes them as having problems with concentration, causing tension and irritation around them, and provoking other children (sometimes a whole class) into turning on them. Although their opinion is contested, several researchers (Olweus; Stephenson and Smith) suggest that one in five victims are provocative.
- Bully/victims are described as both provoking aggression in others and instigating aggressive acts. Perry et al. (1988) found that the most extremely bullied children were often very aggressive, were bullied by stronger children, and victimised weaker children (see also 'Those Who Bully').

Byrne (1999) found that victims of bullying feel guilt, shame, and a sense of failure because they cannot cope with the bullying. They are often worried, unhappy, and fearful, and significantly more neurotic than the norm. Smith (1999) describes bullied children as unpopular and isolated. Because they play less with other children, their social skills tend to be less developed than those of their peers. Their isolation also means that they are targets. Children who are different sometimes get bullied (see 'Racist Bullying, Sexual Harassment, Bullying of Special Needs Children, and Sexual Preference Bullying').

Research has shown that, when surveyed, children can accurately identify those who are likely to be victims of bullying. Such children often stay victims for years, even if they change schools (Olweus, 1993). It is argued that the bullying dynamic dehumanises the victims and makes it easy for the bullies to act without conscience towards them (Troy and Sroufe, 1987; and Perry et al., 1990, both cited in Harachi et al., 1999).

A constructivist approach would challenge the thinking underlying the classification of victims because such classifications focus on individuals rather than dealing with the system. That is, they deal with symptoms rather than addressing the problem as a whole. This is examined more fully in 'Once a Bully Always a Bully? Once a Victim Always a Victim?' (p. 33).

What are Families of Victims Like?

Because children acquire their primary socialisation from the family, some researchers have looked to the family for some of the causes of bullying and victimisation. Sometimes children who are victims come from families under stress (for example, illness, Maines and Robinson, 1998; immigration, large families, Fabre-Cornali, 1999; and marriage breakup, Mellor, 1999). It is relatively easy to see how such life events may make a child sad and withdrawn, or aggressive and angry, and thus open to being victimised.

Some researchers (Minuchin, 1974; Olweus, 1980; Vignes and Auckland, 1980, all cited in Bowers et al., 1992; Bowers et al., 1994) have made causal links between school bullying and the relationship between victims and their families.

It is suggested that children who are bullied tend to be overprotected and do not develop the skills of independence that make them less vulnerable to bullying.

However, although some of these findings may be correct, they are psychological and measurement-based, operating out of a deficit mode that tries to align problems with causes and so to change the behaviour of individuals rather than addressing the system. If teachers assume that such studies are correct, then they may add to the child's predisposition to being bullied by characterising them as overprotected, blaming not only them but also their parents. This also means that teachers do not have to take the bullying seriously.

Other researchers (for example, Rigby, 1994a) have focused on the fact that, when there is support from parents, the negative effects of bullying can be greatly reduced. Clearly, it is more sensible to harness the support that resides in the protectiveness of these families than to blame them for the fact that their children are being victimised.

What are the Effects of Being Bullied?

Research indicates that those who have been bullied severely tend to suffer long-term consequences.

The isolation and exclusion that often accompany bullying not only deny children company, friendship, and social interaction, but also cause them to feel incompetent and unattractive. Those who have been bullied often have difficulty forming good relationships, and tend to lead less successful lives. Even though they may be very capable, bullied children may appear to be incompetent and as a result suffer academically (Olweus, 1978; Parker and Asher, 1987; Kupersmidt et al., 1990; Hazler et al., 1992; Rubin and Coplan, 1992; Batsche and Knoff, 1994).

In an Australian study, Rigby (1994a) found that frequently bullied students were more likely than others to suffer poor health. In a study of over 700 English secondary school students, Sharp (Sharp and Thompson, 1992; Sharp, 1995, 1996) found that 43 per cent of the respondents had been bullied in the past year; of this group 20 per cent said that they would truant to avoid bullying, 29 per cent that they found it hard to concentrate on their schoolwork, 22 per cent that after they had been bullied they felt physically sick, and 20 per cent that they had sleeping difficulties.

Emotionally, victims of bullying may feel any of the following: afraid, alienated, angry, ashamed, depressed, disempowered, hurt, sad, stupid, subhuman, trampled on, ugly, and useless.

Physically, the effects of bullying are often severe: broken bones, broken teeth, concussion, damaged eyes, and even permanent brain damage. Other physical effects include bites, bruises, cuts, gouges, and scratches. The most serious effect of bullying is suicide, instances of which are cited by most anti-bullying researchers (for example, Batsche and Knoff, 1994; Fried and Fried, 1996).

Abraham Maslow (1970) developed a theory that human beings have certain basic (deficiency) needs that must be met before higher order (or growth) needs can be addressed. Our physiological needs are for food, water, and shelter from the elements. Our safety needs require us to protect ourselves from the world at large. Our relationship needs are for social contact, friendship, and love.

Our higher order or growth needs involve gaining the approval and love of others so that self-esteem and self-respect are formed and nurtured. The need to be creative and to be able to reach our potential is achieved only after the other needs have been met.

Maslow's model is useful for explaining some of the possible effects of bullying. If children are bullied, their safety needs have not been met. Instead, they spend their time trying to avoid further bullying, either by escaping the bullies or by finding places in the school and community that feel safer. If they are being emotionally bullied, excluded or isolated, then they are being denied the opportunity of making friends and experiencing the normal interactions of the school years. They are being denied access to the relationship growth that leads to the development of social intelligence. It may also mean that they are being denied access to full cognitive development.

Do Victims of Bullying Tell Teachers or Parents?

Even in the face of unfair and excessive bullying, children tend not to report being bullied. This has to do with intimidation and fear of retaliation (Farrington, 1993) as well as 'honour among thieves'.

Adair et al.'s (1999) New Zealand-based study found that although 81 per cent of those in the study had observed bullying, only 21 per cent had reported it to an adult. In this and several Canadian studies, it was found that children perceived teachers as intervening infrequently in bullying incidents, sometimes because they were unaware, and sometimes because they chose not to intervene (Charach et al., 1995; Craig and Pepler, 1995; Pepler and Craig, 1995; Harachi et al., 1999). If such is the case, it is not surprising that children are reluctant to report cases of bullying.

The level of reporting of bullying is low for a number of reasons. First, the message from the peer group (particularly among adolescents) is that ratting is unacceptable. Second, children tend to believe that bullying will occur no matter what, and that nothing can be done about it. Third, there is a real danger that if anyone tells, the bullies will retaliate. And fourth, the sense of hopelessness that is one of the effects of being bullied makes it difficult for the victim to do anything. This phenomenon can be likened to an iceberg: the incidents being reported account for the tip, but most incidents of bullying lie below the surface.

One of the many messages to come out of the Sheffield study is encapsulated in the title of the British Department for Education (DFE) program, *Don't Suffer in Silence* (see DFE, 1994). The Sheffield study indicated that after an anti-bullying program had been introduced, the percentage of pupils in the project's seven secondary schools who told a teacher they had been bullied increased substantially (32 per cent was the mean, with a maximum increase of 79 per cent). For those who talked to somebody including a teacher, the mean was 38 per cent and the maximum 99 per cent (Smith, 1999, p. 83).

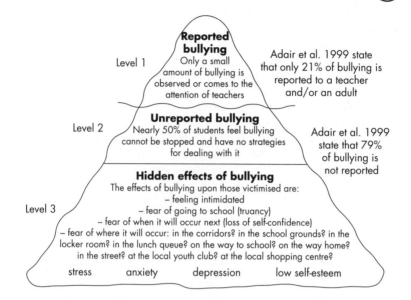

2.3 The Bullying Iceberg

The logical corollary is that when bullying is tackled by a school and reporting is encouraged, bullying decreases significantly.

How is it Possible to Tell if Someone is Being Bullied?

Because the great majority of bullying is not reported, in many cases it is driven underground and the victims are left powerless and trapped. This makes the school, and the world in general, a very unsafe place for them.

It is important, therefore, that we become familiar with the signals that tell us someone is being bullied. A single sign may be nothing more than a temporary aberration, a passing mood or, in the case of teenagers, a symptom of adolescent angst. But if several of these symptoms occur together, then it is very possible that bullying is taking place.

Bullying experts Olweus (1993), Rigby (1996), and Elliott (1997) provide useful information about symptoms of bullying. The following is an overview of what parents and teachers should look out for.

Parents

Symptoms can include the following:
- The child may be anxious about going to school. He or she may find reasons to be late in leaving, or may go to school via some obscure, roundabout route.
- The child may show other signs of anxiety, such as bed-wetting and nightmares, and may develop headaches and stomach aches, particularly in the morning when it is time to go to school.

- The child may come home with books or clothes ripped, or with bruises and cuts.
- The child may appear to lose possessions and ask for (or even steal) extra money.
- The child may receive telephone calls after which they seem sullen or snappy and about which they will not talk if questioned.
- The child may say he or she has friends but never bring children home. The child is never invited to social functions with classmates.
- The child may be irrational and angry with parents, brothers, and sisters.
- The child may seem depressed, sad, and even threaten or attempt suicide.
- The child may be unable to concentrate on homework, and their school work may start to go down hill.
- When asked about what is wrong, the child may avoid answering, make something up, or get angry and refuse to talk about it.
- The child may start doing things that are out of character and get him or her into trouble, such as truanting and getting caught stealing. (Truancy is common with children who are afraid to go to school, and they may steal if ordered to do so.)

Teachers

Clearly, teachers need to know what is going on under the surface. The following could be symptoms that someone is being bullied:

- A child is getting a lot of negative attention, and being teased by a number of people. This can be masked if the children say it is all in good fun and no one minds. A close look will show, however, that the one being victimised is clearly not enjoying it. In fact, the victim may be so churned up that they lose their temper 'out of the blue' and turn their rage on the closest child. On the other hand, the victimised child may be insolent to the teacher. (This can result in their being blamed for bad behaviour—a symptom, rather than being acknowledged as a victim of bullying—the root cause.)
- When a child is consistently sitting alone at lunchtime, or has no friends to play with, and is ignored by his or her peers except to be taunted.

- When sports or classroom teams are selected (such as for a spelling contest), and a certain child is consistently chosen last or only with intervention and persuasion from the teacher.
- When a child does not speak up in class, lacks confidence when forced to participate, and elicits snide remarks when they do.
- When someone seems to be drawn into conflict, but then flounders and appears stupid.
- When there is a deterioration in a child's work.
- When a child is clearly unhappy, distressed, and withdrawn.
- When a child is small and not strong, yet seems to be at the centre of fights and gets blamed for starting them.

6. The Third Parties to Bullying
What Role Do the Onlookers Play in Bullying?

Bullies derive power from a public display. Performing for an audience makes them feel validated. The onlookers, whether directly involved or only present passively, are part of the dynamic. If bullying is likened to a play, the bully(ies) and victim(s) are the actors, the onlookers the audience.

When bullying occurs, the onlookers can choose to passively observe, to become participants in the bullying, to walk away, or to intervene. Adair's recent New Zealand research (Adair, 1999) found that 42 per cent of onlookers to bullying chose not to intervene. She identified three reasons for this: '… the victim was not liked or not a friend; fear of being a target; belief that it was probably deserved' (p. 35). This means that some children will intervene if a friend is being bullied (even if it means risking becoming a target), but those who are not friends or who are deemed to have deserved it will not be helped. This is a highly selective and an entrenched response. Adair et al. (1999) identified a general malaise and sense of powerlessness among many onlookers. This was because they had neither strategies for combating bullying nor faith that it could be stopped.

On the other hand, this same research showed that 32 per cent of students did stand up for victims of bullying and 22 per cent told a teacher or got help (Adair, 1999). Research has shown that those willing to intervene are more likely to be primary rather than secondary students (Vettenburg, 1999), and much more likely to be girls than boys (Adair, 1999; Salmivalli et al., 1998).

Whitney and Smith (1993) found that 80 per cent of students do not like bullying and Pikas (1989) similarly argues that people are uncomfortable with bullying and are eager to find ways of dealing with it. In support of this, results from the Sheffield study (Smith and Sharp, 1994) showed that after bullying programs had been introduced to participating schools, onlookers became more active in trying to combat bullying, with an average of 9 per cent more pupils in the secondary schools reporting that they would not join in bullying. This is an indication that, if schools encourage interventions and have clear anti-bullying policies, more children will feel able to dissociate themselves from the bullying and to offer support to those being bullied. The role of the peer group in objecting to or stopping bullying is potentially very important.

Who Else is Affected by Bullying?

The effects of bullying are obviously felt most deeply by the person who is being bullied. The effects, however, can be far-reaching; bullying creates a ripple effect that spreads outwards to touch other groups and individuals.

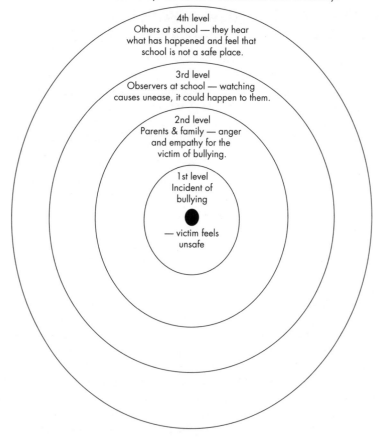

5th level
The wider community – if students are not safe in school, why should they be safe in the wider community? The school is a microcosm of the community.

4th level
Others at school — they hear what has happened and feel that school is not a safe place.

3rd level
Observers at school — watching causes unease, it could happen to them.

2nd level
Parents & family — anger and empathy for the victim of bullying.

1st level
Incident of bullying

— victim feels unsafe

Although bullying most affects those being victimised,
there are second, third, fourth and fifth level effects.
Bullying can be said to have a ripple effect.

2.4 The Ripple Effect of Bullying

The first level: point of impact

The person who is being bullied is a primary victim of bullying, the direct recipient of the physical and psychological harm that is inflicted.

The second level

Parents and family members who see the effects of bullying upon their child or sibling are often angry, and parents in particular feel defensive on behalf of their child. They can be considered secondary victims of bullying as they have to pick up the pieces of shattered self-esteem and are sad, hurt, and angry on behalf of their child.

The third level

Those who observe bullying are also affected by it. They may feel afraid and unsafe, ashamed for not stopping the bullying, or attracted to the meanness and cruelty.

The fourth level

This is the level of the school. Although adults are often unaware of the frequency and severity of the bullying, the peer group certainly is. When bullying occurs in a school it gives the message that this is not a safe school. But when bullying is dealt with, the message is that bullying is not tolerated.

The fifth level

The fifth level is the wider community within which the school exists. If bullying occurs and is neither detected nor effectively dealt with, then there is a sense that those who bully can carry out their bullying in the wider community. This may occur on the way to and from school, in the street, at a youth club, or at a shopping centre. It can also go on throughout life.

7. What are the Dynamics of Bullying?

Once a Bully Always a Bully? Once a Victim Always a Victim?

Up to this point, I have focused on what researchers have discovered about bullying, bullies, victims, and observers. It is important to recognise that these descriptions are only guidelines that give us impressions and can help us to understand bullying and devise ways of dealing with it.

Information on the nature of families of bullies and victims is similarly contestable and variable. In any one family, for instance, each child can be very different. One may be extrovert and have good social skills; another may be popular and very vocal, with good retaliatory and assertiveness skills; and one may be shy and less able to stand up to victimisation. Can it be argued, therefore, that each child is as he or she is because of the family? Or is it more important to use the generalisations as warning signs, but not as hard-and-fast indicators? Perhaps, as with the symptoms of bullying, it is also important to be alert to a combination of several signs, not only to isolated symptoms. To typify a family as predictably producing either a bully or a victim is tantamount to blaming the family, which is not constructive. Research findings on bullying are useful if taken with a large dose of common sense.

Much of our reaction to bullying is, as Slee (1997) suggests, founded in the deficit mode that emphasises faults and weaknesses in the individual, and offers remediation as a solution. This approach tends to deal only with symptoms. A more dynamic alternative is the systems perspective (which Slee uses for his *P.E.A.C.E. Pack*, see Chapter 14) where meaning is seen as socially constructed 'with a strong emphasis on competency, success and individual strength' (Slee, 1997, p. 5). This approach deals with the whole problem in all its complexity rather than only with symptoms.

I have chosen three examples from my own life to show how people can take on different roles depending on the particular situation in which they find themselves. In other words, people's behaviour is determined by their social environment, not predetermined by role. Taking on the role of bully, victim, or bystander did not make me any one of these permanently, yet at particular times and in particular circumstances I was each of these. When I reflect on what was happening to me and my peers on these occasions, it helps me to understand better the dynamics of bullying.

Being a victim of bullying

I was twelve and in my last year of elementary school in Martinvale School in Chomedey just outside Montréal, Canada. It was lunchtime in the middle of winter and I was playing outside where the school's snow-covered baseball diamond was located, far away from the teaching blocks. I was throwing snowballs around with a bunch of friends. He came out of nowhere, attacking me from behind. In a flash, I was propelled to the ground and my face pushed into the snow and I was held in this position, with his knee in my back and his gloved hands on my head, for what felt like an eternity.

The assailant was David Thompson (a pseudonym) who had failed Grade 7 twice and been kept back in elementary school. He was fourteen and much bigger than me and my classmates, and we were rightly frightened of him. Nobody liked him and we didn't think we could do much about his bullying because he was a head taller and had a massive physical advantage over us all.

When he finally let go of the back of my head, I came up gasping for breath. My overriding feeling was not, 'I'm angry and I'm going to get back at you, you bastard', or 'I'm going to tell a teacher about this incident'. It was, rather, 'If Thompson had held me down for much longer, he would have killed me. He could kill me if he chose to on another occasion.'

Whether he would have killed me was not as important as the fact that I was certain he could. No teachers intervened. If they had noticed us they probably would have thought it was only boys messing around.

Being an observer of bullying

During my middle high school years (Grade 9), I can remember another bully called Jacky Cousins who, like Thompson, had failed twice and was two years older than the rest of us. Although he was a good fighter, most of us were closer to his size and he was therefore not as invincible as Thompson. He used to pick on one boy called Brian Harris, who was an easy victim for him.

Brian had flaming red hair and a mass of freckles. His hair was cut in a way that suggested his mother had put a bowl over it and chopped around the edges. He was not good at defending himself verbally and he was physically weak.

Cousins was obviously unhappy at school. Academically, he was hopeless, so he attracted attention by playing the fool, such as charging a ten cents entry fee for others to watch him swallow a goldfish and, of course, using every opportunity available to make Brian look stupid, slapping him around, removing chairs as he was about to sit down, and getting him to do things that sounded reasonable but were actually nonsensical.

I remember feeling sorry for Brian, but I also felt that in some ways he deserved the treatment he got because he did not stand up for himself. To me, he did not seem to have any saving graces. So I was, in effect, a member of the audience that watched when Cousins taunted Brian. Sometimes I felt uncomfortable, sometimes I laughed, sometimes I told Cousins to stop, but I never intervened forcefully.

Being a perpetrator of bullying

In my Grade 11 class (equivalent to the sixth form), I can remember there was a boy, whom I shall call Barry, who was academically very bright but who dressed sloppily, suffered from a skin condition, and had bad body odour. He was socially very awkward. I and two friends, Victor and Mike, used to joke around and play witty verbal games. We would score points off each other and it was all in good fun, but when we turned it on Barry he was unable to retaliate.

Sometimes he said things that were provocative and silly and, when we took him up on these, he lacked the skill to match our verbal manoeuvres and made a fool of himself. Towards the end of the school year the four of us were in the classroom during lunch. We fancifully set ourselves up as future rulers of the universe. 'When we conquer the universe, we'll split it up,' we decided. 'Victor, you can rule Mars, Mike, you can rule Saturn', I said, 'and Barry, we'll let you rule Uranus, because your face looks like an anus.' We thought this was great fun.

Barry had no effective counter and was visibly nonplussed and dejected. Besides, we knew we would easily outmanoeuvre him and cut him down if he came up with a reply. All in good fun, of course! Mike, Victor, and I jockeyed for the upper hand, and made each other the butt of jokes, but when we made acid and cutting remarks, we were evenly matched. For Barry, it was humiliating and cruel. What is more, it clearly underlined his friendless outsider position in the class and the school.

Deal with the behaviour, do not label

If people are honest, many could recite similar tales of being in all three roles at various points in their lives. I would argue that, in dealing with bullying, it is important to focus on changing behaviour and to avoid labelling the participants. This allows people to move out of negative roles as a way of solving a bullying problem. I know of situations where, as a result of such a dynamic approach, former bullies have become defenders of a school's anti-bullying stance. The important points to remember are that:

- Each situation is unique and needs a specific solution.
- In our lives we can be victims of bullying, perpetrators of bullying, and bystanders/onlookers of bullying. A person may be a victim of bullying but not a victim in a general sense. Similarly, a person may bully in a particular situation but not be a bully in general.
- Labels can stick. It is important, when dealing with a bullying incident, to try to find a solution but not to label the participants. The incident should be dealt with, but not by blame and damnation.
- It is important to provide opportunities for people to change their behaviour. If the first strategy does not work, there should be backup responses.

The Downward Spiral of Bullying

To suggest that people who are bullied should stand up for themselves is not only unfair, it is also unrealistic. If they could have stood up for themselves, they would not have been bullied, and the bullying undermines any vestiges of strength that they may have had. The most compelling reason for their inability to defend themselves is the fact that what they are now experiencing is part of a process that has been gradually and purposely created, in which the bully has power and the victim has not. This tends to be self-perpetuating, a downward spiral. I have developed a model to explain this phenomenon, and use a hypothetical example to illustrate how it works (see figure 2.5).

> **Scenario:** It is the beginning of a school year, and students are in the process of re-forming old alliances and starting new ones. The groups students belong to are defined as much by determining who is 'out' as who is 'in'. Those who are 'out' can be subjected to bullying.
>
> A new boy has arrived at the school. He is academically able but quiet and unaggressive. He becomes the victim of serious bullying and this occurs through a five-stage process. The following describes what happens and how the events affect the bully/ies, the victim/s, and the bystanders.

Stage one: watching and waiting

At the beginning of the year, the pupils settle into the school culture. During this early stage, the students are quietly gaining a sense of the characteristics of their classmates and the dynamics of the classroom. Those who will bully are observing and gathering information, picking who will be easy to bully and who will be bully-proof. Those who are prone to be bullied may have no idea that they are being targeted. Those who may become bystanders in acts of bullying may have given signs that they are not easy targets. Research indicates that early in the school year, single acts with bullying potential are visited on a large number of individuals, but that the frequency of these acts decreases as students who may succumb to being bullied and those who are resistant are identified (Perry et al. 1990, cited in Harachi et al., 1999).

Stage two: testing the waters

If, after stage one, a child is perceived as being a potential victim, the next move is for the bully (or part of a bullying group) to activate the bullying in a minor way. He may walk past the potential victim's desk and knock off a pencil case. This is a small but symbolic act that tests the response of the potential victim. If the child is embarrassed and seems nonplussed, and responds weakly or not at all, he gives the message that he is a potential victim. (If he retaliates successfully, he may move out of the potential victim group and be accepted by the main group.)

Stage three: something more substantial occurs

Stage two confirms the existence of a potential victim. When he arrives at school the next day, four boys walk very close to him and jostle him, one grabs his bag, and then they throw it around. He runs from boy to boy, feeling panicky, and they laugh. A teacher comes over and asks what is going on. 'Just having some fun,' the leader says. The victimised boy does not contradict him. He hopes that if he says nothing he will be seen as a good sport.

Stage four: the bullying escalates

More often than not, the bullying goes unchecked and gets worse because there is nothing to stop it. If the boys see they can get away with their behaviour, they may beat their victim up or degrade him in various ways. They can also subject him to bullying outside school and orchestrate a campaign of intimidation. The peer group does nothing, but watches passively, united in their complicity.

Step five: bullying is the status quo

The boy who is being bullied is losing confidence, failing academically, truanting, and, in a worst case scenario, may eventually attempt suicide. Those who are bullying get an unrealistic sense of their power and, as they get older, commit other antisocial acts that are not tolerated by the adult world. Crime and imprisonment can be the results. The bystanders are now immobilised by their inaction and have a negative sense of the world as an unsafe and frightening place in which they are essentially powerless.

The following diagram represents what is occurring for the bully, the victim, and the bystanders. This process is represented as a downward spiral because, as the bullying becomes worse, so do the consequences for all concerned. Further, if the bullying is halted at stage five, for instance, then a person who has been victimised over a long period of time and has truanted to avoid his tormentors, has lost his confidence and is now performing poorly academically, will not automatically recover. All these areas of his life are now in deficit and need to be thoughtfully and supportively rebuilt. It is not an easy process.

The five stages	The person bullying	The victim of bullying	The bystander
Stage 1 **watching and** **waiting**	– getting a sense of classroom dynamics and identifying potential victims.	– settling in and unaware that may be being targeted for bullying.	– settling into school. – gives indications (body language or other signs) that is not prone to bullying.
Stage 2 **testing the** **waters**	– small symbolic acts of bullying. – enlisting support of others.	– does not handle symbolic act well. – is embarrassed and feels uncomfortable but hopes things will not get worse.	– feels uncomfortable but may withdraw or give some support to the bullying.
Stage 3 **something more** **substantial occurs**	– the bullying becomes physical and more serious. – victim is devalued, a non-person.	– feels useless, responsible for being bullied and guilty for not standing up to the bully(ies). – maybe they'll leave me alone. – they're only having a bit of fun.	– feels sense of powerlessness and guilt. – feels responsible for not interfering.
Stage 4 **the bullying** **escalates**	– the bullying becomes worse and the victim is hounded outside the school situation. – bullies are not stopped and get an unrealistic sense of their power.	– the bullying is clearly mean and intended. – growing sense of hopelessness and low self-esteem.	– feels bullying is part of life so best to protect yourself first. – so best to ignore the bullying and not support the bully. – victim is not worth supporting. – society based on fear.
Stage 5 **the bullying becomes** **fully established**	– bullying is extended into the wider world. – bullying is not tolerated, ends in criminal offending and imprisonment.	– the world is a horrible and unsafe place. – extreme and ultimate response is to attempt suicide.	– in society individuals are powerless. Look after yourself.

2.5 The Downward Spirals of Bullying

8. Can School Bullying Be Stopped?

Bullying can be stopped. The schools that do this most successfully are those which act with purpose and thoroughness. Central to effective anti-bullying initiatives is the concept of a whole school approach: all who are affected by bullying are included in developing an initiative and everyone is educated about it at the same time. There are many success stories of schools handling bullying effectively. The next part of this book shows how schools can produce such success for themselves.

Planning, Philosophy, and Policy

*'When everyone in the whole
school community has talked about
bullying, recognised it for what it is,
and decided to work together to combat
it, you can start to deal with it properly.'*

Mark Cleary, Principal,
Colenso High School, Napier

3 How to Create an Anti-Bullying Initiative

Introduction: Adopting a Whole School Approach

Once a school has decided to tackle bullying, it should clarify its philosophy, examine its strengths and weaknesses, and survey the nature and extent of the problem. It then needs to write an anti-bullying policy, and implement and maintain an anti-bullying initiative.

Research has found that when a school wants to create an anti-bullying initiative, a whole school approach produces the best results. Philosophically, the underpinnings of a whole school approach are the notions of inclusivity, ownership, and agreement.

Inclusivity

Although the person most affected by bullying is the victim, a number of other people are affected. It is important to include representatives of all groups in the development and implementation of an anti-bullying initiative (see 'Who Else is Affected by Bullying', Chapter 2).

Ownership

Those who are involved in developing an anti-bullying program are likely to feel that it is theirs. They will be loyal to it and interested in making sure it is well implemented.

Agreement

If schools fully embrace the processes of inclusivity and ownership through discussion, then eventually decisions can be made. The more opportunities people have to discuss ideas, the more chance there is of their arriving at an early consensus and beginning to work on the harder issues of philosophy, policies, and programs.

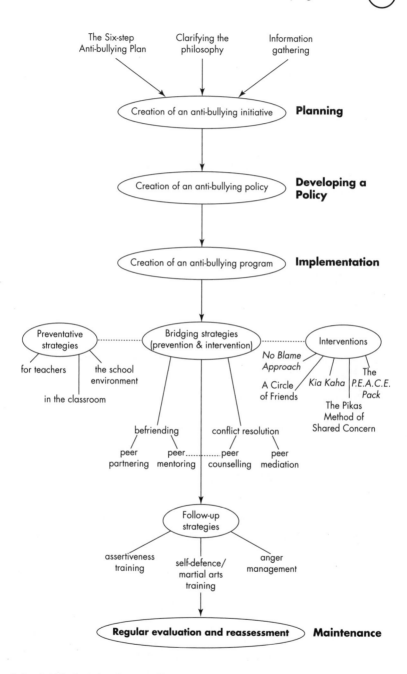

3.1 A Whole School Anti-Bullying Initiative

Summary

A whole school approach is ecological. One entity—in this case, bullying—is looked at not in isolation but in terms of its environment. It is approached consistently throughout the school, by staff and students, and their actions are supported and acknowledged by the wider community of families, community groups, and social services. A whole school approach to bullying may also lead to a decrease in other antisocial and problematic behaviour such as drug abuse and truanting.

The Six-step Anti-Bullying Plan

I have developed a six-step plan to help schools put an anti-bullying initiative in place. Central to this plan is the idea of having both a 'loose' and 'tight' approach. The loose aspect is that everyone who is interested is encouraged to participate and that ideas flow freely. The 'tight' aspect is that each step must be monitored and meet specific goals. The six steps and their components are as follows:

A. Planning

Step one: Preliminary explorations

- defining the philosophy and getting started

Step two: The first meeting, 'What are we going to do about school bullying?'

- the purpose of the meeting
- what we know about bullying
- what we can do about bullying
- establishing the anti-bullying committee
- appointing a working party
- establishing terms of reference
- deciding on a timeframe

B. Developing Policies and Programs

Step three: The anti-bullying working party gets to work

- establishing foundations: carrying out a SWOTSS analysis, a survey of bullying, writing a draft anti-bullying policy
- developing strategies for dealing with bullying: preventative strategies, interventions
- consolidating findings

Step four: Presenting a plan to the anti-bullying committee

C. Implementing the Initiative
Step five: The initiative is put into place
- disseminate the policy widely
- establish the practice

D. Maintenance of the Initiative
Step six: Evaluation and maintenance of the initiative

A. Planning

Step one: preliminary explorations

Defining the philosophy and getting started

Step one is a preparatory step. At this point the school should examine its philosophy and response to bullying. The philosophy is the foundation for all policy and practice in the school (see Chapter 4). This can be done through a meeting of staff and boards of trustees (or their equivalents), focusing on the current school charter as well as identifying the school's underlying ethos and intentions, with the aim of clarifying, redefining, and redirecting beliefs, goals, and values into a conscious philosophy.

A planning committee should organise an initial meeting of the school community to discuss the philosophy and the school's attitude to bullying. This committee should set an agenda and gather basic information about bullying (Chapters 2 and 5 of this book can be used for this purpose). Perhaps the most important consideration at this early stage is the need to generate enthusiasm and support.

It is crucial to cast the net widely, and that every family in the school community receives a written invitation to the meeting. Teachers, school administrators and auxiliary staff, school trustees/governors, and people from relevant community agencies (e.g. religious leaders, community police officers, and social workers) should also be invited.

Information should be sought on what schemes have been developed in other schools, locally and elsewhere. Which teachers or staff are keen to be involved? Are there any parents with relevant skills? Are there any government agencies with useful information or resources? (For instance, in New Zealand, both the Office of the Commissioner for Children and the School Trustees Association have carried out anti-bullying work, and the police have developed *Kia Kaha*, an anti-bullying scheme.)

The purpose of the first meeting will be to raise the issue of bullying in the context of the school's philosophy, and to get support for an anti-bullying initiative involving as many people as possible. Because it is important to keep to this brief, it is essential to find a good facilitator to run the meeting.

The aims of step one, then, are:
- to clarify the school's philosophy, particularly in relation to bullying;
- to gather and disseminate basic information about bullying;
- to get support for and arrange an initial meeting about the intended initiative; and
- to provide an agenda, a guest speaker (if decided), and a facilitator for the first meeting.

Step two: the first meeting, 'What are we going to do about school bullying?'

The initial meeting is very important. It is the first public airing of the school's concerns and it should be well run, with clearly stated aims and objectives. It should have a time limit (between one and two hours), with perhaps a fifteen-minute tea break in the middle. There should be specified times for agenda items, with reasonable gaps in between for people to comment or ask questions. Discussion and the exchange of ideas are very important, and an experienced facilitator will make sure that the items on the agenda are covered, that discussion takes place, that the meeting is not dominated by one or two individuals, that it does not go off on a tangent, and that it finishes on time. A possible agenda for the meeting follows.

The purpose of the meeting

First, the facilitator should explain why the meeting has been called. The concerns of teachers and parents about bullying should be raised, perhaps referring to a recent incident without identifying the participants. There should be a discussion of the school's philosophy on bullying and a clear statement of the school's intention to develop bullying policies and practice which reflect that philosophy.

What we know about bullying

A guest speaker could address the issue of bullying generally, or a teacher could use the information provided in Chapter 2 of this book (some of the diagrams would make good transparencies) to set the scene. This is meant as a brief introduction to issues; it should not dominate the proceedings.

What we can do about bullying

This part of the agenda should discuss what the school community can do to combat bullying and what the next step should be. A fairly open discussion is important here. People tend to have strong opinions about bullying and the discussion may become emotional or heated. Everyone should have a chance to talk. The facilitator must be sensitive to the concerns of irate parents but ensure that the proceedings move along within the timeframe prescribed.

Establishing the anti-bullying committee

An anti-bullying committee should be established from those attending the meeting, perhaps including members of the planning committee. The anti-bullying committee can be fairly large and inclusive. Its purpose is to oversee and support the development of an anti-bullying policy and program, which will be done through a working party. The committee will need to support the working party, to gather information for it, and to liaise with community members.

Appointing a working party

The next item concerns the setting up of a working party to examine the issues in more detail and to develop the ideas further. This tight group is complementary to the anti-bullying committee. Because the involvement of too many people would make the process cumbersome, the working party should be quite small but inclusive of the various groups in the school community. Six or seven members is about right: perhaps a parent, a mature pupil (for intermediate and secondary schools), the school administrator who deals with discipline (usually the deputy principal), a board of trustees/governor representative, and at least two teachers (including a guidance/pastoral care person).

Establishing terms of reference

For a working party to be effective, it must have clear and concise terms of reference, for example:

- to find out what the school's strengths are and what resources are already in place;
- to find out the school's weaknesses and whether more careful monitoring of bullying is needed (see 'Adapting the SWOT Analysis', Chapter 5);
- to find out the extent and kind of bullying in the school (see 'Survey and Questionnaire', Chapter 5);
- to develop an anti-bullying policy that is appropriate for the school;
- to suggest approaches that can be adopted in order to anticipate bullying and to make the school a safe place;
- to investigate what anti-bullying programs are available, how much they cost, and whether they work;
- to investigate what other resources (books, videos, reports) may be worth acquiring;
- to make recommendations about the various schemes;
- to consult widely and form small groups where appropriate for getting specific information (e.g. on the anti-bullying initiatives of other schools);
- to provide the anti-bullying committee with a draft report that outlines the working party's findings, and makes a set of recommendations for policy and program development.

It is also important for the school to give the working party a budget for the purchase of resources and training packages.

Deciding on a timeframe

It is important to work out a reasonable timeframe for the various steps. A draft timeframe should be presented to the meeting.

Although it is often useful to provide a timeline, I feel that each school should decide its own as part of the overall planning. Typically, the whole process may take from twelve to eighteen months.

The aims of step two are:
- to introduce the topic with clarity and enthusiasm;
- to provide opportunities for all to participate;
- to form an anti-bullying committee to provide basic support and information for the working party;
- to form a working party and to develop its terms of reference; and
- to give the working party a mandate to explore issues in depth before coming back to the anti-bullying committee with a draft anti-bullying plan that will include a draft policy statement and a program for dealing with bullying, plus a timeline.

B. Developing Policies and Programs

Step three: the anti-bullying working party gets to work

Establishing foundations

This stage is probably the most intensive and productive. A few individuals work together to develop a clearer picture of the school's strengths and weaknesses, and the nature and extent of bullying in the school. The aim is to draft an anti-bullying policy that addresses the needs of the school. Three stages are needed to make step three work.

Carrying out a SWOTSS analysis. In most schools, some teachers and administrators will have already developed strategies for preventing or dealing with bullying. It is important at this point to evaluate current school policy and practice, to ask such questions as 'What has been done about bullying to date?' 'How effective has it been?' 'What good policy and practice exists?' 'What else needs to be done?' and 'What are the areas of deficiency?' In the business world, SWOT analyses are used to find a company's strengths and weaknesses. The working party can carry out a similar exercise to assess the current state of the school. SWOT analyses are illuminating and will be useful for the school in other ways. I have developed a variation termed a SWOTSS analysis and provide an example of the findings from one school as an example of this exercise (see Chapter 5).

A survey of bullying. So far, bullying has been discussed both theoretically and anecdotally. Carrying out a survey will provide concrete information about the nature and extent of bullying in the school. I have developed a straightforward bullying questionnaire that will help this process (see Chapter 5).

Writing a draft anti-bullying policy. Now it is time to begin writing a bullying policy and to select appropriate strategies for putting the policy into practice. An anti-bullying policy should be based on the following considerations:
- the policy should reflect the philosophy of the school;
- the policy should take into account information about school bullying which has been gathered by the working party;
- the policy should address the legal requirements that the school must meet according to any legislation or binding regulations;

• the policy should be clearly stated, straightforward, and achievable.

Two examples of school anti-bullying policies are provided in Appendix I (and see Chapter 6).

Developing strategies for dealing with bullying

Various strategies can be used to make a school safe. Some of these are preventative, others are interventions, and still others are mixtures of the two.

Within the classroom itself, teachers can introduce programs and strategies to raise pupils' awareness of the dynamics of bullying, help them understand the various roles in the bullying scenario, and suggest solutions. Examples of these strategies are 'On the Bus' and the use of role play (see Chapter 8). It is also crucial for teachers to develop specific pedagogic practices and styles, and create an interesting and safe physical environment.

Within the peer community of the school, four strategies can be used: peer partnering, peer mentoring, peer counselling, and peer mediation. The least interventionist of these is peer partnering, and the most is peer mediation. These can be guided into place and supported by teachers but are run by students (see Chapters 10 and 11).

There are also numerous anti-bullying interventions that can be introduced to the school. These include:
• the *No Blame Approach* (see Chapter 12)
• Circle of Friends (see Chapter 13)
• the *P.E.A.C.E. Pack* (see Chapter 14)
• the *Kia Kaha* program (see Chapter 15)
• the Pikas Method of Shared Concern (see Chapter 16).

And, in cases where follow-up interventions are necessary, strategies such as assertiveness training, anger management, and self-defence are available (see Chapter 17).

Schools should investigate the range of what is available and make their own selection. (A synopsis of further useful programs and resources is given in Appendix II.)

Consolidating findings

The working party should put together a short report providing an overview of the working party's considerations and making a series of recommendations. This is intended to report findings and clarify and consolidate the thinking of working party participants. The report is also a means of sharing this with the wider committee/community and for defining a clear set of directives.

The aims of step three are:
• to examine the issues surrounding bullying and come up with an action plan for developing an anti-bullying policy in line with the school's philosophy;
• to report on the school's strengths and weaknesses in relation to dealing with bullying (a SWOTSS analysis);

- to provide a survey of bullying in the school;
- to write a draft anti-bullying policy;
- to make recommendations about what programs to adopt (preventative and interventionist) and practices to initiate;
- to recommend what other resources, such as videos, books, reports, articles etc., the school should acquire (shortlisted so that a selection can be made according to financial resources available); and
- to provide a short report containing this information.

Step four: presenting a plan to the anti-bullying committee

In this step, the working party reports back to the anti-bullying committee. Their report (see step three) can provide the basis for a discussion about the best course of action for the school. It is essential to debate the report as part of a refining process. For instance, the working party may have made suggestions that are too costly or too complex to put in place. The working party members may want to have the policy ratified and the program implemented right away, but the school authorities and the committee may urge a slower, more considered approach. Such issues must be debated. It is essential to be realistic and selective about goals.

After the report has been discussed, it is important to decide what will be implemented, how this will be monitored, and who will be responsible for the program as a whole and for the individual components. When staff become part of the implementation process, this work must be properly acknowledged as being part of an individual's workload.

The aims of step four are:
- to consider the plan and its recommendations;
- to debate the document;
- to consolidate the policy; and
- to plan for the implementation of the program.

C. Implementing the Initiative

Step five: the initiative is put in place

Disseminate the policy widely

Parents should be informed in writing about what the school intends to do. Alternatively or additionally, a public meeting could be held to provide information and to answer questions and discuss issues. (In New Zealand, Maori and Pacific Island people are much more receptive to an oral rather than a written interchange.) The policy needs to be widely disseminated.

This policy, in effect, becomes the school's contract with parents and pupils about school bullying. The school's obligations are to administer and support the policy and to carry out the letter of it. It is equally important that parents and children support the spirit of the policy. The policy should also be announced and talked about at a school assembly and in classrooms. The anti-bullying programs that have been selected should be introduced and described. It should also be explained how they reflect the anti-bullying philosophy and policy of the school.

Establish the practice

It is vital, now, to put the policy into practice, particularly in relation to already identified cases of bullying. Some pupils may 'push the boundaries' to test the policy and see if the school means what it says. Uniformity of response must be maintained across the staff. This period will be challenging, but if the school is consistent, the policy will retain its integrity.

> The aims of step five are :
> * to establish the policy and program in practice; and
> * to let people know that this is happening.

D. Maintenance of the Initiative

Step six: evaluation and maintenance of the initiative

Although, after a bullying initiative has been put in place, there is a sense that the work has been done and that it is time to move on to other things, it is essential to maintain rigorous support for the program. If not, the same old problems will recur. If a program is maintained, it will continue to work well, even when staff and pupils move on, although each new cohort of pupils and teachers will need to be introduced to the school's anti-bullying philosophy, policy, and programs.

Within the cycle of school management tasks, there should be regular evaluation of the extent of bullying and of the anti-bullying program to ensure that the latter is working and that it is not neglected in the face of concentration on other problem areas such as truancy or the use of drugs. Major evaluations should be carried out after eighteen months and after three years.

It is worth noting that introducing an anti-bullying initiative raises people's awareness of bullying in all its forms. As it becomes safe to report instances of bullying and people understand it better, a survey can give the impression that the rate of bullying has in fact increased. This impression is probably incorrect.

Research has shown that the full process of consolidation, development, and implementation can be long, and that monitoring provides useful feedback on the success of the implementation (see Pitts and Smith, 1995; Smith, 1999).

> The aims of step six are:
> * to maintain and modify the program as appropriate on a regular basis; and
> * to make sure that the school's anti-bullying initiative is explained to new pupils and teachers.

4 Clarifying a School Philosophy

Introduction

Every school has a philosophy about the purpose of education and how to go about delivering it. Often, however, it is implied rather than stated, so it is crucial to bring important philosophical issues to the surface and to encourage debate and make the philosophy explicit.

The nature of this philosophy will determine the school's attitude towards bullying. In setting up an anti-bullying initiative, visiting or revisiting the school's philosophy is the essential first step. In the same way that a house must have strong foundations before the rest of the structure can be built, a school must clarify its philosophy so that initiatives and policies can be developed out of this philosophy.

In developing a school philosophy on bullying, it is useful to look both inwards and outwards. Looking inwards means appraising and discussing the school's existing philosophy, and clarifying it into a general statement or charter. Looking outwards means examining what other schools have done and seeing what anti-bullying researchers and program developers have to offer. This means learning from others' experiences but making decisions for the culture of a particular school.

To assist schools in this process, I have created two models. In the first, I have developed a continuum. At one end is the dysfunctional school, at the other the safe school, and in the middle what I call the conflicted school. The school's philosophy is expressed outwardly in the atmosphere, or ethos, of the school. This model illuminates the relationship between the school's ethos and its approach to bullying.

The second model depicts three different philosophical perspectives on bullying behaviour: the punishment approach, the consequences approach, and the feelings approach.[1]

---

1 Rigby (1996) classifies bullying in a different way. He identifies three approaches which he calls the moralistic, legalistic, and humanistic approaches. Essentially, a moralistic approach attempts to apply moralistic pressures and to get the bully to conform with the moral code of the school. His legalistic classification would include both of my categories of punishment and consequences along a continuum of penalties. The humanistic approach is similar to my feelings approach.

The School Ethos: Identifying and Developing the School's Philosophy

When a school has decided to deal with bullying, it needs to be clear about its foundations—the values or beliefs of the school, its academic and educational aspirations, the nature of the personal relationships it fosters, and the societal attitudes and responsibilities modelled and taught at the school.

Recent bullying research has made an explicit link between the adoption of a whole school policy, the school's attitude towards bullying, and the successful implementation of effective anti-bullying programs. In the Sheffield project, for instance, it was found that the successful schools stood out because the attitudes, processes, and programs within them were consistent, positive, thorough, and well maintained.

In a follow-up study, Eslea and Smith (1998) revisited four primary schools from the original study. In two of the project schools, bullying had reduced further since the project had formally ceased; in one school, things had remained virtually the same; and in the fourth school, bullying had become worse. The authors concluded that the schools where bullying had continued to decrease were those where the policies and programs had been maintained and had even developed beyond the schools' initial involvement in the project.

Similarly, Duncan (1994), when discussing the use of the Pikas Method of Shared Concern in Tayside, Scotland, concludes that the schools where the method works best have a well-developed anti-bullying ethos and do not support a culture of bullying.

So what is meant by school ethos? It is the school's sense of itself as a community of educators, learners, and parents. Outwardly, this is manifested as the policies and programs of the school which, in turn, are grounded in the school's philosophy, its attitudes, beliefs, and values, and its vision of what it hopes to achieve.

The ethos of the school is usually set by its leadership: the principal, administrative staff, governors/board of trustees members, and senior teachers. It is also determined by the nature of the school community. A school's ethos is a fundamental determinant for the rate of bullying, truancy, and general disruptive behaviour. It is made explicit most clearly in the adoption of a whole school policy.

The following model shows how the development of a school ethos works.

Examining a school's philosophy is a useful exercise for a school to go through so that attitudes, expectations, and values are clarified. Without this process, misunderstandings and contradictions are likely to occur. For instance, if a teacher and principal give different explanations of the rules of the school to a pupil or a parent, this is not only confusing but also undermining. It suggests that the school is disorganised and lacks cohesion. It suggests a philosophical void rather than an ethical strength.

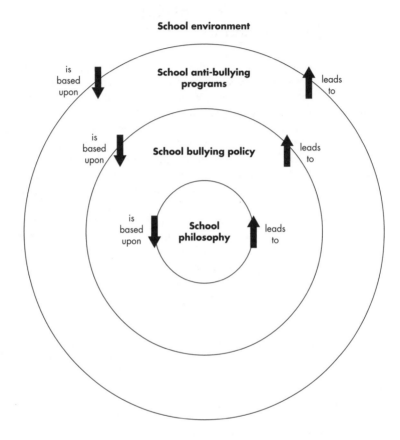

School environment

School anti-bullying programs

is based upon

leads to

School bullying policy

is based upon

leads to

School philosophy

is based upon

leads to

4.1 The Relationship between a School's Philosophy, its Anti-Bullying Policy and Programs, and the School Environment

Examining and clarifying a school's philosophy does not mean that everyone has to think the same or that rules become inflexible and discretion an anathema. What it does mean is that the participants in the school culture agree to play the same game, and that rules can be articulated into bullying policy. When the school's thinking is clear, then internal processes can be constructed and external programs and strategies chosen. The resultant philosophy and anti-bullying policies are consistent. As the processes prove successful, what happens every day in the school will also be founded on the philosophical foundations, policies, and programs. The ethos will inform the ethics, and each will reinforce the other.

Looking Inwards: The School Ethos and Its Relationship to Bullying

Some schools can set up effective anti-bullying initiatives, some choose not to, and some cannot. The following model of three hypothetical types of school ethos provides an insight into the types of issues schools face when they start to deal with a difficult and complex problem such as bullying.

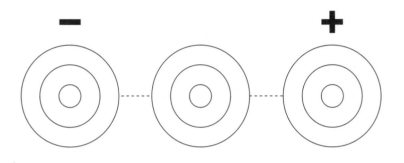

| The Dysfunctional School (The Do-nothing Approach) | The Conflicted School (The Half-measures Approach) | The Safe School (The Whole School Approach) |

4.2 The School Ethos: A Continuum

The Dysfunctional School: The Do-little/ Do-nothing Approach

The school's philosophy

At the negative end of the continuum is the dysfunctional school. A school may be classified as dysfunctional because of a number of characteristics. Research tends to suggest that such schools are located in very run-down areas where the social and economic malaise of the community is matched by the malaise of the school. Although a school in any area may win against the odds because of its philosophy and vision and the commitment of its staff, when it is poorly administered and lacking in morale, it is less likely to remain healthy and more likely to mirror any social problems that are part of the culture surrounding the school.

There may be alcohol or drug abuse and high unemployment in the community, and criminal activity among family members, including some of those still at school. Bullying may occur frequently, but it may be only one of an array of problems. For instance, the school may be subject to a high incidence of physical attacks upon teachers, theft, truancy, and vandalism. Such a school may find it difficult to attract and retain teachers and those who do stay may have low morale. Even young, committed teachers who have chosen this hard posting for idealistic reasons may find that so much of their time is taken up with crisis intervention that they cannot implement any proper change or follow it through.

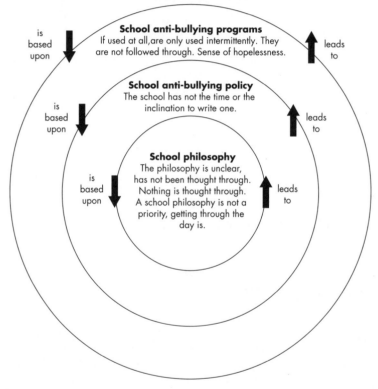

School environment
Children get bullied; high rates of physical, verbal and emotional violence occur. This is not a safe or happy school for pupils and teachers. Survival of the fittest is the rule.

is based upon

School anti-bullying programs
If used at all, are only used intermittently. They are not followed through. Sense of hopelessness.

leads to

is based upon

School anti-bullying policy
The school has not the time or the inclination to write one.

leads to

is based upon

School philosophy
The philosophy is unclear, has not been thought through. Nothing is thought through. A school philosophy is not a priority, getting through the day is.

leads to

4.3 The Dysfunctional School (The Do-nothing Approach)

If challenged, such a school would vilify bullying, but in fact it is dominated by a range of antisocial behaviours that are dealt with haphazardly or not at all. There is no coherent philosophy, and little commitment to developing one.

Developing a school anti-bullying policy
If such a school were to struggle towards a philosophy, it might find that staff are simply not available when they are needed. For instance, a meeting is called and the guidance counsellor cannot attend because there is a crisis elsewhere that she

has to handle. Most long-term members of staff have become cynical in their outlook, and are not prepared to try another 'do-good' effort; otherwise they are simply too overloaded and have low morale. In addition, there is very little will among parents to get involved in the school.

Choosing and implementing an anti-bullying program

The school has been assessed by government as needing extra support because of the difficulties described above, so some extra funding for running an anti-bullying program has been provided. The school buys a program but, although parents and staff are invited to a meeting to introduce it, attendance is poor and ongoing meetings are only sporadically supported. Against the odds, the program works well for the first three months, then loses impetus and eventually fails.

The school environment

For the top dogs, school is fun. The situation for everyone else is essentially survival of the fittest. Children are bullied on a regular basis, most often to extort food, money, and personal possessions, but students are also subjected to emotional and verbal abuse. Some children who have been badly bullied start truanting on a regular basis and eventually drop out. This school is an unsafe place for both pupils and teachers.

The Conflicted School: The Half-measures Approach

The school's philosophy

A number of schools I have come across in the last few years could be described as conflicted. This takes two forms:

- Different staff members in the school take conflicting positions.
- What the school says it believes in and what it does are contradictory.

In the first instance, the principal may not think there is a bullying problem in the school. This is because he believes that learning to stand up to bullying is character-building, and that the preoccupation with bullying is out of all proportion to the reality. He therefore thinks that it is not a major problem and that, if he waits, this misplaced concern will disappear. Several of the teachers think there is a bullying problem in the school, and want to do something about it. The principal, reluctantly bending to pressure from the teachers, allows an investigation and the development of an anti-bullying policy.

In this situation, anti-bullying initiatives could be undermined in the following ways:

- The principal could allow insufficient resources to be allocated to bullying so the job will not be done properly.
- He could allow meetings to be arranged to set up a bullying policy, but make them voluntary and out of teaching hours, not committing himself or other administrative staff to attending. This would give the message to the rest of the staff that the initiative is not important.
- In handling bullying, he could use different strategies than those decided by the anti-bullying team or suggested in the adopted anti-bullying program.

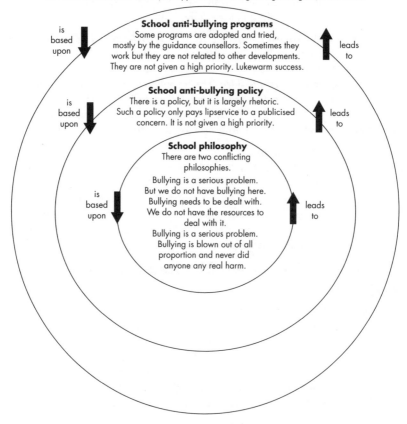

School environment
There is an awareness of bullying, but pupils feel that if they tell adults they will not
be safe from retaliation. The school appears to be doing the right thing but it is not safe.

School anti-bullying programs
Some programs are adopted and tried,
mostly by the guidance counsellors. Sometimes they
work but they are not related to other developments.
They are not given a high priority. Lukewarm success.

is based upon

leads to

School anti-bullying policy
There is a policy, but it is largely rhetoric.
Such a policy only pays lipservice to a publicised
concern. It is not given a high priority.

is based upon

leads to

School philosophy
There are two conflicting
philosophies.

Bullying is a serious problem.
But we do not have bullying here.
Bullying needs to be dealt with.
We do not have the resources to
deal with it.
Bullying is a serious problem.
Bullying is blown out of all
proportion and never did
anyone any real harm.

is based upon

leads to

4.4 The Conflicted School (The Half-measures Approach)

In the second instance, an anti-bullying stance is taken which is supported by policy, but contradicted by practice. Some conflicted schools rely very much on their academic or socio-economic standing and, while paying lip service to innovations and staff development, prefer to keep their culture intact. Such a school may handle bullying incidents when they arise in a piecemeal, unreferenced, and often ineffective manner but, if challenged about their interpretation of the event or their handling of it, will close ranks and write off the challengers (usually parents) as interfering, ignorant, or overprotective.

Such a school exhibits the following belief syndrome. *Ideologically*, the school does not approve of violence or cruelty in any form. *And because of this*, there is no bullying in the school. Redefinition of the event denies the existence of the phenomenon. Bullying only exists 'out there', in other 'bad' schools.

Developing a school anti-bullying policy

In the first instance, the school may go through the motions of developing an anti-bullying policy, and this process may be driven by one or two people who see bullying as an important issue. Here, the job of coordinating the initiative may be regarded as a voluntary activity, and in this way the school hierarchy signals that the initiative is not a priority. Teachers who in other circumstances might have become involved do not do so because the school leadership does not place enough value on the process. It is also difficult for teachers to fit it into their busy schedule. Such a policy is not fully embraced by the school.

In the second instance, the school may fully support the idea of developing an anti-bullying policy and involve the school community in doing this.

Choosing and implementing school anti-bullying programs

For the first school, the principal may provide money for staff training or the purchase of an anti-bullying program but perhaps not enough to develop the program fully. It will eventually fall to the guidance counsellor, the deputy principal, or a teacher to handle all cases of bullying and they may become overwhelmed and unable to act effectively because of other demands on their time. The bullying program may lose support because it is not considered important in light of other developments. If the guidance counsellor asks for more bullying resources the following year, she may be told, 'We did bullying last year and will be working on truancy this coming year'. Pupils may be encouraged to report incidents of bullying and begin to do so, but then find that the bullying is not handled properly and the bullies retaliate. In other words, if there is no thoroughly developed and implemented program for dealing with bullying, the initiative will probably fail in the long term.

For the second school, an anti-bullying program may be adopted but, when bullying occurs, it is usually ignored or handled badly. Only extreme cases of physical bullying are treated seriously.

The school environment

An outsider looking into these schools may see institutions that seem to be performing well. They may be located in affluent middle-class areas and, by the perceived important criterion, academic success, they do very well. There may be no immediately obvious signs of bullying, but physical and verbal bullying and bullying by exclusion are occurring just below the surface. The schools collude in pretending this is not the case.

Pupils know that, more often than not, teachers will dismiss reports of bullying. As a result, most students do not tell. They feel that, if they report an incident of bullying, it will probably not be resolved and the bullies will get back at them. Despite appearances to the contrary, for some pupils such schools are not safe places.

Some staff may feel disaffected because their extra work in the bullying program has not been appreciated or supported. Others may feel confused, defensive, and uneasy.

In some ways, a conflicted school is worse than a dysfunctional school because it makes the right noises and appears to be doing the right thing. Not only is the school's philosophy mixed and uncertain, but so are the messages, the policies, and the safety of pupils.

The Safe School: The Whole School Approach

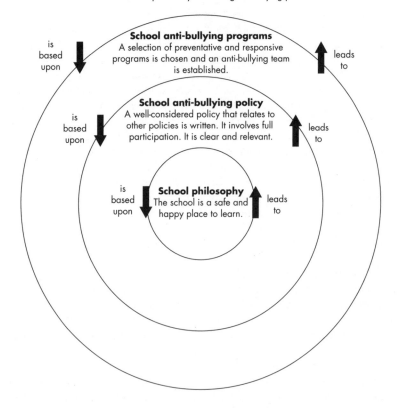

4.5 The Safe School (A Whole School Approach)

The school philosophy

The safe school is one that has adopted a whole school policy based on the philosophy of creating a school that is safe from bullying and supporting the development of each person towards their potential. Research indicates that, when a school takes the issue of bullying seriously and develops a thorough and inclusive anti-bullying initiative, it is most successful in combating bullying. In the whole school approach, everyone in the main and extended school (administrators, teachers, students, parents, and the community) is involved in all processes, from the early discussions, through the development and implementation stages. Everyone knows what the rules are because they have participated in generating them and so own and feel responsible towards them.

Developing a school anti-bullying policy

The development of an anti-bullying policy is a realistic set of understandings and expectations flowing directly and logically from the school philosophy. The policy will be clearly written and will relate, in its tone and intentions, to policies designed for other similar areas that put people at risk, such as alcohol and drug use, disruptive behaviour and fighting, and truancy. In other words, school policies will be integrated.

Choosing and implementing school anti-bullying programs

The logical follow-on is that the school develops and chooses a set of preventative and intervention strategies to implement. These programs should reflect the values and beliefs of the school community and the policies of the school.

The school environment

As a result of having a carefully prepared and implemented policy, the school will be safe from bullying. It will be bully-proof. The teaching staff and pupils will know what the rules are and will not be afraid either to intervene or to get help when bullying occurs. Pupils will be able to concentrate on their work without fear of being intimidated or bullied and there will be a culture of awareness. The school will understand that it is acceptable and expected that students can either intervene or tell an adult if bullying occurs.

> **Comment:** Smith, in a discussion of the interventions in the Sheffield project states, 'Generally, schools which put more time and effort into anti-bullying measures, and which consulted widely in whole school policy development, had the best outcomes in reducing bullying. Success in taking action required the commitment of at least one member of staff as coordinator of interventions against bullying, and the clear support of senior management for that person' (1999, p. 82).

Looking Outwards: What Approaches to Bullying Have Been Developed?

Three Ways of Dealing with Bullying

Essentially, three distinctive ways of dealing with bullying have been developed in recent years: the punishment approach, the consequences approach, and the feelings approach. The first two derive from a deficit perspective, which seeks to change behaviour rather than systems, and the third is an example of a constructivist perspective, which instead attempts to alter the ecology of the bullying environment and rid the system of the bullying dynamic. I will describe each of them and discuss their advantages and disadvantages.

The punishment approach

The punishment approach as a response to bullying reflects the criminal justice system. In the latter, if an offence is committed and the person is found to be guilty, he or she is punished by doing community service, paying a fine, or going to jail. The equivalent punishments in a school context are detention, extra homework, tasks around the school and, if the behaviour persists, suspension and expulsion. When I interviewed Angela Glaser, a counsellor at the London-based anti-bullying organisation, Kidscape, she clearly favoured this approach. She spoke to me about the horrific results of bullying that she had seen in some London schools. She felt bullying had to be dealt with harshly to make it clear that it would not be tolerated and that a punishment suiting the crime would follow. Several other people with whom I have discussed this issue have held similar views.

Bullying courts are an example of a punishment-based approach. Whereas in most of these approaches it is the school that metes out the punishment, in this case the peer group is put in the position of judge. The bully court concept was introduced in the UK by Laslett (1980), and brought to prominence by Michele Elliott, director of Kidscape (Elliott, 1989). In the bully courts, perpetrators of bullying are brought before a panel of their peers (with some teacher representation) and 'put on trial', as in a court of law. If they are judged to be guilty of bullying, a sentence is passed, e.g. staying in for an hour after school every day for a week and picking up litter in the school grounds. The intention is to let the bully know that, if they choose to bully, they will not get away with it but will be punished. It could be described as a short, sharp shock approach.

The consequences approach

When I spoke with Delwyn Tattum of the Cardiff Institute of Higher Education's Countering Bullying Unit, he described an approach to bullying that he calls crisis care (see Tattum and Herbert 1993, 1997). This is typical of what could be termed the consequences approach: if a student chooses to bully, then there have to be consequences. The distinction Tattum made between this approach and punishment-based responses is that consequences should be educative rather than punitive. In other words, rather than just listening to the circumstances surrounding a bullying incident and then punishing the bully, the intention is to let the bully know that there will be consequences (which may or may not be specified) if the bullying does not stop. The following is a description of crisis care:

I believe it's adults' responsibility not only to look after the children but also to introduce them to the difference between right and wrong. We've got to give them moral precepts, and if we don't say that certain behaviour is wrong then the chances are that while they might think it causes a little bit of distress, it's not too serious. We disagree with the whole idea there. The idea that we have, which is crisis care, is really a structured approach to gathering data and then supporting the victim and getting the bullies to change their behaviour because they see it is in their best interest [to do so].

We gather the data on a proforma ... on the nature and the extent of the bullying and the perceptions of the persons involved. ... [The proforma] is not a questionnaire which is [meant]to [provide a] survey in a school to get a profile of the school, but rather is to deal with any particular cases. ...

[Here is an example of how it would work.] You're the deputy head, and it's come to your attention that somebody is getting bullied and you've got to find out as near as you can the truth of the matter. You can't assume [anything but should investigate further]. After making some initial enquiries, let's say there is a girl and three young girls are making life miserable for her, you get the girl who is the victim to fill in the proforma about what happened, where it happened, these sort of things. And then quite separately you get the other three girls who have been making her life miserable, independently to fill in the same thing and to sign it and to date it. And then you look at it and ... make a decision about whether there are conflicting bits of information between the three girls. ... [Then] you get some of [the onlookers] to fill in [a proforma] so you get as detailed a picture as you can.

Once you've got that and you're convinced in your own mind that you've got a bullying case, you then meet the girl who's the victim and you say, 'Look, we'll give you all these different strategies for dealing with it. If things are a bit difficult to deal with at playtime or whatever, go somewhere else. Go to the art room or whatever'. ... The self-confidence of youngsters is sadly damaged by bullying because they can't cope, so the best thing is not to force them to try to cope unaided but to say, 'Get out of the situation if you can't cope. On top of that, we'll help you through every day, so come and see me at the end of every day, and if everything's gone OK, just give me a nod or a thumbs up or whatever, so you're not giving yourself too much trouble.' If it goes well for a fortnight, you can say, 'Come and see me at the end of the week'. And, hopefully, then their self-confidence is beginning to be restored.

Then as far as the bullies go, say, 'Look, I've got to monitor your behaviour. I'm going to monitor it in all kinds of ways and at the moment I want you to change your behaviour because what you're doing is quite unacceptable in the school. But I don't want to make life impossibly difficult for you by punishing you or by bringing your parents in or anything like that. But I want you to change your behaviour just as the victim is trying to change her self-image, self-confidence, self-esteem.' You want them to say to each other, 'Well, there's no mileage in this, let's leave her alone. There's lots of other things we can do.' The threat must always be twofold: one, 'The report will remain in your files and it will follow you through the school, but if after twelve months there is no repeat of this, then we'll destroy it. We won't damn you for the rest of your school career.' It is a sort of contract without being written down. 'If there's a repeat we'll send for your parents and we'll take it further. [We'll have you up] before the governing body and all kinds of other things so that your reputation will be a bad reputation and that is something you won't want.'

It won't work in every case, but the teachers and schools which have adopted it say that with the less serious cases of bullying it works. With the more serious cases which have been going on for a long time, and they are hard cases, it won't work. I think then you have to use all the forces you can muster (Tattum, pers. comm., 16 November 1995).

The feelings response

A third way of dealing with bullying can be termed the feelings response. The philosophy here is that, rather than punishing or providing consequences for bullying, it is more effective to appeal to the better nature of the bullies and to alter the bullying system. One of the characteristics of bullying is that those who bully usually see their victims as worthless, as non-people, a picture that the victims, in their despair, probably share. With a feelings approach, a major concern is to 'rehumanise' the situation. This means not only stopping the bullying but also aiming to change the behaviour of the perpetrator so that he or she empathises with the victim, feels what it is like to be bullied, has a sense of remorse, and comes to the realisation that it is wrong to bully. This change comes about not because of a fear of punishment or a wish to avoid inconvenient consequences, but because humanity is restored to the relationship.

Another important dimension of this approach is that tapping into feelings often extends to the peer group. It is not left solely to the one doing the bullying to learn how to empathise, but the supporters, reinforcers, and larger peer group are also drawn into the process of change.

George Robinson provides a useful overview of this perspective in the following description of some of the features of the *No Blame Approach*, which he developed with Barbara Maines (see Chapter 12).

The *No Blame Approach* sees the victim as an individual, but does not bring her in front of the group. It offers help and support. The *No Blame Approach* in no way blames the victim. The victim must never be expected to be able to change the behaviour so that the bullying stops. The victim may need lots of support and they may need to learn some social skills, but this is not part of the process of dealing with the bullying. If you are learning to drive, you aren't put on the motorway straightaway, you are put in a safe place, and that is the same with bullying. The victim has first to be put in a safe place, and not in the most difficult and stressful area of your life which is the dynamic situation you find yourself in with bullying.

The *No Blame Approach* isn't just sitting down and having a chat but uses a whole series of processes. When you talk to the young people who are involved in the bullying, who are part of the group, they say things like, 'I knew we weren't being very nice but we really didn't know the effect it was having on the person'. They show genuine surprise. And the other thing that comes over is that because you're clear about there being no punishment and no blame, the level of their fear and anxiety passes, and rather than being in a situation where they don't want to help they are now in a position where they do want to help. So I don't think it's just bringing a group of kids together for a little chat, it's also all the messages you are transmitting. If you all sit in a circle, then the symbolic message is that we're all here in a circle to talk about this and there is no power base, we're all equal, and we're here in this circle to sort it out (Robinson, pers. comm., 7 November 1995).

Discussion

I considered the above descriptions and thought, if I were a member of a group in a school whose job it was to decide on how to develop an anti-bullying initiative, what questions would I ask?

> I have read these descriptions with interest but would like a critique that describes the pros and cons of each approach. More specifically, what are the underlying characteristics of each approach?

The punishment approach
1. The bully must be punished for bullying, by detention, suspension, or expulsion (also known as exclusion) from the school, or by some other form of punishment.
2. The punishment is meted out by an adult with power (with the exception of the bully court).
3. The victim of bullying does not have any role to play, although he or she may have reported the bullying.
4. The intention of this approach is to make bullies stop bullying because they will be punished in an escalating fashion if they do not.

The consequences approach
1. The bullies must be made to change their behaviour or face the consequences, which could include a written record of the bullying and other punitive responses.
2. The consequences are meted out by an adult with power.

3. The victim of bullying is rescued by the adult running the program.
4. The intention of this approach is to make bullies stop bullying because there will be escalating consequences if they do not.

The feelings approach

1. The victim of bullying is encouraged to describe in some way how it feels to be bullied.
2. A group of peers including the bully is helped to understand how it feels to be bullied.
3. Rather than attributing blame, it is more important to find a solution.
4. The intention of this approach to make the bully stop bullying because the peer group suddenly understands what has been happening and learns to empathise with the victim. The dynamics of the situation change so that it is no longer easy or acceptable for the perpetrator to victimise others.

Are these three perspectives really distinctive and different from each other and, if so, how do they differ?

Clearly, there are differences between these three approaches, philosophically and fundamentally, and also in terms of the atmosphere they create and the outcomes they produce.

The punishment approach relies on an authoritarian figure upbraiding a bully and providing a punishment for the crime of bullying. When a person comes from a dysfunctional family where they receive mixed messages and do not feel loved, or a situation in which attempts to get the bully to empathise have not worked, then laying down the law may be a way of teaching right from wrong in a clear and structured way. It could be argued, however, that this approach is essentially the same as the act of bullying itself: it involves a person in power in some way hurting a person with less power.

The consequences approach also gives a clear message about the unacceptability of a certain type of behaviour. It is less authoritarian than the punitive approach, but is similarly static. Someone in power (often the deputy principal) has to deal with bullying as one more form of disruptive behaviour in which the perpetrator must be sorted out.

Both these approaches are essentially behaviouristic, that is, they both take a gamble on the chance that bullies will give up their antisocial behaviour because they know if they do not they will be punished, in the first instance, and face consequences in the second instance.

The only real difference between these two approaches is one of degree: punishment is immutable; consequences may, in the case Delwyn Tattum cites, be later removed from the record. In the first, the victim is avenged; in the second the bully may be redeemed. In both, behaviour is controlled through threats and manipulation.

Programs that use a feelings approach are grounded in an understanding that bullying is a dynamic situation, that there is room for manoeuvre, and that if the dynamics can be changed then it may be possible for the bullying to stop.

When I spoke with George Robinson about the relative merits of the different approaches, he suggested that it is often the parents of bullied children who want punishment and consequences, even revenge. They are one step removed from the bullying and see the effects of the bullying upon their child. Robinson argues that what the children want is for the bullying to stop.

If there is punishment or there are consequences for an incident of bullying, it is arguably only the symptom of the bullying rather than the bullying itself that is being addressed. This type of response also exposes bullied children to retaliation and revenge.

The feelings approach gives bullies a chance to understand what the effects of bullying are, to empathise, and to personalise. It also involves the onlookers, and makes it clear to them that they have the choice to support, to counter, or to do nothing. If the purpose of bullying someone is to gain peer approval, then the withdrawal of this approval will immediately undermine the bully.

In effect, the first two approaches deal with the events in isolation from the overall context, although getting a clear picture of what has occurred is important before making a decision about what punishment or consequences should follow. They take the situation as given and then attempt to change the behaviour of the bullies. The feelings approach is essentially a systems approach. The underlying intention is to change the dynamics of the situation, to raise awareness of the participants about bullying, and to support the peer group in taking responsibility for the bullying.

> **Do I really have to choose only one approach, or can I use whichever one seems most appropriate to each situation?**

Although I feel more attuned to programs based on the feelings approach, bullying is complex and comes from a much wider range of behaviours than those I have experienced personally. Therefore I may sometimes need a strategy that, although not my first choice, may provide a better solution to the particular problem. At the same time, however, I need to pay attention to my philosophical stance (or ethos) on human interaction and relationships. This is where my preference for the feelings approaches comes from: the accord with my ethos, and the consistency between my philosophy and the program that makes the most sense to me.

In some cases where a child needs to be given clear structures and boundaries, a behaviourist consequences approach may work well. The feelings approach is, however, more humane and problem-solving, and regards bullying as a dynamic that can be changed. Implied in this approach is an encouragement for people both to empathise with others and to take responsibility not only for their own actions but also for the actions of others in their peer group. It is potentially empowering, and presents what, to me, is a better paradigm of social interaction and the type of society I would like to live in. It has also produced many more useful anti-bullying materials than the punitive and consequences approaches.

5 Planning and Information Gathering

Introduction

The school can expedite the process of developing and planning policy first by examining its strengths and weaknesses, and gaining a clear, objective picture of itself; and second by gathering information about the nature and extent of bullying that occurs among the school population. It can achieve the first of these aims by running the educational equivalent of a SWOT analysis; and the second by administering a questionnaire throughout the school.

Adapting the SWOT Analysis for Planning and Policy in Schools

A SWOT analysis is a useful business tool that has been developed for strategic planning (see Thompson and Strickland, 1990) so that a company can examine itself closely in order to improve its competitive edge. Using the SWOT analysis process, a company can examine its strengths and weaknesses, and develop a strategy to minimise or change the weaknesses, and to build on and extend the areas of strength.

SWOT stands for strengths (S), weaknesses (W), environmental opportunities (O), and threats (T). SWOT analyses not only focus on the characteristics of the company itself, but also examine the environment in which the business is required to function. Strengths and weaknesses are internal characteristics which, when fully recognised and strategically altered, can improve the company's competitive advantage. A threat, on the other hand, is a condition or characteristic of the larger environment that can work to undermine the business's potential. An environmental opportunity is an aspect of the surrounding environment that, if harnessed, can enhance the company's strategic planning and improve its performance. In a school, the environmental setting as a competitive entity is less significant than in the business world, but it nevertheless remains a valid perspective.

An adapted SWOT analysis gives a school an objective picture of itself and helps it to identify its areas of strength and weakness. The school can then plan to build on its areas of strength and to correct its weaknesses. Because it is an empirical analysis, it can, for example, be used to look specifically at the physical environment of the school, the creative use of space both in buildings and in playgrounds (see Chapter 9), and the ratio of staff to students. And because it is also an impressionistic analysis, it gives access to such aspects as a sense of the character of relationships between peers and others in the school, the morale of teachers, and the role of parents.

In schools, a SWOT analysis can be usefully adapted to plan for the future, either on a large scale or, in this particular instance, in deciding how best to prepare for an anti-bullying initiative. For these purposes, I have added a step to the SWOT process that focuses on providing strategies and solutions (SS), which then makes it a SWOTSS analysis.

A SWOTSS analysis can be carried out in schools either by an individual or by an anti-bullying working party.

A Case Study of a SWOTSS Analysis

Here is an example of a SWOTSS analysis used to develop an anti-bullying initiative.

Te Aroha Nui School (a fictional name) stands on hilly farmland on the outskirts of a medium-sized New Zealand city. It is an area school with a population of approximately 300 students, fourteen full-time teachers, and three administrative staff. The school has a small kindergarten and full primary and secondary sections. Although the school does not appear to have a bad bullying problem, the teachers are aware that bullying occurs in all schools and that it is often not reported. There is a particular worry about the school's special needs children, some of whom are being bullied. The school has decided to find ways of improving its systems so as to create an environment that is not conducive to bullying, and to find better ways of detecting and monitoring bullying.

For the purpose of this SWOTSS analysis, I have included the greater school community, parents as well as teachers and students, in the school's internal environment. The external environment is the wider community and the larger social and political environment.

Strengths: internal and potential internal strengths

The school is small in population, considering it spans the years from the start of early childhood until the end of secondary school. It consists of smaller than average class sizes and has more voluntary parent participation than is normal. From the perspective of developing an anti-bullying initiative, the following strengths were identified:

- There is a positive school ethos. Students are taught responsibility with kindness, which means many older students take care of and have good relationships with younger children.

- There is an interesting and friendly school environment, with many diverse spaces and mini-environments in the school.
- The teachers are largely devoted to the children's well-being, have good intentions and are committed to their work.
- Several of the teachers have demonstrated skills in dealing with difficult issues such as bullying and are well liked by the students.
- The classes are smaller than the national average (twenty-two rather than thirty students).
- The school structure minimises stress for students at transition points: entering the early childhood sector, entering primary school, beginning intermediate school, and starting secondary school. At these times children can be vulnerable and at risk of being bullied. Having all sectors in one school largely removes the stress.
- Some teachers at the school use cooperative learning. By working together in a cooperative fashion, children learn to appreciate diversity.
- The school can afford to purchase anti-bullying resources. The school has an annual fair that raises money to support developments at the school. Some of this money could be used to buy anti-bullying resources.
- The teachers are involved in the school's decision-making processes, and are very democratic. Tasks are shared out among staff in an equitable way.
- There is strong support from parents, many whom are involved in the school on a voluntary basis, and can be called on to help monitor the playground and provide specialist resources to the school, e.g. acting, dance, music, and photography classes, and sports training.

Weaknesses: current and potential internal weaknesses
- The school is hard to patrol. It is spread out over a large area of varied terrain, and there are a lot of potential blind areas, nooks, and crannies, with many buildings. This means that there are many places where bullying could take place.
- The staff are not trained to deal specifically with bullying.
- Because there is no policy on bullying, it is difficult for teachers to be sure about what constitutes bullying, what the school's stance is in relation to bullying, what teachers should do to handle it, who people can approach to formalise a complaint about bullying, and what to do about contacting parents.
- The kindergarten, primary, and secondary sectors of the school are largely independent, making it hard to coordinate efforts. This would make it more difficult to implement an anti-bullying initiative consistently and thoroughly.
- There are a large number of competing demands on teachers' time: meetings, new initiatives, preparation and marking, speaking with parents, and time in the classroom.
- The school has good intentions but is often slow at getting things in place. This is partly a result of the school's democratic nature.
- Special needs children are bullied behind the teachers' backs.

Opportunities: current and potential external opportunities

- Some funding may be available to support the development of an anti-bullying initiative from the Ministry of Education, and grants can be applied for from charities (such as the New Zealand Lotteries Board). These could be investigated.
- Several parents are skilled in anger management training, anti-bullying work, assertiveness training, and counselling, and have contact with social agencies and knowledge about effective programs. They have been approached by the school and are willing to help develop an anti-bullying plan.
- There is a growing awareness of bullying in the greater school community. Partly because of recent media attention, most parents are aware that bullying is occurring in all schools. It is therefore an opportune time to develop an anti-bullying initiative and any efforts are likely to receive parental support.
- A lot of time, effort, and money has gone into research about bullying and to develop anti-bullying programs for schools. Using money from the school budget selectively to purchase books on bullying and kits for dealing with bullying would provide a useful resource base for the school.

Threats: potential external threats

This dimension was the least relevant of the four because, unlike businesses, schools are only minimally in competition with each other. However, the following external issue was identified:

- If the school addresses bullying, it could be thought that it has a bullying problem. Rather than being seen as proactive and responsible, the school could be labelled as a 'bullying school'. Since funding is directly related to the number of students in the school, bad publicity could have a detrimental economic effect if parents choose to send their children to other schools.

Strategies and solutions

Preventative measures

- Peer support. A class-to-class buddy system could be developed using the wide age range of the children within the school. For example, Class 5 could develop a caring relationship (buddying) with Class 1. This would be a beneficial and learning process for the children in both classes.

    This relationship could be maintained throughout the children's school careers. From a bullying point of view, it would mean that a younger child who was being bullied would have someone they could turn to for advice (see Chapter 10, 'Peer Strategies: Befriending'). Mount Roskill Grammar School in Auckland, which was voted the best New Zealand school in 1998, is well known for its buddying system.
- School policy on bullying. Clearly, it is important to develop and write a whole school bullying policy that outlines the importance of making the school a safe environment for all of its members, and identifies the rights and responsibilities of the various groups.

- More teachers in the playground. To make sure that the opportunities for bullying are minimal, it is important for teachers to be more visible and involved with children out of the classroom. Because the school grounds are spread out, teachers need to patrol widely so that potential danger spots are not overlooked.
- Monitor system in the playground. It was suggested that selected senior students be given responsibilities for playground and classroom supervision of younger children. This could operate in a similar fashion to bus monitors, which is already a success. Bus monitors note and report misbehaviour and reinforce good behaviour. (This recommendation was made with a note that it needed to be examined more carefully before being introduced.)
- More combined outing activities. There was a suggestion that more activities be arranged in which different classes go out and do activities together, such as beach outings, sports days, and walks. This concept is already in place but could be greatly expanded. In 1998, for example, four Class 12 students with outdoors skills took part in the week-long bush camp of Class 8 students.

- Allocate funds for an in-service course in cooperative learning, which encourages children to appreciate the particular skills and differences of others. It was suggested that teachers with cooperative learning experience share this with other teachers and that the possibility of in-service training in cooperative learning be explored.

- Parent involvement in lunchtime activities. Parents could become involved with generating and running interesting activities, such as teaching children games, and taking small groups for various indoors and outdoors activities. It would be important to consider what and who is appropriate.
- Address the anti-bullying requirements of the special needs children. There should be a consciously constructed program for teaching and demonstrating to children how to behave with people who have various disabilities. This could be done in class or through assemblies. Some of the children with disabilities have been mercilessly teased, largely because some of the others have not been taught how to relate to them. It would also be useful to invite visitors who have struggled to overcome a disability to speak to an assembly.
- Creating foundations of mutual support with the parents. Early networking and discussion could prevent later problems with issues such as bullying.

Interventions
- Adopting the *No Blame Approach*. The *No Blame Approach* video and booklet have been shown to the teachers and have been discussed (see Chapter 12). It will be recommended that the school adopts this as a major strategy. Even though it is an overseas program, the school regards it as its first choice after having considered several others. There was some concern that the program would be too old for kindergarten children and that a similar program should be found for them.

Conclusion

A number of strategies and solutions have been suggested as a result of using the SWOTSS process. At this point an important consideration is how best to continue. Is it better to plan to introduce a number of strategies over a specified period of time, or to adopt only one strategy and do it thoroughly and well, before moving on to another?

Survey and Questionnaire

As well as a clearer picture of its strengths and weaknesses, a school needs to have some idea of the nature and extent of its bullying before it can plan for appropriate policies and initiatives. The results of a questionnaire, once collated, are an important record of the state of the school at a particular time, and can also be used to support the argument for a whole school policy and an anti-bullying initiative. Once an initiative is implemented, the collated first survey can be used for comparative purposes.

A questionnaire should be designed not only to elicit information about who bullies, where it happens, when it happens, and how often, but also to outline the types of bullying there are and therefore educate children about what is and is not bullying. A questionnaire must be clear and simple for ease of understanding by those taking the survey; for ease of generating statistics, for those who have to add everything up; and for ease of interpreting, when the information is presented to parents, staff, students, and trustees/governors.

The following questionnaire was written with secondary students in mind, and can be altered and adapted for younger age groups as necessary. Once the questionnaire has been completed, the same basic form can be used to record the total responses to each question for statistical purposes.

Questionnaire About School Bullying   **Form/Grade_____**

Introduction: This school takes bullying very seriously and we wish to know how much bullying is taking place in the school. Bullying can be hitting, kicking, or the use of force in any way. It can be teasing, making rude gestures, name-calling, or leaving you out.

Bullying means that these things happened more than once and were done by the same person or persons. Bullying means to hurt, either physically or so that you feel very bad.

This is an anonymous questionnaire. This means that you can answer the questions but you don't have to let us know who you are. There is a blank for your name, however, so if you are having a problem with bullying you may wish to put your name in so that we can help you to sort it out. If you do this, it will be kept confidential. We will not give any information to anyone or do anything without your agreement.

Name: _____
(give your name only if you wish)

1. Are you a boy or a girl? (circle one)   boy   girl

2. How old are you? _____

3. Which form/grade are you in? (circle one)

   3rd   4th   5th   6th   7th

4. Since I have been at school, I have been bullied (circle one of the following):

   never   once in a while   about once   more than
                                  a week   once a week

5. I have been bullied in the following ways (tick ✓ yes or no for each category):   Yes   No
   –hitting (punching, kicking, shoving)
   –a knife or a gun or some kind of weapon was
     used on me
   –mean teasing
   –purposely left out of things
   –had my things damaged or stolen
   –was horribly sworn at
   –had offensive sexual suggestions made to me
   –had a nasty racial remark made to me

–received nasty (poisonous) letter(s)
–someone said nasty things to make others dislike me
–had untrue and mean gossip spread about me
–I was threatened
–had rude gestures or mean faces made at me

–anything else (write it in here) _____

6. Since I have been at school, I have bullied someone (circle one of the following):

    never   once in a while   about once   more than
                                   a week   once a week

7. I have bullied someone in the following ways (tick ✓ yes or no for each category):   Yes   No
    –hitting (punching, kicking, shoving)
    –use of a knife or a gun or some kind of weapon on
      someone
    –mean teasing
    –purposely left someone out of things
    –damaged or stole someone's possessions
    –swore at someone
    –made offensive sexual suggestions to someone
    –made a nasty racial remark about someone
    –sent nasty (poisonous) letter(s)
    –said nasty things to make others dislike a person(s)
    –made up and spread untrue and mean gossip about
      someone
    –I threatened someone
    –made rude gestures or mean faces at someone

    –anything else (write it in here) _____

8. Since I have been at school, I have seen bullying take place (circle one of the following):

    never   once in a while   about once   more than
                                   a week   once a week

9. I have watched or have heard about the following types of bullying (tick ✓ yes or no for each category):   Yes   No
    –hitting (punching, kicking, shoving)
    –use of a knife or a gun or some kind
      of weapon on someone .
    –mean teasing
    –someone purposely being left out of things
    –someone having their things damaged or stolen

−someone being horribly sworn at

−someone having offensive sexual suggestions made to them

−someone having a nasty racial remark made to them

−someone receiving nasty (poisonous) letter(s)

−someone having nasty things said to make others dislike them

−someone having untrue and mean gossip spread about them

−someone being threatened

−someone having rude gestures or mean faces made at them

−anything else (write it in here) _____

10. Tick (✓) all places where you have been bullied or have seen bullying take place:

	have been bullied	have seen bullying take place
−in the playground		
−in the corridors		
−in the classroom		
−in the locker room		
−in the toilets		
−on the way to school		
−on the way home from school		
−on the bus		

−anywhere else (write it in here) _____

11. Where are the 'danger spots' where most bullying takes place? Please list these:

1. _____

2. _____

3. _____

4. _____

5. _____

6 A School Policy on Bullying

Introduction

A written anti-bullying policy is a very important document, the school's equivalent of an act of parliament. It states the school's intentions and how it will enforce and uphold its rules and processes; what teachers', students', and parents' rights and responsibilities are; and what procedures are in place. It is, in effect, a contract between the school and its community.

After the school has clarified its philosophy and gathered information about itself and the bullying that occurs in the school, the next step is to create a school policy on bullying. Several stages will be necessary: consultation, discussion, and writing a policy. Once the policy is written, the stages of implementation, and monitoring and maintenance will follow.

In this chapter, I will discuss how to go about creating a school policy, what and who should be included in the various stages, and the steps that follow. I will also provide a school policy generated from this process (see Appendix I for examples of two school anti-bullying policies).

Stage One: Consultation

In order to be effective, the policy has to be a whole school policy. All groups and individuals who will be affected should be consulted, including those identified by the ripple effect (students, teachers, parents, and the greater school community). The implementing, running, and maintaining of the school's anti-bullying initiative will largely be the responsibility of the teachers (and, in the case of peer programs, the students with support from teachers), and policy development is the time and place for parent and community input. Consultation can be done through group meetings, interviewing individuals, surveys, and through carrying out brainstorming sessions in focus groups. Part of the consultation process should be to educate people about bullying so that the suggestions and advice are based on a good understanding of what bullying is.

The Students

Students do not report most of the bullying that occurs so, if they are asked to contribute to the development of a bullying policy, it shows them that the school is serious about stopping bullying and that their input is valued.

Students can be asked, in classes or smaller groups, to discuss and think about bullying. This can be done through self-selected or nominated groups, structured sessions, or through the use of questionnaires. Ideas and issues that arise can be used to keep the momentum of discussion going. It is important (perhaps through school assemblies) to keep the whole student population informed of the process. There should be several helpful outcomes:

- the students, who know most about bullying, can contribute to the process;
- a clear message that the school really cares is the first step in creating a safer environment; and
- some very useful ideas and information are likely to come out of this process.

The Teachers

Teachers' input is as crucial as that of the students, for several reasons. Teachers will be generally responsible (the classroom teachers) and specifically responsible (the counsellor and the deputy principal) for dealing with bullying when it occurs, and for running any anti-bullying programs adopted by the school. They will be seeing that the school policy is implemented, and constructively and consistently supported. They have a good knowledge about bullying in general and where it is likely to occur. They understand how students interact and have specific knowledge about the relationships among their student population. They often know who is likely to bully or be bullied. They are also familiar with the school's regulations and requirements.

The Administrators and Governors

The people who run the school, either as part of the management team or as a member of the board, are ultimately responsible for the school meeting its responsibilities to its community and to government. In particular, their expertise should be used to consider the legal implications of a bullying policy. It is also their job to make sure the school has the resources to put any program in place. By being involved in the development process, this very important group is better able to support and understand the intentions of the policy.

People who are elected to boards usually have prestige and status in a particular area (accountancy, law, medicine, or public administration, for instance), but in educational terms they tend to be generalists. Although they are valued for the specific skills they bring to the school, their role as overseers of school policies is even more valuable. They can make sure there is consistency with other school attitudes and responses when initiatives such as an anti-bullying policy are introduced, or when they are consulted on specific incidents of bullying.

The Parents

Parents must be involved in the process from the start. In the ripple effect of bullying, they are described as secondary victims of bullying. They are usually willing to become involved in making suggestions if their child has been bullied, but it is better that their involvement occurs earlier, when policy is being developed.

In a multiethnic school, parents can also present perspectives from other cultural points of view.

The Wider Community

Within the wider community, there may be experts who can contribute their knowledge to the policy-making process. Some social agencies may deal with bullies who get into trouble elsewhere, and offer useful resources such as anger management programs which can be used to deal with a bullying problem. This means, too, that the community knows that the school is handling bullying in a positive and proactive way, which can help agencies outside the school.

Others from outside the school are also important in the process. In a multi-cultural school, for example, representatives of the different cultures may want to be involved. In New Zealand, a kaumatua (elder) from a Maori student's tribe may be willing to help with a bullying problem. (A similar process of tribal involvement and responsibility has been introduced in the criminal justice sector.) In many Pacific Island communities, if one person transgresses then the family as a whole takes responsibility for the misdeed. Therefore the involvement of such people and their presence as resources for the school are critical. In a multicultural setting, building on cultural knowledge is both helpful and essential.

Stage Two: Discussion

The working party can discuss the various perspectives and results that come out of consultation. They can also refer to work other schools have done, and to theoretical work from other sources (e.g. Sharp and Smith, 1994; Rigby, 1996). The school may already have a policy on bullying that needs revision or a related policy on disruptive behaviour. All relevant matters should be thoroughly discussed before moving to the next stage. This can be done by an anti-bullying working party (or individuals given this task) and taken to the larger anti-bullying committee.

Stage Three: Writing an Anti-Bullying Policy

Once all the information has been gathered, it is possible to write a clear, straightforward, and useable policy document (after Rigby, 1996).

A statement about bullying and the school's intention
This school believes that, in order for students to learn to the best of their ability, they must have a safe and friendly environment in which to spend their time. In order to do this, we declare the school to be a no-bullying zone.

We have discussed matters thoroughly with the school's community—students, teachers, parents, trustees, and the wider community—and, in order to make the sort of school we all want, we have created an anti-bullying policy. In this policy, we have made a statement about what bullying is and what people should do when they experience it or see it happening or hear about it.

A Definition of Bullying

Bullying is a conscious and wilful repetitive act of aggression and/or manipulation by one or more people against another person or people. It is also an abuse of power by those carrying out the bullying, which is designed to cause hurt.

Bullying contains the following elements:

- harm is intended;
- there is an imbalance of power;
- bullying is often organised and systematic;
- bullying is repetitive, occurring over a period of time; or it is a random but serial activity carried out by someone who is feared for this behaviour;
- hurt experienced by a victim of bullying can be external (physical) or internal (psychological).

Bullying can be either physical or non-physical:

- Physical bullying can include biting, hair-pulling, hitting, kicking, locking in a room, pinching, punching, pushing, scratching, spitting, or any other form of physical attack. It also includes damaging a person's property.
- Non-physical bullying can be verbal, which includes abusive telephone calls, extorting money or material possessions, intimidation or threats of violence, name-calling, racist remarks or teasing, sexually suggestive or abusive language, spiteful teasing or making cruel remarks, and spreading false and malicious rumours.
- Non-physical bullying can also be non-verbal, which includes making rude gestures and mean faces; manipulating relationships and ruining friendships; purposely and often systematically ignoring, excluding, and isolating someone; and sending (often anonymous) poisonous notes.

Bullying can be any one of the above or a combination of them. It includes racist bullying, sexual harassment, bullying of special needs children, and the bullying of children with a different sexual orientation.

Rules and Regulations for Dealing with Bullying

Rules for students

Students have the right not to be bullied in any way or by anybody. Bullying is harmful to everyone, in both the short and long term. No one has the right to bully anyone else. All cases of bullying brought to the school's attention will be taken very seriously and all necessary steps to stop it will be taken.

In order to stop bullying happening, it is important for students to know that it is not only all right to tell, but also important to do so. The unwritten rule of the code of silence for many students is 'Don't tell adults about things that are occurring in your group', 'Don't rat on your mates'. The best weapon bullying pupils have is their misuse and abuse of this code of silence. No one has the right to be protected by their peers when they physically or psychologically abuse others.

If students are being bullied or know of instances of bullying, it is important to tell somebody. Bullying only gets worse if it is not stopped, so it is important to do this right away. You can do this by asking to speak to a teacher, by taking a friend in trouble to a teacher, by making an appointment with the deputy principal or another person you trust, or by asking your parents or a close family member to help you follow things up. All incidents of bullying brought to the school's attention will be investigated and will be taken seriously. In dealing with such matters, confidentiality for those concerned will be safeguarded.

A strong anti-bullying stance by students contributes in a major way to making the school a safe place. Another major weapon of those who bully is that they are sometimes 'tougher' than their peers, and individual bullies often have a small group who support and encourage their bullying behaviour. If most students decide that bullying is not acceptable and support each other in letting adults know or in intervening assertively and showing their disapproval, much of the bullying will stop.

What parents need to know

If you know or suspect that your child is being bullied, contact the school immediately. You can contact your child's teacher, the deputy principal, or the guidance counsellor. We take bullying very seriously. All matters will be thoroughly followed up and appropriate action taken. We will also assure confidentiality in our contact with you. When the school knows or suspects that a child is being bullied, they will contact the parent(s) of the children involved, seek their advice, and support and keep them informed of progress with the handling of the bullying.

What teachers need to know

Bullying can grow to become very serious or it can be nipped in the bud. If teachers know of bullying or suspect that it is occurring, they should report this first to the deputy principal. After discussion, it may be decided the teacher can handle the bullying satisfactorily. A brief report is important so that the matter is on record: if another incident flares up later it can be seen as part of a pattern, not an isolated occurrence. This is not intended to label people as victims or bullies but it is important to track bullying behaviour.

Because teachers cannot be everywhere at once and because bullying is often a clandestine activity, it is important for teachers to encourage students to tell about bullying.

The Process

The process for dealing with cases of bullying is:

1. The bullying must first be reported to the deputy principal.
2. A brief report will be made detailing the nature of the bullying, who was involved, and what happened. This should go on file.
3. It is important to inform parents that bullying has occurred and that it is being dealt with.
4. The teachers of those involved and the deputy principal or guidance counsellor should discuss how best to find a solution to the bullying. Together they can devise a strategy which may call on a program that the school has adopted.
5. If, after adopting a course of action, the bullying has been resolved, a report should be written and put on file.
6. If the bullying is not resolved, those trying to find a solution will need to meet again to decide what should be done.
7. When a solution is found, a report should be written. At this point it should be decided if backup strategies are needed (e.g. anger management, assertiveness training, self-defence or martial arts training, see Chapter 17).

Stage Four: Implementation

An anti-bullying policy should clearly outline the school's attitude and intentions towards bullying. Teachers, students, parents, and the wider community should be informed about the policy, and their help in developing it should be acknowledged. When it has been accepted, it must be implemented and become the reference point for the handling of all cases of bullying in the school.

There may be teething problems at first. The policy may be challenged, for instance, by those found to be bullying, or their parents. It is important to adhere to the policy so that students can see that if they do take a stand, then they will be fully supported by the school and will not be at risk of retaliation from the bullies.

Stage Five: Monitoring and Maintenance

Policies are developed and written on the basis of information available at the time. When they are being implemented, changes will need to be made to accommodate unforeseen circumstances and dynamics. A policy should be a living document, that is, refined and updated on a regular basis. If a policy and program have been well thought through and are seen to be working, this momentum will keep them going; however, it is also important to maintain and support them, and to continue the process of monitoring and evaluation.

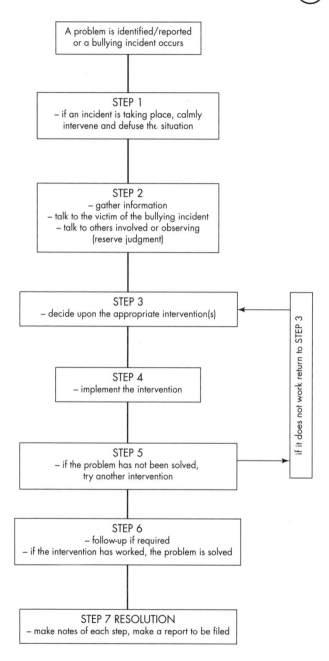

6.1 A Step-by-Step Guide to Handling a Bullying Incident

part 3

Preventative Strategies

'If you can understand the system, then you can understand everything. This is about the mirror. If I am the bully, then you are the victim. This has been the bilineal process that has dominated our society for centuries. Now our society is changing. While I am the bully and you are the victim, there is another there, the onlooker. Now what needs to happen is for this third person, the onlooker, to involve themselves.'

Paddy Paltridge, psychodrama
practitioner and teacher

7 Strategies for Teachers

Introduction

This chapter examines strategies teachers can use to help them understand the social relationships in their classrooms; to encourage prosocial functioning at the individual, group, and class level; and to find answers to problems that arise. The strategies discussed in this chapter are reflective practice, Circle Time, cooperative learning, and the use of sociometry. First, I will examine recent research which indicates that many teachers do not understand how bullying works and fail to deal effectively with it.

The Teacher as Ineffective Practitioner

Several international studies show that the great majority of bullying is not reported to teachers or is not noticed by them. A Canadian study which video-taped children playing at school (Craig and Pepler, 1995; Pepler and Craig, 1995) indicated that duty teachers were aware of only a small percentage (17 per cent) of the playground bullying observed by the researchers. What is more, for the incidents they did witness, they chose to intervene only 23 per cent of the time. This means that, overall, teachers intervened in only 3.9 per cent of the bullying. These observations are supported by evidence from another Canadian study (Bentley and Li, 1995) in which 31.5 per cent of children who were victims of bullying reported that teachers almost never tried to stop it.

As a first step in handling bullying, it must be clear that the school will intervene and that it has strategies for dealing with bullying. Because teachers are often the first point of contact for bullies and their victims, it is crucial that teachers know what to do and are supported by their schools in doing so. It is not helpful if teachers and schools do not respond when bullying occurs, or if teachers completely ignore instances of bullying and say they 'don't want to know', or if they respond to those who have sought help by telling them to sort things out themselves.

Sometimes, when teachers do intervene, the outcome is not successful. There are many reasons for this, some of which are the responsibility of the teacher.

Failure is most frequent when teachers respond irresolutely and half-heartedly to a problem that needs to be thoroughly followed through. This may be because they do not fully understand what bullying is, or are swayed by the deceit and lies that are part of the bullying culture.

In one case, a fourteen-year-old girl whom we shall call Tania was harassed every afternoon on the school bus by two younger boys aged eleven and twelve. They made lewd remarks and gestures that grew more obscene every day, until eventually she lost her temper and let loose with a tirade of swear words. Although she had retaliated and left the boys stunned, Tania was very upset and told her parents about the boys. Her parents contacted the boys' teacher who said that Tania must have identified the wrong boys, that one of the boys in particular was very well behaved and always pleasant and would never indulge in such rudeness. The teacher also stated that, because Tania had sworn at the boys, she was a guilty party and had to accept some blame.

Tania's parents pointed out that, whatever their daughter had done, she was not to blame for the incident on the bus. They decided to go to the principal to get the incident properly dealt with, and even he said that Tania must have made a mistake: the ringleader would never behave like this. Her parents insisted that she had not and asked the principal to follow it up. He did, with the two boys, and the boys' parents, who were very upset with Tania's parents for involving the school. The boys did not trouble Tania again.

Six months later, an incident occurred in the school playground when the ringleader viciously attacked a younger boy. He was dealt with very severely by the duty teacher. Several other children then came forward to say he had been bullying them. Soon after this his parents removed him from the school.

In this case, the victim was not believed because the boy she accused of bullying had convinced all the teachers at the school that he was a 'good boy'. Tania was also held responsible for the unpleasantness of the incident and its follow-up because she had sworn at the boys. It was only because her parents fully supported her that anything was done, although the school espoused an intolerance of bullying, and some teachers went as far as to say that there was no bullying in the school.

Sometimes teachers contribute directly to the bullying dynamic themselves, in two main ways. They misunderstand the symptoms exhibited by bullied children and treat them as annoying or wilful; or they are not fully empathetic to bullied children (and in some cases blame them for their victimisation), thus exposing them to further victimisation.

A common occurrence, especially in girls' bullying, is that children are systematically isolated from the group. Besag (1989) observed that such children are not only most at risk of being bullied at school but are also most likely to be misunderstood by their teachers. She states, 'The shyness or confusion of such children can lead to them being thought of as stupid or, in some cases, disobedient' (p. 117). These children are then the victims of both the social world of their peer group, and of their teachers. If teachers choose to ignore such children or treat them as stupid or disobedient, they reinforce the behaviour of the peer group and condone the bullying of that child.

Another way in which teachers can contribute to a bullying culture is when they do not feel truly empathetic towards the child being victimised and in fact think that the child is at least partly to blame for the victimisation. In one case, a teacher waited until the girl in question was away from school, and told the class that she was having problems, had no friends, and needed them all to be nice to her. She told some of the girls she thought it would be helpful if they gave their erstwhile victim 'smiling lessons' and 'making friends lessons'. When the girl returned to school, she was distressed to hear what had happened, was treated to patronising and bossy do-gooder behaviour for two or three days, told that her only problem was that she did not wear 'label' clothes, and was then mercilessly excluded and ridiculed all over again. The teacher had stripped her of any remaining defences and exposed her to the group (see Sullivan, 1998).

Some teachers control their classes by using their greater verbal and intimidatory skills to bully some children, in effect role modelling bullying behaviour to the class and inviting others to ridicule a child as the teacher has done.

The Teacher as Reflective Practitioner

Teachers must not only deal with the academic needs of the children in their care, but also understand what goes on in their classroom so that it is a safe environment for everyone.

Central to education today is the concept of the teacher as reflective practitioner (see Schon, 1983). This means that, when teachers are faced with small or large problems (both in learning and children's peer relations), they call on their problem-solving skills, reflect on their teaching experiences (or refer to a more experienced colleague), and use current educational research which focuses on their problem area. By using reflective practice, teachers can construct their classrooms in such a way that they anticipate and prevent bullying, or deal with it effectively when it does occur.

Tapping into the Experience and Common Sense of Teachers

In the case study of a bullied child in a New Zealand school (see Sullivan, 1998), the nine-year-old passive victim of bullying (Sarah) was found to be systematically isolated and ridiculed with very mean intent by her peer group, and either patronised or rejected by her teacher. When her parents spoke to the principal, he brought in the class teacher and the deputy principal. Together they closed ranks and said that Sarah had been a worry to all her teachers since she was a new entrant, and that it was a psychological rather than an educational problem. The school put what was an act of bullying by a group of nine- and ten-year-old girls in the too-hard basket. They called in an educational psychologist who observed Sarah's isolation and unhappiness, and the principal told her parents that the case was outside the school's spectrum of expertise and therefore not its responsibility. They also reframed this concerted and long-standing act of bullying as caused by the victim herself. Supported by the educational psychologist, the parents decided to move the child to another school.

I decided to carry out a piece of quasi-action research by presenting Sarah's case to a recognised expert-teacher (whom we shall call Mary) in the area of children's social relationships. She had fifteen years' experience as both a full-time and part-time teacher and as a mother. In Sarah's original school, she was identified as having psychological problems. Mary reframed this as a *learning* problem, recognising that a bullied child is traumatised and needs to be safe from bullying before she can change her learning behaviour. Mary identified several strategies she would use to support the child in dealing with the bullying:

- Quality time. Having five minutes of quality time at a set time each day with a bullied child helps to provide a sense of continued concern and create a safe place. It is important to deal with the trauma of bullying first and then to move gradually towards academic support.
- Role modelling. If the group is told to treat the bullied child in a more respectful way, they may do this in front of the teacher but not behind her back. It is important to change the group dynamics by role modelling how to treat the victimised child.
- Putting the child into situations in which she is seen to be successful. The teacher supports her success and gives her positive and public feedback.
- Effective classroom management. If the teacher is thoroughly prepared and in control of her teaching, then she can deal successfully with the children's relationships. This requires effective classroom management.

These strategies are examples of what can be done through creative problem-solving that calls on experience and a dash of common sense (see also Carr, 1989; Pollard, 1996; Pollard, 1997).

Action Research

Action research is a practical and useful approach that teachers can adopt for problem-solving (see Elliott, 1991). Unlike most other forms of research, action research is designed to involve those whose best interests will be served by solving the problem at hand, and is easy to use.

For example, if a teacher has discovered that a small group of children is picking on other children in the class, she can tell them, 'I notice we have a problem with bullying in this class at the moment, and several children have expressed their concern about it. I am not completely sure why this is happening, but it is making some children unhappy. What I would like to do is for us to work together as a class to investigate this and come up with some ideas for solving the problem.' The teacher could add, 'Bullying occurs all over the place. The point of carrying out this research project is to find a solution in our classroom. We don't want to blame anyone for the bullying. We just want to stop it happening.'

The children can then be asked to observe and record bullying incidents and report to the class with their findings. This means that children who are known to have bullied, have been bullied, or have witnessed bullying will be involved in gathering information. These findings can be compiled, and focus groups can work on solutions and recommendations.

Action research is particularly useful because it contributes to finding solutions, empowers teachers and students, encourages cooperation, and can create better student-teacher and peer group relations.

Circle Time

Circle Time[1] is a regular activity in which students and their teacher spend from fifteen to thirty minutes a week sitting in a circle participating in games and dealing with more serious issues, such as bullying. Its major purpose is to encourage the class to work as a team rather than being only an alliance of cliques. It means that a teacher and a class of students can share time together and get to know individuals they may not normally have contact with. It is also a way of having fun together as a group and of increasing mutual support, breaking down barriers, and encouraging the group to deal with difficult issues. From the teacher's perspective, it provides an extra dimension to their relationship with their students, and gives them a lot of information about the individuals in their class. For the students, it gives them a chance to develop and practise relationship and communications skills.

A number of recently developed resources provide information about the underlying philosophy and intentions of Circle Time, describe how sessions can

---

1 Circle Time is not the same as quality circles, which are a problem-solving/creative thinking technique that has been adapted from the business world for use within the classroom by Helen Cowie and Sonia Sharp (Sharp and Cowie, 1994). It is also an excellent tool for teachers to consider.

be structured, and suggest building blocks that provide variety and interest (see references for this chapter).

Developing Circle Time (Bliss et al., 1999) provides details about content and structure of Circle Time sessions. *Circle Time. A Resource Book For Infant, Junior and Secondary Schools* (Bliss and Tetley, 1999) explains the processes and provides a resource bank of games and activities to use with Circle Time. The video, *Coming Round to Circle Time* (Bliss et al., 1995), illustrates how Circle Time works. It also supports the claim that it is a strategy that can be used with children from three years old through to adults. It does this by filming in six settings: three primary school classrooms (including a multiethnic setting), a secondary school, and during a teacher training session. The video shows how the process works in the school, teaches the adults by taking them through the process, and provides explanations about meanings and intentions. It makes the Circle Time strategy very accessible.

Circle Time warms people up, deals with the issues that are central to the particular session, and then brings the session to a close. The following steps can be used to construct a Circle Time session.

Step One: Preparation for Circle Time

It is recommended that, if possible, Circle Time occurs in the classroom as it is important to connect the positive interactions with this environment. It can occur on a regular basis at the same time each week (fifteen to twenty-five minutes is recommended for younger children, and thirty to forty minutes for older children). It is important to clear a space in an orderly fashion, to lay out seats in a circle, and to invite the children to sit there. As with other classroom activities, the teacher will need to plan both the structure (sequencing) and content (what topics will be covered).

Step Two: Starting the Session

In starting the session, it is important to welcome the children and to state what the ground rules for Circle Time are:
- we listen to whoever is speaking and will also be listened to;
- we listen to what the person speaking has to say;
- we don't laugh, giggle, or make comments;
- everyone has the right to pass (although it is important to return to those who have passed when you've gone round the circle. Usually people will then contribute but are under no obligation to do so).

An activity such as the naming game can be used to start off the circle. In the naming game, the student introduces the person to their right, then themselves, and finally the person to their left. This process goes right around the circle.

Step Three: Mixing Up Games

This game is designed to get people to stand up and move around and to sit next to someone they do not usually have much contact with. The mixing up process can be done two or three times by saying, for instance, 'All people with younger brothers stand up and change places'. If the group has been asked to number off, the even numbers can be asked to stand up and change places.

Step Four: With a Partner

Now the group has been moved around the circle and students are often sitting next to someone they do not spend time with and may not know. They are given a small task involving talking with the person they are now partnered with. For instance, the group can be asked to talk about things they like or enjoy, and to find two interests they have in common. The teacher can then go around the room asking the pairs to identify these two common interests.

Step Five: Encouraging Eye Contact and Touch

This step is intended to get students to have closer contact with other class members than they normally would. This helps to provide the glue for the bonding and reaffirmation of the group. Two examples of games played are provided in the video: in one, a smile is passed around the circle, and in the other the whole circle holds hands and a squeeze is passed around the circle.

Step Six: Joining In and Following Instructions

The teacher can then play a game that requires students to work together to carry out the same set of instructions. The example used in the video is of the group together making the noises of the wind and rain and, through the loud stamping of feet, to the delight of all, they produce thunder.

Teresa Bliss states, 'Having fun together does actually generate a team spirit and it does bring people together' (*Coming Round to Circle Time*).

Step Seven: Discussing Personal Information Safely

The games are the foundation of Circle Time. In the video, Teresa Bliss says,

> We start by playing the games to encourage empathy and trust amongst the children. Once they are used to working in that way and that is established, they can then take it on to deal with more serious issues.
>
> We ... move on to more personal information and perhaps more sensitive things. Circle Time isn't a therapy group. It's not a time when we're asking children to bare their souls, but just small amounts of personal information come up and it is important that it's kept on a fairly light level.

Potentially difficult issues can be handled during a well-established circle process. If a sense of safety and trust has been built up, then issues such as bullying can be probed using a variety of techniques, the most non-threatening of these being the silent statement.

This involves the teacher saying something like, 'Stand up and change places if you know bullying has taken place in this school'. This can be followed by, 'Stand up and change places if you know bullying has taken place in this class'. The number who get up and move gives an indication of the severity of the problem.

Once students are involved in a way that means they do not have to admit personally to being bullied or bullying, a more specific strategy can be used such as a sentence completion exercise. In the case of bullying, this could be as follows: 'A child who has been bullied might feel …', 'A child who is a bully might feel …'.

Step Eight: Making Positive Statements About Others

The intention of this step is to allow each person to make a positive statement about others in the group, emphasising the positive qualities of everyone, even those who may normally have been dismissed as having few redeeming qualities.

For example, in an infant school scenario, a child is very upset because his parents' marriage has broken up. This is being acted out through very bad behaviour at school. When he is outside the room, the children in the class all make one positive remark about the child. The teacher writes these down and when he returns each child tells him the positive thing. This is very good for him to hear (and probably helps the class to be more tolerant of him).

Step Nine: Making Positive Statements About Themselves

In this situation, students work with the person next to them. Often people are too embarrassed to make positive statements about themselves, and the partner can make a positive statement about the person they have been working with.

Comment: Circle Time can be used as a preventative tool for bullying in that it encourages children to get to know others outside of their normal groups. This means that, as with cooperative learning, it teaches children to value diversity, including those from minority groups, those with disabilities, and anyone who is different in some way. It supports the development of self-esteem and mutual appreciation on a one-to-one basis. It encourages the class to have a positive sense of itself as a whole and of the individuals within it.

Discussion

A number of benefits can come out of Circle Time. It allows the teacher to interact with his or her class as a group in both a fun way and in a serious fashion. It allows the class to see itself as a whole rather than only as a collection of cliques. It encourages tolerance. Teresa Bliss identified the following benefits:

> Circle Time is not a magic wand. Circle Time is something which takes a while to build up and develop. I've used it in schools where there have been, for example, social and ethnic divides. It's very gratifying to go back a few months later and talk to teachers and discover they're saying things like they notice children are choosing children outside their normal social group in PE, and they are playing with children away from their normal group in the playground.

Cooperative Learning

Cooperative learning is a well-constructed process in which the success of the group depends on the true cooperation of its members. In normal classroom situations, some children who are isolated and prone to bullying are dismissed by most of the class as lacking in value. In a cooperative learning situation, hidden talents emerge and class members learn to value diversity and to be more accepting and supportive of their peers in general.

Johnson et al. (1994) identify three basic types of learning: competitive, individualistic, and cooperative. Competitive learning is when students in a class compete against each other through tests, examinations, and answering questions, with an understanding that only a few will get high marks. The logical corollary is that those who do best will succeed not only in school but also afterwards in life. Individualistic learning is when students work by themselves to reach goals unrelated to others in the class. This is seen as more humanistic than competitive learning because it is criterion-referenced: individuals are competing against themselves rather than against a norm. By competing against their past achievements, students can gain a sense of success rather than being failures compared with those who have outperformed them.

Cooperative learning is also criterion-referenced but differs from individualistic learning in that its aims are group-focused. The groups are small (two or three people), and they aim to accomplish shared goals. There are three types of cooperative learning groups: cooperative base, formal, and informal groups:

- Cooperative base groups are long-term groups (lasting for a year at least). They are usually mixed and are designed for members to provide mutual support, help, and encouragement so that everyone succeeds academically, makes progress, and develops healthily, both cognitively and socially.
- Formal cooperative learning groups function for a shorter period of time (one lesson or over several weeks). The same learning and social themes run through the group processes but, as members will not be as familiar with the rules and processes, the teacher is required to play a larger role in terms of lesson planning and evaluation, and overseeing the group.
- Informal cooperative learning groups use a cooperative approach to encourage students to organise, explain, summarise, and integrate materials

into their existing conceptual frameworks during direct teaching. It is a method that is used, for instance, in university lectures when a lecturer asks students to discuss what they are being taught or to discuss a question being asked. It helps to focus attention, to set expectations about the coverage of a topic, to supply a space for processing material, or to close a lecture. It can last a few minutes or longer, but does not extend beyond the class period.

The Characteristics of Cooperative Learning Groups

Cooperative learning groups have the following five defining characteristics:

1. Positive interdependence. The efforts of each group member benefit both themselves and the group and maximise learning for all members. This creates a commitment to the success of others as well as oneself. Individuals recognise that, in working cooperatively, all members must work fully together, and that, individually, they can work to a better level by working together. If one fails, they all fail; if one succeeds, they all succeed.

2. Individual and group accountability. The group is responsible for meeting its goals and no one can expect a free ride. The group must be clear about its goals and able to measure progress and the efforts of its members. Individual accountability means that each person honestly assesses their efforts and results and reports back to the group. Those who need help are given it by the group so that all members (each with different strengths and weaknesses) can benefit and, through group support, can perform better as individuals.

3. Face-to-face promotive interaction. Students provide support at both an academic and a personal level. When students explain how to carry out a procedure or argue against a proposition, they are accomplishing a cognitive and a social task and, through promoting each other's learning at a face-to-face level, also become more committed to supporting each other's learning.

4. Teaching students interpersonal and small-group skills. Cooperative learning is more complex than normal class work as it requires students both to learn the academic subject at hand (taskwork) and to develop skills to work effectively as part of a small group. This includes building trust, communicating well, dealing with conflict, learning how to lead, making decisions, and being motivated to learn all of these. Johnson et al. (1994) suggest that teamwork skills need to be taught as clearly and thoroughly as academic skills.

5. Group processing. Cooperative learning is regarded as a social growth process which has an evaluative component to make sure things are working well. The group needs to have effective ways of monitoring and adjusting its work, checking how well goals are being achieved, and maintaining personal relationships. The group must be objective about which actions are helpful and which are not. A careful analysis of the group's processes helps to improve working relationships and academic outcomes.

As a result of these efforts, the group becomes greater than the sum of its parts, everyone performs better academically than they would if they worked alone, and their social intelligence is increased in the process.

> **Comment:** Cooperative learning is a well-planned and rigorous approach to learning. It is often confused with other, quite different types of group learning. If students work together on assignments and gather information together but are still individually assessed, this is not cooperative learning. When information is gathered jointly and shared between the group but there is little motivation to teach each other what has been learned because of the emphasis on individual assessment, this, also, is not cooperative learning. In these cases, mutual help and sharing of information are minimal. Those who are conscientious put in a lot of effort whereas others are able to get by on the efforts of others and with minimal input themselves. In such situations, learning can be exploitative rather than cooperative.

Positive Effects of Cooperative Learning

In an examination of cooperative learning, Slavin (1983) found that it increased students' self-esteem and their feelings of happiness, that children named more people (and were named more) as friends, felt more successful academically, and actually achieved higher results.

In addition, it is argued that cooperative learning is a way of gaining a healthy understanding of conflict. Johnson and Johnson (1994) point out that, if a conflict situation is approached competitively, one of the parties in the conflict must win, and the other lose, whereas cooperative learning stresses that what is important is solving the problem for the benefit of everyone. Having this ethos in a class provides the basis for dealing with conflicts and potential conflicts that may result in bullying. Cooperative learning is an approach that can be used by teachers in conjunction with more traditional approaches.

Sociometry

Sociometry can be defined as the measurement of social relationships. For teachers, it is a useful tool for mapping out the dynamics of relationships in a class and for providing answers to such fundamental questions as: 'Who is in?' 'What is the nature of the various groups (the cliques)?' 'Which clique is dominant?' 'Who is the most popular pupil?' and 'Which pupils are isolated?' This section discusses how teachers can use sociometry to better understand the relationships in the class and can use this knowledge to anticipate potential problems and prevent bullying.

A number of researchers have used sociometry in their work. For me, the early work of Hargreaves (1973) still stands out as a landmark for its incisiveness and clarity. In this section, I will refer to Hargreaves's work and Cleary's unpublished adaptation of McLean's (1994) sociometric model. Hargreaves's work provides a useful overview of sociometry, and Cleary uses sociometry as a tool for better understanding of peer relationships and bullying. I will also refer briefly to the creative use of sociometry in anti-bullying research in Finland (Salmivalli et al., 1997, 1998).

In the 1960s, Hargreaves carried out research with five fourth form classes at a streamed male secondary school in the north of England in order to develop a better understanding of the social systems within schools. He created a map of the social relationships of the groups in each of the five classes, determined the status of each pupil, and provided an analysis of the values and norms of each class. He identified that each of the fourth form classes he studied had their own particular micro-culture, and that the norms and values varied from class to class, as did the norms and behaviours of the various cliques within each class.

The A stream class most represented the aspirations of the school, and the boys in the class exhibited behaviour and took on norms that reflected mainstream and prosocial values. In the lower streams, on the other hand, the norms were almost reversed. These leaders tended towards antisocial behaviour, were good fighters, and maintained their status by their ability to control through bullying. In all classes there were several cliques, each of which shared values and behaviours and an agreed set of norms. The cliques were defined by those who were 'in', those 'on the periphery', and those who were isolated ('out').

Hargreaves mapped out the social relationships in the fourth form classes by using three measures: a friendship measure, a power and status measure, and the academic achievement measure of each pupil. He also gathered information through interviewing students and staff at the case study school. He triangulated this information to provide a very useful reading of the dynamics of each class. The academic status of each student was obtained by teachers ranking students according to past examination results. The information on friendship measurement and the informal status hierarchy was gathered in the following fashion:

- All students in a class were asked to name up to five children they went around with most when they were at school. If they went around with just one or two people, they were asked to name only these individuals. By compiling this information, Hargreaves created a sociometric diagram to show the friendship groupings: who is in which group, who is most popular, who is isolated, who is on the periphery of a group. Hargreaves also asked students to name up to two people they disliked, and to name the student they most disliked. They were also asked to identify the person who was their best friend.

- In order to develop an informal status hierarchy, students were given a list of all students in their class and asked to place the names in one of three boxes. In the top box, they were asked to write the names of all students who were leaders (those who others admired or followed, those who led, those who were the bosses). In the bottom box, they were asked to place the names of those who did not get much attention, who were largely ignored, who got teased and picked on, who were unpopular, who did not take the lead, or who followed what the others did. All other names were to be placed in the middle box. By assigning a mark to each box and adding up the numbers, the informal status hierarchy is created.

Hargreaves stressed that, when students put names in one of the three boxes, their choice should not be determined by whether or not they liked the person but by whether or not they were leaders. This is an attempt to measure power and influence rather than preference and popularity. If those with the greatest social power can be identified, then so can the norms that are dominant in each class.

Researchers today are very concerned about the ethics of asking questions about who is liked and disliked. Maines and Robinson (1998) warn that filling out sociometric questionnaires can result in discussions in which students name their choices, with unpleasant results. I would suggest that if teachers use such measures to anticipate and identify bullying, this is the greater good. If such measures *are* used, however, they should be administered with sensitivity, confidentiality, and forethought so that as little harm as possible is caused.

In order to demonstrate Hargreaves's method, I have provided a friendship analysis for an imaginary class, Class 7. Each person in the class is represented by a number and the friendship links are represented by lines. Solid lines indicate a reciprocated choice, and broken lines an unreciprocated choice.

Class 7

Class 7 is a mixed class of twenty-four eleven- and twelve-year-old children in a primary school in a middle-class Auckland suburb. The teacher, Mrs Wright, has given the class a friendship question, asking them to name up to five friends. She has also asked them to name their best friend and up to two people they do not get on with (or leave it blank) and to name the person they do not get on with most in the class (or leave it blank). She has asked the class to place everyone into one of three leadership classifications (essentially, leader, neutral, rejected). She has put together her marks for the mid-year assessments and has ranked the class academically. (The school does not emphasise academic differences but still tracks each child's academic progress. The children themselves are in no doubt about who the academic leaders are.) Mrs Wright has tabulated the results, and generated the sociogram in figure 7.1. She has done a detailed analysis of her findings. Here is an excerpt.

In terms of social relationships, Class 7 consists of four cliques, a pair, two isolated students, and a new girl.

Clique A is the dominant clique of the class and it seems to set the norm for the class overall. Emma (child 18) is the dominant person in this group and the leader of the class. She has an informal status rank of 1, is the top student academically, and has a very pleasant personality (although she can be very mean to those who cross her). The average informal status ranking for the clique as a whole is 6.5 and academically the average is 5.

Emma was nominated the most times in the class as friend (nine times) but she nominated only three people as friends: Claire, Annabel, and Penny. The two other girls in clique A, Kate and Jane, seem to be constantly seeking Emma's approval but she keeps them at a distance. When Emma makes negative remarks about someone, these two girls are the ones who make a point of being unpleasant to that person (Melanie has been isolated by this clique). This group works hard and also participates in school sports.

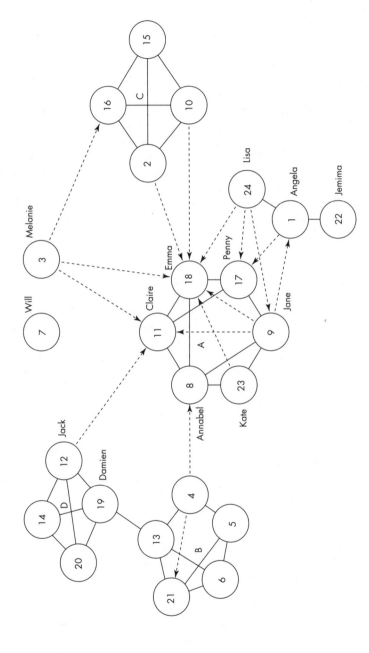

7.1 A Sociogram of Class 7

Clique B is made up of five boys. They are dominant among the prosocial boys in the class but are not as articulate as the girls in clique A.

Clique C is the academic clique of the class. It is made up of two pairs of children (2 and 10, 15 and 16).

Clique D is made up of four boys. They all chose each other in the friendship question and all chose Will as the person they most disliked in the class. Will used to hang around with the group but two of them, Damien and Jack (19 and 12), were caught stealing earlier in the term and they think Will was responsible for telling on them. The boys in the group are pleasant individually but as a group are becoming more and more disruptive. Although it has not been proved, they are thought to be responsible for the recent outbreak of vandalism and graffiti in the school, and they are suspected of intimidating some of the younger children from other classes. It seems that they are making things difficult for Will but it is unclear how. Academically, this clique fares the worst of all cliques: 18.5 is an average placing. They are about 12.5 in terms of their informal status placing.

Child 7 (Will) and child 3 (Melanie) are isolates. They have been chosen as friends by nobody in the class. Melanie (who wrote down three unreciprocated friendship choices) arrived from another school towards the end of the previous year. When she first arrived, she was adopted as a novelty by clique A. After about two weeks they stopped playing with her and they now make snide remarks about her clothes and her intelligence. Emma makes the most cutting remarks and the other girls follow her lead, particularly Jane and Kate. They were once challenged about this by the teacher but laughed and claimed it was all in good fun.

Will is disturbed and very withdrawn. He has run away from home several times and performs very poorly academically. He has a tendency to lose his temper and most kids steer clear of him. Will was friends with 19 and 12 of clique D for a while at the beginning of the year, but after they were caught stealing from a local shop they blamed him for telling on them.

Angela and Jemima (1 and 22) have acted as a self-contained unit for the past three years, and are not members of any cliques. They prefer it this way and consider themselves to be 'alternative'. They have been friends since they were small, but also have friendly and confident contact with many of the children. A new girl, Lisa, seems to be moving in on this relationship (and was also named by Angela as a friend). She has been spending a lot of time with Angela to the exclusion of Jemima.

So what use is this information?

This information is useful in several respects. It gives the teacher specific information and insights. It allows her to see how the various cliques operate and how they perform a number of useful functions—they provide a sense of identity for their members, and they solidify friendships. In terms of bullying and the potential for bullying, they suggest several areas of concern about the 'at risk' condition or potential of at least three children in the class. For instance:

- Melanie cannot possibly keep up with the fashion demands of clique A, nor should she. They accepted her into their ranks to have a look at her and then rejected her. The more she tries, the harder they make it for her, and she becomes increasingly isolated, low in self-esteem, and a poor academic performer. The girls in clique A, however, are everyone's favourite pupils. They are the epitome of success, good-looking, articulate, and well-groomed, whereas Melanie is quiet, unsure of herself, shy, and easy to ignore. Is this class a safe place for Melanie? No, it is not. What should and can the teacher do to make things better?

- Girl 24 (Lisa) has come from another school (where she was asked to leave). She has a history of disruptive and antisocial behaviour and is very articulate and powerful. She seems to be breaking up the close relationship of Angela and Jemima. Should the teacher step in? Is it her business? What should be done?
- Will is surly and uncooperative. He appears to ask for trouble and is becoming seen by the school as a troublemaker. A closer examination shows that he is disturbed and it is not clear exactly why (although there are rumours about abuse at home that should be referred to the guidance counsellor for investigation). He is being subjected to bullying by clique D, particularly by Damien (student 19). Whereas it first seemed that Will was the troublemaker, it is now apparent that he is being set up by Damien and other members of this clique (and a few boys from another class).

Other Useful Information

Hargreaves provides the following useful background information:

- Small groups (cliques) that interact regularly and frequently are united by common values and group norms. These define the criteria for membership and expected behaviour, and determine who is 'in' and 'out'.
- Cliques control their members by constantly exerting pressure to conform to central norms through punishing or rejecting those who deviate. A clique has less control over its members when the norms are weak.
- Cliques can influence a member's sense of identity, and control or regulate group behaviour. Members differ in the extent to which they conform with or deviate from the norms. Those who conform are more acceptable than those who deviate.
- Group members usually have different status that is dependent on length of membership, the esteem in which they are held, their assistance with group goals, and the extent to which they conform. Within the group, leaders are held in high esteem, and those with low prestige have low informal status.
- When groups form, similarities tend to develop between members in behaviour and communications, acceptance of group norms, and the expressions of the group's values. As the person's group membership indicates an acknowledgment of the norms, clique members can predict within reasonable limits the behaviour of their co-members.

As a cautionary note, Furlong (1984) argues that relationships are not as rigid as in Hargreaves's model, and that students move in and out of what he calls interaction sets, which are determined by context. My sense is that both interpretations are right to a degree (and that interaction sets are probably a particularly useful measure for secondary schools as the number of groups individuals participate in tends to be much greater than in primary schools) and that both approaches can be used sensibly and with caution.

Here is an example of a questionnaire that could be used to generate a sociogram:

CONFIDENTIAL

Name _____

Friendship question
1. Which pupils in the class are your friends?
2. Which pupils are the most likely to bully and hurt others (physically and emotionally)? You can name from 0 to 5 people.
3 Which pupils are most likely to be picked on and hurt by others? You can name from 0 to 5 people.

Informal status question
4. You have been provided with a list of the pupils in your class. Place each name within one of the three boxes below.

Definitely a leader	Part of a group	On the outside of things

An Application of Sociometry

Using student-based leadership to reduce bullying in the classroom: the junior leadership program

Mark Cleary, Principal of Colenso High School in Napier, has developed a strategy that he calls the junior leadership program for use with third and fourth form students. Cleary argues that if potential leaders can be identified in the first and second year of secondary school, taught leadership skills, and encouraged to take on prosocial roles, then teachers can create classrooms which espouse cooperation, acknowledge diversity, and have the potential to become bully-proof.

In developing this program, Cleary has combined aspects from three sources:
1. The *No Blame Approach*, which is based on the philosophy that, rather than blaming those who bully, they should become part of the solution along with the more prosocial students (the philosophy).
2. The senior students' leadership program. The school has an established program to teach leadership skills to senior students which Cleary decided to adapt to use with younger students (the program).
3. Strathclyde's anti-bullying program (see Appendix I), which provides a relationship map that Mark has used creatively for identifying actual or potential

class leaders who are invited to undertake the leadership program (the means of identification).

Near the beginning of the school year, form teachers are asked to use the Strathclyde Relationship Maps (see McLean, 1994) to identify four students (two girls, two boys) in their class who are genuine leaders with power and influence. To qualify as leaders, the students need only be active and influential among their peers. Academic success, popularity, or even positive social skills are not prerequisites for selection. This process can be called the social mapping of a class.

It works as follows:

- There are three components to social mapping (see Figure 7.2). Diagram A is the social map. Diagrams B and C respectively help to interpret what the mapped characteristics mean in terms of the individuals' likelihood of being assertive, aggressive, or passive (the assertiveness map); and what type of role they are likely to take on in a bullying situation (the bullying map).
- The first step is to create a scatter diagram on the dual axis social map, diagram A. The horizontal axis is a continuum consisting of passive behaviour at one end (to the left), and active behaviour at the other (to the right). At the passive end are located the very quiet, withdrawn children, and at the active end are located the most extrovert children. In using the continuum, the teacher gives each child in the class a number and places them at a point that seems about right along the horizontal axis (McLean suggests doing this quickly and instinctively).
- The vertical axis has accepting behaviour at the top and rejecting behaviour at the bottom. Accepting behaviour means being supportive and being able to see others' points of view; rejecting behaviour is domineering, hostile, and self-centred. Having plotted each pupil first on the horizontal axis, the teacher then moves them up and down the vertical axis. When this is done, the teacher will have a scattergram representation of the class.
- Diagram B consists of a triangle with assertive, aggressive, and passive behaviour descriptors located in its three angles. When this diagram is made into a transparency, it can be placed over the scattergram (diagram A) to give a sense of which pupils will fit into which category.
- Diagram C predicts which pupils are likely to bully or be victims of bullying, which are likely to be able to resist or not be a target of bullying (bully-proof), and which are likely to be bystanders. When this diagram is made into a transparency, it can be placed over diagram A. As a rough guide, McLean suggests that 5 per cent each of children in a class are likely to be located within the bullies, bullied, and bully-proof ellipses of the diagram, and that most others are in the large in-between area.

Reduced versions of the three diagrams are shown in figure 7.2. Full-sized versions are given in Appendix III.

Cleary suggests that, in selecting four students from the class, the teacher should identify those with prosocial leadership skills (bully-proof and assertive), and those who use their leadership skills antisocially (aggressive bullies). The leadership program is intended to build further the skills of the prosocial students and to teach those who express their leadership antisocially to do so in a prosocial fashion.

Diagram A: The social map

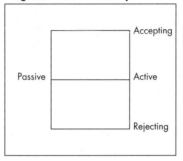

Diagram B: The assertiveness map

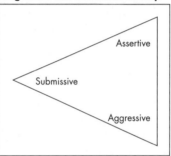

Diagram C: The bullying map

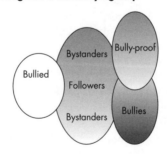

7.2 The Strathclyde Relationship Maps
Source: McLean, 1994.

For many students, selection as leaders will come as no surprise. They will always have had their leadership acknowledged by adults and will be comfortable with their position in the peer group. They will have developed sound people skills, and will typically be empathetic to their fellow students. In terms of the relationship map, they will be classified as assertive.

For others, this might be the first tangible recognition of their leadership potential. They will have been aware of their influence (as are their peers) but will not have had it recognised by adult members of the school community. In particular, those leaders who are self-centred and who lack empathy (labelled aggressive in the Strathclyde Map) will be more used to having their peer group power challenged by adults. They will have become skilled at being subversive and maintaining their position in spite of adult attempts to change their behaviour. Often these students will not have been successful either academically or in extracurricular activities and so will be even more determined to hold onto the status they have established over the years. Both groups of students have much in common. They tend to be active, and are used to having followers, influence, popularity, and status.

Sociometry as a Creative Tool for Teachers

As Hargreaves and Cleary have illustrated, sociometry can be used creatively to understand the social relationships in a class. Salmivalli et al. (1997, cited in Salmivalli et al., 1998) have used sociometry in a very innovative fashion to map out the peer networks, children's participant roles, and bully/victim relationships in a typical class. They suggest six roles that individuals can take on in a bullying situation: the victim (V), the bully (B), the assistants (A), the reinforcers (R), the defender (D), and the outsiders (O). The following is an illustration of a typical school class (the circles represent girls, the squares boys):

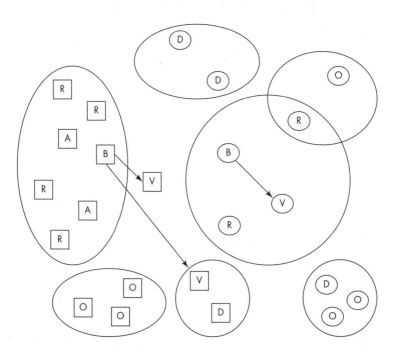

7.3 A Typical School Class
Source: Salmivalli et al., 1998.

8 Interactive Strategies in the Classroom

Once a school decides to adopt an anti-bullying initiative, it may find it useful to initiate classroom activities that give students a better understanding of the dynamics of bullying. One activity is an innovation developed jointly by Mark Cleary, a New Zealand secondary school principal, and me, called 'On the Bus'. Another is role play. This chapter deals with both of these.

'On the Bus': A Program Designed to Raise Students' Awareness About School Bullying

The 'On the Bus' program was developed to be used by secondary school students and their teachers. It is a straightforward and useful, action-based resource. This account is based on Mark Cleary's use of the method with a group of Class 9 students at a Hawke's Bay secondary school.

How It Works: The Eight Steps

The eight steps of the program are designed to give students a better understanding of the nature of bullying, leading to the development of solutions for the particular bullying scenario, and the creation of a summary statement that provides deeper knowledge and an overview. In this example, the students chose a scenario on a bus, and this is used here to illustrate the method. Another scenario could be used and the same steps followed.

Step one: the teacher and students jointly develop a bullying scenario

The class was encouraged to discuss the various types of bullying situations that they had experienced or seen, and the type of bullying they felt most uncomfortable about. They identified being on a school bus going to or from school.

Being subjected to bullying on a school bus can be very intimidating. Once a student is on the bus, he or she is trapped until their home stop or school.

Comment: This first step is intended to start students thinking about bullying and to make it have personal meaning.

Step two: the scenario is discussed

Once a type of bullying was identified, a hypothetical scenario was created in order to explore what was happening on the bus and what could be done about it.

Scenario: Kristy is called names every time she goes on the school bus but she does not tell anyone because she is afraid of retaliation. She cannot see any way out.

The students then discussed what was happening. They were asked, 'What should Kristy do?'

Comment: This scenario emerged from the discussion about bullying and the concerns of this particular group of students. If the bus scenario is inappropriate or triggers little response, then another scenario can be suggested and analysed instead. In order to focus the discussion, it may be useful to record on a large sheet of paper or on a board the points the students make.

Step three: strategies and/or solutions are suggested

The students suggested that Kristy could:
- tell someone, tell her parents;
- see the principal about it;
- make sure that the bus driver knows what's going on;
- sit with a friend or friends;
- tell the bullies to stop calling her names;
- look them in the eye and tell them that she doesn't like them calling her names, that it makes her feel bad;
- ignore them;
- catch another bus.

From the list of suggestions, three strategies were identified: tell an adult, stand up to the bullies, or avoid the bullies. In all three instances, the onus was on Kristy, the victim, to find a solution. This seemed an unsatisfactory conclusion.

Comment: Having discussed the scenario, and called on their own experiences and observations of bullying, students suggest some possible solutions. These are written down.

Step four: feedback and extra information are provided

In order to explore this scenario further and as a way to stimulate discussion, the class was told that recent New Zealand research (Adair et al., 1999) revealed that only 20 per cent of students who had been bullied had sought some kind of help. This information caused the students to reconsider Kristy's position. They knew that telling somebody about the bullying or standing up for herself were theoretically good things to do. They realised, however, that for many people, and certainly for Kristy, these strategies would probably not work and would end up making her even more isolated and at risk than she already was. For instance, if she told someone, would she be safe from retaliation later?

> **Comment:** This first set of solutions is a good start but it is now up to the teacher to take things further. He or she can provide extra information about bullying which builds on what the students have said and addresses the underlying issues so that a deeper understanding is reached.

Step five: improved strategies and solutions are developed

The students reconsidered the situation and decided that the only realistic and safe strategy was for Kristy to catch another bus and so avoid the trouble. This strategy still placed the onus on the victim to find a solution.

The next step was to come at the problem from another direction, to use an innovative process to harness the students' interest and momentum to take things further and to seek better solutions and strategies.

> **Comment:** From these further discussions (with the teacher's critical input), a further set of strategies or solutions is devised. If the teacher feels that this does not really solve the problem, he or she can suggest that the students explore the issues further.

Step six: steps four and five are repeated until the participants are satisfied with the strategies/solutions

The students now had a better understanding of Kristy's predicament and had dismissed two of their original strategies. They felt that the bullying problem had been skirted around rather than solved: the strategy of catching another bus could bring short-term relief for Kristy, but it would not end the bullying.

They thought that the next time Kristy met the bullies, they would bully her again, knowing that nobody has stopped them before. Kristy would be living in fear. If she stopped taking this bus, then somebody else would take her place as the victim of the bullying group.

Another approach was used. Rather than repeating the previous strategy of providing more information, Cleary used visual stimulation.

An examination of the dynamics on the bus

He drew a picture of the bus on the board to recreate physically and graphically where these acts of bullying were taking place. He wanted the students to think about the dynamics of the situation. He focused first on where the various actors in this scenario would be located.

Where would Kristy be sitting?

The group unanimously agreed that Kristy would be sitting at the front, close to the driver.

Where would the name-callers be sitting?

Everyone agreed that they would be sitting at the back of the bus. Having established where people were sitting, discussion turned to the nature of the name-calling.

What would happen to Kristy on the bus?

- When Kristy gets on the bus, going from school to her home, the bullies would jostle her and call her names. They would push past her, and keep making derogatory comments about her hair, her weight, her clothes, the fact that she wears glasses, etc. When she climbs onto the bus at her home stop in the morning, she will again be met with derisory and raucous comments.
- The group would consider these throwaway remarks as 'a bit of fun', 'a good laugh'.
- The other students on the bus would be expected to join in and would, in fact, laugh along.
- Kristy would take her seat, dishevelled and humiliated.

These findings were explored further. Those who were the bystanders to the bullying, seen as sitting in the middle of the bus, were brought into the equation.

> **Comment:** At this point the teacher can provide his or her analysis of the situation, with input from the students, who have become very involved in trying to understand what is going on. They want to find a solution that will work. The teacher can ask questions at this point to focus on those involved in the scenario: Kristy, those doing the bullying, those observing, and the driver—the only adult on the bus. The purpose of this exploration is to examine the foundations upon which the bullying occurs.

The teacher asks, 'So, what is happening here?'

For the one being bullied, Kristy?

Those who are close to the driver may feel they are under her mantle of protection, but her job is to transport children. She may choose to control as best she can what goes on in her bus, but she usually wants only minimal control so that no accidents happen. The driver does not see it as her role to protect children, understand the dynamics of peer relations, or stop anyone from getting bullied. In fact, it would be dangerous for her to pay too much attention to what is going on, since she is driving.

If the back-seaters have chosen their victim well, Kristy will not respond at all, or will respond only passively and ineffectually. She may seek refuge by trying not to be noticed. Typically, her body language will reinforce her passivity. She may sit down low in her seat, hunching her shoulders and trying to pull her body inwards to make herself appear invisible.

Those doing the bullying, the back-seaters. What's in it for them?

By sitting at the back of the bus, the bullies are locating themselves as far as possible from the adult in charge of the bus. This is where they are most likely to be able to be disruptive, to be objectionable, or to bully, because the adult's main job is to drive the bus.

The back-seaters support each other in their abuse of Kristy. They are like a group of actors on a small stage (the back of the bus) who rely on the middle-seaters, their audience, to appreciate the play they are presenting. Their bullying is a demonstration of power over a person who is much less powerful than they are. Among the back-seaters, one student is probably the ringleader, initiating proceedings, and controlling the group.

The back-seaters take the laughter and compliance of others on the bus as an affirmation of their actions. It tells them:
- everyone agrees that it is funny and fun;
- no one is really getting hurt;
- that they are popular, cool, and have lots of friends on this bus; and
- that they should keep doing it.

They act confidently and swagger in their success.

Those who are on the sidelines. What does this mean for them?

The middle-seaters are physically, and symbolically, in the middle of the conflict. Their feelings are probably mixed. They may be:
- slightly embarrassed, with perhaps a twinge of sympathy;

- mainly pleased that it is not them who is the butt of the derision; and
- excited by the bullying, but aware that it is sadistic and that they are weak not to intervene.

The role the middle-seaters choose to adopt is pivotal in determining whether the taunts will die away or escalate.

> **Comment:** At this point, the students are much clearer about what is going on, and reframe the situation so that the onus for solving the problem is no longer on the victim of the bullying.

Step seven: a statement of final recommendation is made

These various ways of examining the 'On the Bus' scenario enabled the students to draw on their own experiences and understandings and to work as a group to find ways of dealing with the bullying. They agreed that most students on the bus did not like the name-calling, yet their shared passivity gave the impression that they all condoned it.

Cleary and the class brainstormed what to do to create solutions that were more acceptable. They came up with the following suggestions:
- When the bullying starts, it is important that the middle-seaters ask Kristy to sit with them.
- If anyone feels uncomfortable with the name-calling, they should either challenge it then and there or, if they do not feel strong enough, they should talk about it with someone else on the bus.
- Middle-seaters should not support the behaviour by laughing.
- The middle-seaters should let Kristy know (off the bus) that what is being said about her is not true.
- They should take Kristy to see the teacher.

None of these suggestions requires the victim to take responsibility for the situation. Having realised what is happening, the peer group—the observers—decides to bring a halt to the bullying. It seems that the class has now found a good way to stop the bullying. As important as the solutions they have come up with is the process of deep learning they have gone through. What they have learnt can be applied to other bullying situations.

> **Comment:** A final set of recommendations for a solution is reached and presented as the culmination of the problem-solving part of the exercise.

Step eight: an analysis and commentary are given

This final step is a summary and analysis of the whole experience. This is a very important exercise because the students have gone through a process of reflective thinking and group problem-solving and, in the process, clarified issues they had sensed but not articulated. In providing a joint written analysis, they can integrate more fully what they have learnt. (The teacher could summarise the thinking, type it up, and present it to the class the next time they meet.)

The following analysis and commentary are given as an example of what can be added to the 'On the Bus' case study.

The following set of dynamics makes the bus an unsafe place:

- The name-callers, hearing the laughter, get confirmation that they are popular and funny and that everyone (except for Kristy) is enjoying themselves.
- The bystanders get the message that there is nothing they can do and that none of them feels any sympathy for Kristy.
- Kristy gets a clear message that she is on her own.
- The driver hearing the name-calling dismisses it as 'a bit of harmless fun'.

Although it is obvious that Kristy is not enjoying what is going on, many people still think that the old saying, 'Sticks and stones may break my bones but names will never hurt me' is true. It is not!

If the bullying is not handled, things will only get worse. Those who feel uncomfortable but powerless will withdraw and find ways to justify their inaction. The back-seaters will continue their bullying and make increasingly outrageous comments as no one is there to oppose or stop them. The laughter will increase as the others desperately try to justify their inaction and cover up their discomfort. The bullying behaviour could escalate into attempts to humiliate Kristy physically or even sexually. Her feelings will not be considered, no one will empathise with her—they cannot afford to.

The driver will get fed up with the raucous behaviour and start shouting at everyone (indiscriminately) to keep quiet. She will tell the back-seaters to behave and that she has her eye on them. Kristy, increasingly alienated and miserable, will become more withdrawn, isolated, and fearful. Desperate to maintain their power, the back-seaters will increasingly threaten Kristy, safe in the knowledge that she will not tell. A culture of intolerance and lack of respect will have become embedded.

What is happening under the surface?

In situations like this there is a gradual buildup of aggression. The taunts are symbolic, meant to test and challenge what Kristy, as well as the other students and the bus driver, will accept. There is also a set of other variables, some of which are known and some of which are unknown.

Among the knowns is the fact that, although the middle-seaters are going along with the situation, they feel very uncomfortable. They feel unsafe and do not want the negative energy to be turned on them. Things are out of control for everyone, perhaps even some of those taking part in the bullying. Kristy is very unhappy and feels inadequate and isolated. This will affect everything else she does—for her the world has become an unsafe place. If Kristy is being bullied on the bus, then she is probably being bullied at and outside school.

It is unknown whether there are individuals on the bus who would be prepared to stand up for Kristy. It was felt that most of the students on the bus would decide not to support her because the risk is too high and her status is too low. Kristy's initial reaction will have established her status, and her passive response will confirm to the others that she is not worth taking the risk for.

If the peer group is strong, however, and tells the bullies to stop, then the bullying dynamic will be altered. How this happens and how the bullies will respond are issues for consideration. The risk of confrontation is reduced as more students choose to reject the bullying. There is less risk for four girls taking Kristy's part than two, for instance.

How This Exercise has been Beneficial

The teacher and students have gone through an exercise to solve a bullying problem. The incident is imaginary and non-threatening, but real enough for them all to relate to it. Carrying out this exercise has produced the following useful results:

- It has helped students to clarify some of the issues and dynamics around bullying, which they can use in other situations.
- It has led to a discussion of some of the long-term effects of bullying and an understanding of the social dynamics involved.
- It has underlined the fact that the peer group has a choice either to support or to stop bullying.
- It has shown that the students (with facilitation from the teacher) can find their own solutions to bullying problems.

  Practical outcomes of the scenario itself are that:

- Everyone is a winner if bullying stops. Kristy will no longer be bullied, she may make friends with those who support her, and they will feel good about their prosocial behaviour. The back-seaters will channel their energy elsewhere and might develop more positive ways of relating.
- The driver will no longer need to keep one eye on the students and can concentrate on the road.

Role Play

Another way of confronting the issue of bullying is through role play, which can be used with all age groups. Role play gives young people a better understanding of how bullying works by allowing them to get inside the roles of bully, bullied, and onlooker in a safe environment. Young children enjoy the opportunity to act things out, and much of their play is based on pretending to be other people. As they get older, they do this by echoing the behaviour of those they admire. A well-directed role play can be a challenging and powerful experience for the participants, as well as a stimulating learning experience.

Research suggests that some children who bully at school lack empathy and are violent because this is how they are treated at home. In other words, they do not empathise because they have not learnt to do so. If such children are placed in a victim role, they can learn to empathise with victims of bullying. Role play is an excellent way of making the experiences of others real; if awareness about bullying is raised, a no-bullying culture is encouraged.

Creating a Role Play

In order to create a role play, it is important to have a suitably sized group. It must be big enough for all the roles to be filled and for there to be an audience. But it needs to be small enough for everyone to be totally involved. A group of ten students plus two adults is a good size.

Ideally, one adult should be either a drama teacher or a counsellor with psychodrama/role play experience (the director), and the other adult should have acting ability and experience and be able to help develop the students' role playing (the auxiliary).

The room should preferably be soundproof or isolated from the rest of the school, and big enough to split the group into two.

Step one: preparation

Before embarking on a role play session, the adults who will be involved should meet and discuss what they are going to do. They need to be aware that a role play is a theoretical reproduction of a scene of bullying, so it is important that they do not plan to make individual students act out only their own predominant roles straightaway.

Scenarios must be pitched at the right level for the age of the children. Teachers can either invent various scenarios or use the ones suggested in this chapter.

In preparation, the adults should act out the scenarios themselves so that they can see if they work and what the participants are likely to experience. The auxiliary should take on one of the roles and act it out fully in order to practise drawing student role-takers further into their adopted roles.

Step two: meeting with the class

Once the group is selected, the adults need to explain the process and purpose of role play and what they will all be doing. If the children have done 'On the Bus', they can be told that role play is another and more direct way of understanding how bullying works. The group needs to know that role play is a way of allowing them to generate solutions to bullying, that its purpose is to be educational, experiential, fun, informative, and practical.

At this point, the ground rules need to be negotiated with the group. For instance, students must respect one another and not put each other down. When someone is talking, others must not interrupt. If the rules come largely from the group, they will tend to support and respect them.

Some students will find the idea of role play very difficult, particularly if they lack self-confidence. They should not be pushed but allowed to move at their own speed. On the other hand, it is essential to unblock barriers by 'warming people up' (this is similar to warming up the body before doing strenuous exercise so that muscles are not damaged). Such strategies as ice-breakers (see Appendix IV) can be used for this. It is not a good idea to get students to talk about bullying experiences. Role playing is action-based and focused on getting in touch with the feelings around bullying; discussion is intellectual and can stop this happening.

Step three: getting to work

Now the group is ready to work. This can happen immediately after the meeting, or in another lesson if the role play process is taking place as part of a social studies unit. At this point the adults can act out a simple, pre-arranged role play to demonstrate how the process works. Afterwards, two or three scenarios can be suggested, or students can invent their own.

Step four: acting out the chosen role play

A group that is warmed up will have plenty of volunteers to take on the various roles. They all have a contribution to make; there are no stars. The two main roles are the victim and the bully. On the sidelines are the observers (three), and the others (five), whose role is to watch and provide feedback (the audience). Two groups of five works well, with each a distinct unit. They take turns playing out the bullying scenario and being the audience.

The students will be developing a scenario and creating a script for it. The adults describe the events one step at a time, and the students provide the words. If this is difficult for the students, the director and the auxiliary need to contribute more. Perhaps the students are not quite sure what is expected of them. The director will pick up on this and demonstrate how to do things. She may say to the auxiliary, 'Sue, I want you to go in and pick up the role of the victim'. Sue stands alongside the 'victim', mirrors his stance, but develops the role, makes it real, even exaggerates it. She talks to the victim as if they are allies, even as if they are parts of the same person, and as the victim responds to her affirmations, her promptings, and her questions, the drama takes off with its own momentum. For those watching, Sue's acting is very real, and they grasp the depths of the roles.

It is a good idea for students to comment on their own role playing and that of others in the group. It should be emphasised that there is no right way to play the roles, just different interpretations. Students who think a role could be done differently can be asked to show how they would play it.

The role play will thus take shape and develop its own integrity. When people take on the roles they will, to some extent, become the people they are playing. It is essential that, after a role play has finished, the director takes the participants out of their roles or a residue can remain with them. This should be done publicly. The director could say something like, 'Thank you, James. You played the role of Beavis the bully very well. You must now come out of that role. Turn to the left three times, close your eyes, and count to ten. Good! You are now James again.' When this is done the director could say, 'Welcome back, James'. The adults may also realise that a student has taken on a role they commonly play out in their lives and this may need to be followed up with the student after the session.

Comment: Step four is the most important. Here the students go into the role and put their energy into developing the characters being portrayed, feeling what each is like and playing them through.

Step five: discussing the process

After the role play, there should be a discussion in which the students talk about how it felt to be in the various roles. Because of the vulnerability and power of the roles, it is very important that this discussion be as honest as possible. Some students may make outrageous or implausible statements in order to feel less exposed. Boys may feel less inclined to be honest about their feelings than girls, but this interaction will be most open if the play has been fully acted.

The students should be asked what they saw happening. It is important to record this on a board in order to elicit further discussion. (If resources permit, it may be a good idea for students to have a copy of what is recorded.)

The bully should be asked how it felt. (Powerful, happy. I enjoyed being in control. I didn't enjoy it. It felt wrong.)

Next, the person being bullied should be asked how the role felt. (I felt desperate, sad, unhappy. I felt frustrated. I felt scared. I wanted to do something to stop the bullying.)

And finally, the person observing should be asked. (I wanted to join in. I felt uncomfortable. I felt ashamed. I felt like doing something to make the bullying stop.)

The people acting the roles should then be asked, first, what the person being bullied could do to improve things and, second, what the observers could do. Realistic solutions should be sought.

The observations of the audience are very important since they have objectivity and distance that the players do not.

As with 'On the Bus', the first set of solutions may not provide an adequate solution. The students playing the roles should try out the suggestions and ask for ideas from the audience.

If students from the audience have suggestions, they should explain, and then, with the help of the director, show the others what they mean. The 'observers' and 'bullies' can, staying in role, say how each suggested interaction feels. Does it feel better? Or is there yet another way of doing it? Can this be shown? Will the role players do it again and see how it feels? For the one observing, does it appear better? For the person in the bully role, how does it feel? How do they feel the bully would react with this change of tactic? (The bully and observers will need to be coached.) The bully needs to stay in role while the others are asked what his or her likely response to the new approach will be.

Although the director wants the answers to come from the participants, they sometimes need directing or shaping. As with the 'On the Bus' exercise, it is important for the teacher to have a flexible script and timeline in directing the course of the role play. The director must supply the shape, but it needs to be given life by the students.

In 'On the Bus', students went through three stages before they found good solutions to the bullying problem. A similar process is needed here, by discussing, eliminating, or modifying the suggestions played out in the role play and its follow-ups.

Step six: reflection and learning

At this point the role playing has gone through several stages:

- Watching and listening. At the beginning the students watch the director and the auxiliary to get a sense of what role play is about.
- Trying it out. Next, they take on roles and start to feel what is happening dynamically. Does the victim feel weak and sad, the bully cynical and powerful, the observer confused and guilty?
- Acting it out. The students now act out a more fluent version of the role play, perhaps the first group followed by the second group.
- Finding better ways of responding. The fourth stage is about trying to find alternative ways of doing things, seeking solutions, trying these out, and seeing if they feel better than the previous bullying situations.
- Reflection and learning. Step six focuses on this stage. Using different approaches, the director and the auxiliary explore other problem-solving mechanisms, extend the discussion, and bring all the approaches together in a recapitulation that endeavours to make sense of the whole experience.

A series of questions can be asked:

- What did students feel about the scenarios when they were being played out?
- What was going on for the students playing the various roles (in terms of feelings, motivation, sense of control, etc.)

  –for the victim of bullying?

  –for the bully?

  –for the observer?

  –for the students in the audience who were outside the event?
- What have they all learnt about the dynamics of bullying, and how it feels for everyone involved?
- What rules about bullying can be made for the students, the class, and the school?
- How can bullying be stopped?

Step seven: turning the role play into a drama for presentation to a larger audience (optional)

Students at Selwyn College in Auckland, New Zealand, recently put together a moving drama to illustrate the negative effects of bullying. Creating such a drama is very challenging, but it can have a powerful effect on both the actors and the audience.

If a group creates a powerful and well-acted role play, they may be willing to perform it before a bigger group of students, in front of the whole school, or for other schools. A graphic way of presenting such a bullying role play is to show 'before' and 'after' scenarios.

Summary

Using a bullying scenario as a structural basis for understanding how bullying works is useful in several respects:

- Having the scenario as a sketch around which students develop the role play and fill in the blanks allows them to call on their own experiences. It also allows them to 'own' the process and the results. If a student has a tendency to bully and is part of a role play group that rejects bullying, he or she may cease to find bullying an attractive way to behave.
- When students role play, they feel what it is like to be in all the roles. This usually encourages empathy and understanding, and a cessation of the bullying.
- One of the major loopholes in the bullying dynamic is the fact that one bully has so much power over such a large group, which could in fact intervene and bring a stop to the bullying. The potential power of a group of students acting against bullying cannot be overestimated. Acting together to solve a problem not only gets students thinking about what is happening and coming up with answers, but also shows them that together they can be strong and combat bullying.

Four bullying scenarios have been developed, with background information and commentaries to provide a selection of real-life situations that can be used for role play. These can be adapted for use by various numbers of actors. The scenarios of the physical beating up of a boy in the school grounds, and the harassment of a gay/effeminate boy, are intended for use in secondary schools; the scenarios of the racist bullying of a Maori boy, and the isolation of the young girl, can be used in primary/intermediate settings. Other bullying scenarios can be generated using the format provided here.

Four Bullying Scenarios

Scenario One: Physical Bullying. The Beating Up of Ben by Shane and His Friends

In the playing fields of a large secondary school, far from the main teaching blocks, Ben, aged fourteen, marches towards a prearranged spot with a look of determination in his eyes. When he gets there he is surprised to find a crowd of about a hundred teenagers restlessly milling around. It seems as if everyone has heard about what is about to happen and has come to watch. Soon, a self-assured and slightly older and bigger boy called Shane arrives with a group of his friends who are sniggering among themselves.

When the fighting starts the crowd becomes noisy and there is a sense of excitement in the air. Some of the boys yell out to encourage Shane ('Come on, Shane. Give him what he deserves') or to discourage Ben ('Go home, loser!'). The verbal support fans Shane's aggression, and almost immediately it is apparent that he will win. He is obviously a much better fighter and has many other advantages—more weight, more confidence, and the support of friends. Ben is knocked to the ground and Shane's friends start to kick him. He tries to protect himself by contracting into a foetal position and covering his head with his arms. Shane and his friends then walk off with a sense of camaraderie, of a job well done. As they leave, they make taunting and threatening remarks to Ben such as: 'Fucking wimp! 'Piece of shit!' 'Well done, Ben!' 'Tell anyone about this and you're fucking dead!' The crowd disperses and leaves Ben lying on the ground, alone, humiliated, and hurt.

Ben knows better than to go to the school authorities, first because, despite the savageness of his beating, he would be transgressing the ultimate taboo of 'ratting on his peer group' but, perhaps more important, because even if the school supported him over this incident, he knows Shane and his friends will get back at him and that in the long term his prospects will be very poor.

Here are several useful pieces of background information to this incident

- It is a close representation of a real event.
- Ben has been bullied by one boy in particular, Shane, who has been supported by a group of boys (a type of bullying sometimes referred to as mobbing).
- The bullying of Ben started off in a low-key way, with one of Shane's group accidentally-on-purpose tripping Ben as he passed him in class and making low-grade insulting remarks, such as 'Who cuts your hair, your mummy?' As Ben was unable to counter these attacks successfully, things have gradually got worse, and the bullying has escalated.
- With some encouragement from his father that he should stand up for himself, Ben decided enough was enough. He responded to Shane's challenge to fight him.
- Unlike so many Hollywood movies when the good guy stands up for himself and the bully, who is always a coward, either runs away or loses the fight, Ben does not have the skills or support to do anything but lose and lose badly.
- The school's principal will defensively state that bullying does not happen in this school. He will agree that there is some rough play: 'All right, there may be odd incidents, but boys will be boys! Besides, it's character-forming to have to learn how to stand up for yourself. It's a good preparation for life.'

What observations and inferences can be made about this incident?

- This school is not a safe place for Ben or, by implication, for other pupils.
- Many people were watching the fight. Some came to see what was going on and some just happened to be there. They vastly outnumbered the bullies, yet nobody intervened or provided any vocal or physical support for Ben.
- Those involved in the bullying treated Ben as a 'non-person' and did not seem aware or to care that they could do Ben serious, long-term, physical and psychological harm. They lacked a sense of empathy towards him.
- The principal may have acted defensively in response to the suggestion that there is a bullying problem at the school. He may also truly believe that bullying does no harm but is character-forming. In either case, he lacks adequate strategies for dealing effectively with bullying, as does his school.

Scenario Two: Jamie is Bullied Because He is Gay

Jamie is average in many ways: average height, average weight, average academically. One attribute which has set him apart from his male peers ever since he started school is that he is effeminate in the way he talks and moves, and many people think that he is probably gay.

Jamie has been teased from an early age, and is frequently beaten up. He seems to be without any aggressive tendencies and does not have any real friends. Some of the teachers are ambivalent about him and treat him as if he brings his victimisation on himself.

Jamie tries to avoid the other children at lunchtime by going to the library. There is a teacher on duty and a few children are scattered through the room working. While he is sitting and making notes in an alcove by himself, two boys come in to look for him. They signal to some other boys down the corridor, then go past the duty teacher and make their way to the alcove where Jamie is sitting. They sit down on either side of him. The door to the library opens and closes again, and they know their friends have arrived. These boys sit down in the next alcove.

The first boy grabs Jamie by the knee and pinches hard. Jamie pulls away and looks as if he may cry. The boy then pats him on the head and says, 'There, there, cry baby. Isn't mummy here to blow your poofter nose?' The other boy giggles. Jamie looks from one to the other and feels trapped. The second boy pulls the book away from him. 'What ya reading, freak? Trying to find out how to bugger boys, I bet.' He pushes Jamie hard so that he falls against the other boy.

The boys in the next alcove are watching and listening. They start to mutter, 'Faggot, faggot', and to make sarcastic comments: 'Come on, queer, haven't you got a life', 'Come on, Jamie, you disgusting freak', 'Yer fucking faggot, go fuck yourself. Nobody else will.' They laugh. The first boy pushes Jamie back so hard that his head slams into the wall behind him. 'Poofter, poofter, his brain'll be mashed,' he jeers. 'If he's got one,' says the other boy. They grab the pages on which he has been writing, scribble over them and screw them up.

The duty teacher calls out, 'What's all that noise? No noise in the library or you'll be thrown out'. 'Yes, sir, no sir,' chorus the boys. They giggle again. The two on either side of Jamie hiss, 'Teach you a lesson, homo freak. Just go die somewhere', and one punches him hard in the solar plexus. The others file past and stare at him with disdain. A couple make obscene gestures.

Jamie stays still and silent until they have gone, gasps for breath, and then tries to wipe his face, straighten out his clothes and his pages, and get ready for the afternoon.

Here are several useful pieces of background information to this incident

- It is a close representation of a real event.
- Jamie feels very confused about his sexuality, especially in light of the disgust with which he is treated. He lives with his mother who is a solo

parent. She loves him and supports him, but is low in self-esteem herself and does not have many resources for helping Jamie to survive in the world. He never sees his estranged father who detests the idea of having 'a poofter' for a son.

- Children of gay or lesbian sexual orientation are likely to be bullied. Rivers (1995, 1996) carried out research with 140 gay and lesbian teenagers and reported that over 80 per cent had been teased about their sexual orientation and over half had been physically assaulted or ridiculed both by other students and teachers.

What observations and inferences can be made about this incident?

- In this school and community, there is clearly a sense of homophobia.
- The pupils treat Jamie with scorn and hatred. This is not stopped by the school.
- The adults know that what is happening is wrong but are ambivalent about Jamie themselves, and directly and indirectly condone the bullying.
- This school is a very unsafe place.
- Jamie's self-esteem and confidence have been poor for a number of years. He starts to truant regularly to avoid school. Though he is obviously intelligent, his academic work suffers. Jamie eventually unsuccessfully attempts suicide because he feels so bad. Shortly after this, he will leave school early. He will be put in touch with a central city organisation that is active in supporting gay rights. They will find him a job and a place to live, and arrange counselling for him.

Scenario Three: Racist Bullying. Rangi Replies to Harassment and Racist Teasing with Violence

Rangi is working by himself in the classroom. The door opens. 'What are you doing, Maori boy?' taunts David. 'Did ya fall in the shit, black boy?' He struts closer. 'Are you reading something? I didn't know you could read.' 'Hey, nigger,' the other boys say as they start to filter in and see Rangi on his own.

Instead of ignoring these taunts and provocations (as he has done four or five times over the last month), Rangi loses his temper. He turns on David. The two boys fight and Rangi is clearly a better fighter and is winning. David's friend Jim steps in, grabs Rangi around the neck and pulls him away from David, throwing him on the ground. He helps David up. The duty teacher arrives, and David and Rangi are taken to the deputy principal's office. David has been crying and says that he was just having fun and that Rangi went 'psycho' and really hurt him. When questioned, Rangi is surly and insolent and is suspended from school for a week for fighting and being rude to the deputy principal. David's friends back him up and say that Rangi went 'psycho' for no apparent reason. David is given a warning about fighting but is largely seen as the innocent party.

Rangi is identified by those in authority as the aggressor. He is not listened to. Instead, the boy with more credibility in the school is believed.

Here are several useful pieces of background information to this incident

- It is a close representation of a real event.
- Rangi is one of only a few Maori children in this South Island school.
- Rangi is seen as having a bad attitude. He is regarded as violent, with a tendency towards bullying.
- Rangi has shown he is tough and can stand up for himself and people do not generally mess with him.
- The school sees Rangi as being to blame for the situation.
- The school authorities believe racism does not exist in their school.

What observations and inferences can be made about this incident?

- Although there is a strong element of racism in this scenario, the school authorities believe the aggressors and discipline the victim.
- These boys will probably not bother Rangi again.
- Rangi, however, will probably harbour a grudge against the boys, will be angry at the racism, and will turn against the school because of its inability to address the problem justly.
- It may set him on a path to antisocial acts based on a sense of grievance and injustice towards society at large.
- The other boys will turn their attention to somebody else they can victimise more easily.
- The other boys may grow to think racism is acceptable.

Scenario Four: Psychological Bullying. Rachel's Exclusion by Charlotte and Her Peer Group

Rachel is nine. She is playing in the school yard by herself. Four girls from her class, led by Charlotte, come up to her. 'You can't play here. This is our area,' says Charlotte. They push Rachel aside, purposely ignoring her as they do so, and start to chalk in hopscotch squares. She does not resist, even though she is taller than they are.

'Can I play?' asks Rachel.

'No, you dress funny and you're too dumb and ugly to play with us,' replies Charlotte in a sweet voice that contradicts her words. It seems to be a bit of a joke, as if perhaps she does not mean it, and even Rachel laughs. Charlotte flashes her winning smile at her friends as she says this. They all giggle at her comments.

'You can come over to Anna's house after school, though. We're going to watch a video,' Charlotte says condescendingly, giving a knowing look towards the circle of admirers. Rachel's instincts tell her things are not as they seem but she really wants to go to Anna's house; she wants to be accepted.

Rachel walks to Anna's house after school and knocks on the door. No one answers the door. She knocks several more times. She sees the curtain move and hears the quiet giggling of several girls on the other side of the door. Her heart sinks. After a few more quiet knocks and no response, Rachel gives up and walks home despondently. Later that evening, Rachel answers the telephone. 'Hello, this is Rachel,' she says. Someone laughs at the other end of line, says, 'Weirdo freak', and then hangs up.

Here are several useful pieces of background information to this incident

- It is a close representation of a real event.
- The school in this scenario is in an affluent neighbourhood. It is academically very successful and much value is placed on material possessions.
- Charlotte's father is a successful lawyer who is well known in the school community.
- Charlotte is an attractive child, she smiles a lot, does well at school, and is highly thought of. She is her teacher's favourite pupil. She is widely recognised for her leadership skills, and is seen as having all of the hallmarks required for success at school and in the world at large.
- Rachel is unusual in her dress and thinking. Although she is creative, interesting, and intelligent, she is also introverted, quiet, and whimsical, and sometimes appears to be sullen. She is not popular with the teachers. She is an average achiever and her teacher feels ambivalent about her. She either does not notice or is willing to overlook teasing or exclusion of Rachel by Charlotte and her friends, not only in the playground but also in the class.
- Becky, one of the girls who is part of Charlotte's circle of friends, once invited Rachel to play but told her not to tell Charlotte or the other girls. Becky was invited to Rachel's house several times but she never came.
- Events like this happen to Rachel almost daily. It has become routine and nobody seems to notice.

What observations and inferences can be made about this incident?

- The crowd of girls around Charlotte has no empathy for Rachel, nor do they feel in any way responsible for what is, in fact, an act of bullying.
- This sentiment is echoed by the teachers. They do not consider the purposeful exclusion of Rachel by her peer group to be bullying, they do not take it seriously, and they see it largely as Rachel's problem.
- Although not subjected to physical abuse, Rachel is still the victim of bullying. It is manipulative and cruel, and could have as detrimental an effect on Rachel as physical bullying has on Ben.
- This school is not a safe place for Rachel.

9 The School Environment

Introduction

Although there must be a strong emphasis on strategies, students, and teachers when examining anti-bullying procedures, it is also important to consider the physical environment of the school.

In class, children are in a small, defined group with established peer relationships and a teacher in charge. There is also usually a formal learning task in hand, with specific processes and goals. Because the classroom is a closed unit within a structured timeframe, it is generally a safe environment. But bullying can occur in the classroom if the teacher is not vigilant.

When children are out in the corridors and playground of the school, the structures and rules are less defined and the chance of being at risk is greater. From a finite set of relationships, the children move into a mass where different rules apply, where the social groupings are fluid and ever-changing, and where there is little supervision.

And it is during this important time that bullying occurs most often: in the playground, and elsewhere in the school between classes (see Chapter 2, 'Where Does Bullying Take Place?'). Dealing with these areas is a management issue that requires creativity and vision.

There are two major ways of tackling bullying in the school environment: by extending control over areas where bullying is likely to occur, and by creating a stimulating and enjoyable school environment. Control over the school environment can be both psychological, that is, children are taught to monitor their own behaviour and that of others; and physical, that is, teachers, and possibly parents and students, may be asked to patrol areas of the school outside class hours. The creation of a stimulating school environment as a way of combating bullying is more a matter of architecture, gardening, landscaping, and using the imagination, ingenuity, and resources of the school community.

Extending Control Over Areas Where Bullying is Likely to Occur

In less controlled situations children can be bullied opportunistically. This can occur on a large playing field or in an enclosed space. For example, a group of girls find themselves near a girl alone in the playground. They think she is 'a bit of a loser' and notice that she is wearing a new jersey. They run past her, yelling abuse, and one of them grabs her sleeve as she runs and keeps hold of it until it rips. They call out, 'Sorry about the lovely jersey', and run off laughing. A group of older boys comes upon a single smaller boy in the toilets. No one else is around so they decide to have 'a bit of fun' by teasing him, and then they start to push him around and force him to give them all his money.

The open spaces of the playground, and the corridors, toilets, and other public areas of the school, are also perfect environments for more systematic forms of victimisation. In the playground, relative anonymity and the general hurly-burly of play provide covers for this sort of bullying. In the unlikely event that it will be noticed by staff, it can readily be passed off as 'fun'. Bullying some- times occurs as an out-of-class pastime when a group of bullies plan to 'get' their victim, and stalk him or her down. Such children often live in fear of going to the canteen, having to go to the toilet, and walking down corridors. They are almost always alone, and they are targeted by bullies.

Extending control over these areas is the first step in discouraging and finally combating bullying. If a school adopts a whole school approach, then one of its aims will be to encourage children to respect others, and to report bullying, both experienced and witnessed. In addition, it is important that bullying danger spots are identified to make proper patrolling of the school more efficient and to help create a safe school environment.

There Should be an Appreciation of the Rights of Others

In the playground, if there is a large group of children and only one or two teachers, all the teachers can manage is damage control. The law of the jungle prevails, and the stronger children dominate. In an unsafe playground, a number of trends occur:

- Boys' exuberant games tend to take up a large area and expand as they need to, dominating everything else. Girls, although half of a coeducational school's population, can be pushed into a small corner of the available space.
- In single-sex schools, this type of disparity occurs between the dominant, physical children and the passive, quieter children.
- Children who are isolated from their peer group, and special needs and ethnic minority children, are vulnerable to bullying either from peers or groups of older children.
- Children who have been marked out to be victimised can be separated from the group and bullied in an unpatrolled area.

- The creating and breaking of rules that is part of children's growth and learning can be subverted into destructive behaviour that focuses on victimisation.

Because this is a potentially anarchic environment, it is crucial that the school develops a clear set of rules about what is and is not acceptable. Concerns about bullying and not considering others should be part of a wider aim of making the playground safe. It is imperative that these rules stress the need to respect the rights of others. If these rules are grounded in a whole school approach to bullying, then they are more likely to have some effect.

If the school has a play area with equipment, it is easy to encourage children to develop their own rules for the use of this area, in junior as well as secondary schools. These playground rules, for example, were developed within an American junior school after it designed and funded its own play area:

1. One person at a time on slides and poles.
2. Use the playground on your day. The first graders use it on Monday, second graders on Tuesday …
3. Go down the slides.
4. Try not to disturb others.
5. No throwing snowballs, wood chips, or rocks.

For more information about this school and its play area, see http://www.needham.mec.edu/NPS_Web_docs/Hillside/main/playground.html

Part of this approach, which attempts to provide ground rules about behaviour and attitudes in a whole school policy, stresses the importance of students letting staff know if they experience or see bullying. The acceptance of this rule is the most effective way of defeating a bullying culture.

Identifying the Danger Spots

Within any school there are danger spots—areas where bullying is more likely to occur. These may be places where people rarely congregate (a passageway or corridor), which are isolated (the periphery of a large playing field), or which are enclosed and not patrolled (certain toilets or the cafeteria).

Carrying out a survey of danger spots with students will give an accurate sense of where bullying occurs most frequently. This will also involve students in an anti-bullying measure, and may be a first step in signalling to bullying students that the school will no longer tolerate bullying, and will handle it rapidly and thoroughly if it occurs.

A survey can be successfully carried out by providing students with a photocopied map of the school and asking them to mark on it where bullying occurs (a) very often, (b) quite often, or (c) sometimes. By putting these responses together, an overall picture of a school's bullying danger spots can be drawn. Included in this survey should be questions about going to and from school (either on foot or by school bus or public transport).

The students can be shown the results of the survey and asked how to deal with these problem areas. It may be useful to show the video, *Bullying: Don't Suffer in Silence*, in conjunction with this work (DFE, 1994), and to use the danger spots survey and a discussion of the video as a way to begin changing the school culture. Students may suggest that they patrol the danger spots, or that teachers or parents do. They may suggest altering them physically so that they lose some of their peripheral or enclosed nature. But, most important of all, if they start to think of the danger spots differently, they will start to feel responsible about what occurs in them. If this process is repeated throughout the school, the danger spots may cease to be perilous places.

Patrolling the Playground

Boulton (1994a, b) argues that putting more people on duty and thereby increasing the policing is not enough. It will not stop children excluding each other, bring an end to vicious remarks, halt obscene gestures, or stamp out physical bullying. It may deter some instances of intimidation and victimisation, and increase the amount of reporting, but it will not make children feel more empathetic or socially responsible.

Better and increased patrolling is, however, an immediate and practical response to out-of-class bullying, especially when the danger spots have been identified. And there are policing methods that are more effective than simply having larger numbers of adults moving around the school in breaks and at lunchtime. For instance, a teacher recently told me that areas of his school were habitually not patrolled because teachers felt unsafe there. It became apparent that this was because they patrolled alone. The solution was that, rather than giving up this space to a gang of intimidating students, two teachers should patrol together.

In Chapter 8, I discuss Cleary's method of identifying class leaders. One of the tasks allocated to class leaders could be to help maintain order in the playground. Allied to this approach is the use of student monitors. In a school that encourages peer strategies for dealing with bullying, the appointment of monitors from the group of trained peer counsellors or mediators to act as playground monitors will work well (see Chapters 10 and 11). Alternatively, students who have shown an interest in the danger spot survey or who are directly involved in an anti-bullying initiative may make successful monitors.

There are also ways to involve the community in playground monitoring. In some schools it is appropriate to ask for parent help in patrolling playgrounds at lunchtime. This can be done with minimal training and, in a school that is operating an anti-bullying initiative, can be part of the plan for a whole school approach.

Community initiatives can also be adapted to the local needs of schools. For example, in New Zealand, the Tu Tangata (standing tall) program (see Puketapu, 1988) has been developed by the Maori community but is not directed only at Maori students. It brings the community into the classroom through placing adults alongside students, and these same adults could also fulfil the role of playground patrol as part of their contribution of time and commitment to the school. The adaptation of the program should be relatively straightforward and could be suggested at preliminary meetings that involve the school community in the setting up of an anti-bullying initiative.

Creating a Stimulating and Enjoyable School Environment

There are a number of ways in which a school can be made a better environment for children, by thinking out the use of space, and by introducing playground activities. This can involve specific professionals and tradespeople such as architects, builders, and landscape gardeners, but it can also rely on the ingenuity and resources of the school population. It involves a change not only of the physical, but also of the psychic and temporal, environments.

Time Management

School playgrounds vary enormously. Some are very small and overcrowded, some are massive and barren. There are practical ways of managing the use of space and providing the best conditions within the limitations of the school. For example, if the playground area is small, or there is a problem with overbearing and raucous play, lunch hours can be staggered so that there are fewer children in the playground at any one time.

Alternatively, classes can be rostered to use the playground at different times. This will relieve overcrowding and give the children a sense that it is a privilege to be allowed time out of class. For example, in a school with five different grades, one grade could be allowed to use the playground one day a week at lunchtime, and during breaks the class whose teacher is on duty could be allowed to use specific play equipment or to play in a specific area. This may simply be an extension of the rule that allows only a certain number of children on play equipment at any one time.

Rethinking the Structure and Aesthetics of the Playground

Children can be involved in modifying the space. When I was setting up a community centre in Montréal in the 1970s, I involved the potential users in designing the centre, getting community donations of paint and furniture, and decorating it. The teenagers had good ideas and created an environment that they liked. As a result they enjoyed, respected, and policed what they had created. School children, too, can be involved in beautifying and planting playground areas, thus feeling a sense of ownership.

There are numerous examples of the involvement of students and school communities in the beautification and development of playgrounds. In Australia, the Tidy Schools Competition attracts many entries in several categories, and encourages children to take pride in their school environments and to find ways in which they can improve them. The *Detroit News* of 21 October 1997 reports how 425 children at Gompers Elementary School in Detroit raised $10 000 to create a new play area in a barren west-side playground. One of the parents at the opening ceremony said, 'I'm hoping it will calm the neighborhood. Kids should feel safe at their playground. ... It will teach the kids to take care of stuff. You got to respect your own stuff before you get self-respect.'

Alternatively, the driving force behind environmental change can come from regional or national agencies with local and voluntary input. In the United States, for example, many schools have been upgraded by urban development initiatives and Federal Work Programs. Jordan High School in New York has been totally transformed through a Federal Work Program which beautified an ugly wasteland of the Old Erie Canal and created a baseball diamond, gardens, and playing fields for the school.

Environments can be changed architecturally and spatially with imagination, little cash, and a lot of hard work. In the school population, there are often parents with architectural, building, or landscape skills who may be persuaded to help with such a venture. Alternatively, it is a good idea to ask the children what they want in their ideal playground and then to get students from a local architecture, design, or recreational studies tertiary course to take on the project as an assignment. In some cases this will lead to the creation of detailed plans that can then be implemented with community help, and sometimes to the building or partial building of the design at a minimal cost through the use of grants or subsidies. People from a government-funded job scheme can also be invited to participate.

If a play area is worn out and ugly, students can be asked to suggest ways of making it pleasant and stimulating again. Gardening and painting involve only minimal cost (and local businesses may donate plants and paint). Students can be asked to decorate areas of barren asphalt with games, roads, and world maps, for instance. When graffiti has appeared, it could be painted over but a designated 'graffiti wall' created. Rusty, broken equipment can be painted and repaired. If children do the work themselves, with help, then they are more likely to take pride in the area and look after it.

Sometimes space is at a premium. Even then, there are usually ways to increase and improve space. All it may require is imagination and lateral thinking. When I was a member of the management committee of my children's primary school, the school made a creative decision to provide more playing space. A limited area was available, but, by lateral thinking and a great deal of ingenuity, the school was able to build a multilevel adventure playground in a bordering city council gully, using parental support and only minimal funds.

In designing how best to use the space, it is beneficial to survey what various children do or would like to do. It is important to create spaces, both inside and outside, for all weather, so that all children are catered for, both those who love exuberant play and those who enjoy quieter activities.

If children have access to the Internet at school, they may want to see what playgrounds in other schools and other countries are like. A useful address is http://www.kidlink.org/KIDPROJ/Bridges/playgrounds.htm

In a whole school environment, cooperation between parents, students, teachers, and the community is crucial. Although it may require out-of-school time and energy, it builds strong foundations that should make a resilient school resistant to bullying. Many side benefits result from working together like this.

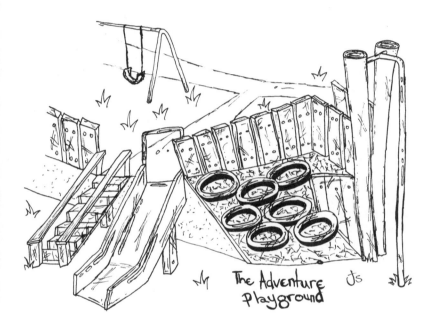

The Adventure Playground

Beating Boredom

Many children are bored in school playgrounds. One result of the television age is that children often become passive and unimaginative, and do not know how to play creatively. If a school becomes proactive in its management of recreational time, there may be a reduction in bullying simply because there are more interesting things to do. For example, teachers can introduce children to traditional games for outside play (see Opie, 1993; Opie and Opie, 1969, 1998) and to board and other games for inside play. This has the very important added advantage of giving teachers and children a way of getting to know each other and building stronger connections in a less formal setting.

If children have access to the Internet at school, they can contact other schools to share descriptions of popular playground games. For example, there is a web site that describes various games and includes and invites contributions from schools around the world. The address is: http://www.whitehall.waltham.sch.uk/game.htm

It is worth considering the creative involvement of parents in both the recreational and academic functions of the school. Although in some schools it is common for parents to help with reading and other classroom tasks, for some parents the school exists behind a kind of imaginary barricade. An Israeli project in which I was involved (Lichman and Sullivan, 1999) had the larger intention of building bridges between Jewish and Arab children but was also designed to bring parents into the school by getting children to ask their parents and grandparents about games they played as children. The parents and grandparents then came to the school and showed the children how to play the games. This benefited everyone concerned, giving the children something to do in their lunch hours and breaks, giving parents (sometimes for the first time) access to the school, and endowing the children and teachers with often lost cultural knowledge.

Playground time, as Briggs (1994) argues, can be seen as an educational opportunity.

Concluding Remarks

This chapter suggests ways of preventing bullying in the school and playground by being innovative and inclusive, and by making the children the proud custodians of their school environment. The suggested readings explore this topic further.

part **4**

Interventions

'"There is nothing wrong with
conflict," one eleven-year-old
explained to me. "It's what we do with
it, how we handle it." "And the same for
anger," piped up another. As the young people
explain it, it is "cool" to resist violent confrontation
and settle disputes in a non-violent way.'

('Cool Schools…', *Broadsheet*, Spring 1994, p. 24)

10 Peer Strategies: Befriending

Introduction

The potential for using the peer group to solve bullying conflicts is enormous. Although adults, teachers, and parents may have the best intentions in the world, the power of the peer group, from an early age but especially from adolescence onwards, is very great. This power is often a cause of bullying, but it can also be used to find solutions.

Within many schools, two worlds exist: that of the teaching staff and that of the pupils. These worlds come together in the classroom, where the teacher has the authority, owing to his or her position and role. Outside the classroom, the teachers are numerically overwhelmed and these worlds exist side by side, often with very little interaction and overlap. Although teachers may be able to deal with occasional outbreaks of antisocial behaviour outside the classroom, most of what goes on there is usually unseen, not reported, and beyond teachers' control.

Most bullying is not reported to adults, partly because of fear of retaliation and a belief that nothing will be done, but also because of peer group pressure. Whatever it is called—narking, grassing, ratting, snitching, splitting, or telling tales—the unwritten rule is that children should not tell on their peers. Loyalty is to the peer group, not to the adult world; to ask for interventions from that world is not considered 'cool'. If students go against the accepted code of conduct, they risk rejection not only by antisocial members of the peer group but also by the more prosocial members.

There are, however, counters to this peer group pressure. Pikas (1989) argues that the peer group is not comfortable watching bullying but feels powerless to do anything about it. So, if these students are provided with a way of stopping the bullying, then they are likely to respond positively.

And, most important of all, if the culture in the school rejects bullying and supports its students in telling rather than suffering in silence, then the greater good of a safe school will win out over fear of reprisals, rejection by the peer culture, or tyranny.

One of the ways in which a school can create a safe culture is through the adoption of peer support strategies. Such strategies, which include peer partnering, peer mentoring, peer counselling, and peer mediation, are among a school's best weapons for combating bullying. If the students are fully involved in the solutions, then they have a very good chance of working. Peer strategies can be supported from within the curriculum, or by interventions from the outside that are embraced by a whole school approach. In this chapter, I will discuss two forms of peer support under the general heading of befriending: peer partnering and peer mentoring.

Peer partnering and peer mentoring, both based on one-to-one relationships, take place as a result of a school initiative or a school policy (in the case of a buddy system, for instance). Peer partnering is essentially about sharing time and providing support, whereas peer mentoring is about helping to solve a problem by giving positive feedback and the benefit of experience.[1]

Peer Partnering

Peer partnering is a form of befriending in which an individual is chosen to provide companionship and friendship for a student who has been identified as needing support or who appears to be at risk. Once a befriending project is started, there should be an adult to oversee and monitor it. This approach, which is suitable for use in primary or secondary schools, aims to provide helpful and friendly support, to encourage confidence, and to widen the befriended student's cohort of friends.

Peer partnering can be used when individual students arrive at a new school, or speak a foreign language, or when a child seems to have low self-esteem, is isolated, or has been bullied. In recent years, peer partnering has been used in the UK context with refugee children who have experienced traumatic life events, are lonely, and perhaps do not have the support of their families (Cowie and Sharp, 1996, p. 65).

A school may use peer partnering on a larger scale. It can be used to make sure, for instance, that a cohort of new third formers is integrated into the school. In New Zealand, third formers are often referred to as 'turds' by older students and subjected to verbal and physical abuse. To avoid this, in a number of schools third form students are buddied with seventh formers. They are befriended, made to feel safe, and welcomed into the school community. The support they receive from the older students signals to the rest of the school that they are accepted and included, and shows clearly that the school culture does not accept the victimisation of younger students.

Befrienders should be chosen because of personal qualities and their willingness to help. To learn the qualities and skills required, trainees will need to

---

1 It is important that children who agree to befriend or mentor others are acknowledged for this, perhaps with a certificate or a book with an inscription inside. These are very small items in a school's budget and it is important that these students are not overlooked.

attend a course. Ideally, this should take place during one day on a weekend, with several follow-up sessions to reinforce what was learnt. Cowie and Sharp suggest that part of the training should focus on team-building exercises, and that for such schemes to work well it is important that befrienders meet regularly so that they can debrief, get feedback, and so increase their effectiveness.

The supervisor will need to meet with both the selected peer partner (the befriender) and the individual needing partnering (the befriended) to help them set up a contract and an agreement to work together in a particular way for a specified length of time. If a general buddying system is created for a new group of third formers, they can be talked to together.

Children are often bullied because they stand out in some way. Those chosen as befrienders must be helped to acquire a high level of tolerance and understanding so they can appreciate, rather than feel uncomfortable about, difference. They need to be taught the difference between supporting and befriending, on the one hand, and being patronising and 'rescuing', on the other. They should expect something from the relationship too; the relationship should involve give and take, rather than being one-sided.

When the peer partnership is coming to an end, a transition out of the relationship should be sensitively arranged, or the relationship should be deformalised. It is important that students are not befriended for a short while and then dropped. If this happens with children who are isolated from their peer group, they can end up feeling worse than before. On the other hand, children who have been chosen for partnering because they are isolated, and who continue to be isolated after a period of peer partnering, may need some other form of intervention to accompany this strategy.

Peer partnering is a preventative approach designed to stop a problem such as bullying from starting or growing. It is a temporary arrangement (usually for a term). (See Demetriades, 1996, on peer partnership in action.)

> **Comment:** Peer partnering is relatively undemanding but can be a very effective form of peer support. New Zealand schools that have a buddy system say it works very well in helping third formers to settle in. It is a prosocial intervention: because third formers are new to the school and are the smallest and weakest pupils, they are the most prone to bullying.

Peer Mentoring

Victims of bullying are not the only ones who need help. Bullies are often in trouble in other areas of their lives and may be on the verge of being excluded (expelled) from school. For both victims and bullies, having a peer mentor for discussion, feedback, and support (often in concert with another program) can be very beneficial.

Peer mentoring[2] is a one-to-one approach based on the pairing of a more socially skilled student (usually of the same sex) with someone of their own age or a little younger who has a problem with bullying. It is appropriate for use in secondary schools.

It is important to identify the aims of the scheme (written down as a statement of intent or policy) and to run a clear program that can be monitored and evaluated.

Peer mentoring has three elements:

- befriending, being a friend or providing companionship to someone, sharing activities with them;
- talking about life in general, and discussing all the unwritten rules and understandings of the school; and
- supporting the person by discussing their particular difficulty (as a victim of bullying or a perpetrator of bullying) and helping them to find a solution.

Introducing the Program

A peer mentoring program could proceed as follows.

Announcing the scheme

The school should let students know that a peer mentoring scheme has been developed to help sort out bullying problems. It should be made clear that bullying occurs in all schools and that nobody has the right to bully another person. Students should be told that the purpose of the scheme is to work with those who are having trouble with bullying, either as victims, as perpetrators, or as bystanders. The point is to find ways of reacting to bullying that support and create a safe school environment. It is important to say that, if someone is being bullied, it is not their fault; that it is a problem the school will help to solve. Similarly, students must understand that, if they are being bullied, or feel hopelessly caught in the middle when bullying occurs, or if they know of someone who is being bullied, they should let a teacher or counsellor know.

Information about peer mentoring should be given initially at a school assembly. The guidance counsellor or deputy principal (or whoever is in charge of the program) should then visit individual classes to provide more details.

Selecting peer mentors

It is best to use students who are at least in the fourth form (for a Form 3 to 7 secondary school) or in the ninth grade (for a Grade 8 to 13 high school), as they will have had enough experience of secondary school to be helpful.

---

2 The idea of peer mentoring came to me during my brief period as a guest tutor at Oxford University's Department of Educational Studies in 1995. Central to their postgraduate certificate in education was the involvement of expert teachers as mentors for trainees. This seemed to work well for all concerned (see McIntyre, 1997). Peer mentoring is similar to befriending as described by Cowie and Sharp (1996, pp. 13-19), and could be characterised as a further development of this concept.

Peer mentors can be self-nominated, or nominated by teachers or counsellors. When choosing mentors, it is important to be inclusive so that peer mentors can be matched with their clients. They should come in all shapes and sizes. Students can be kept 'on the books' and called on (and trained) as the need arises. Preference may be given to those who are enthusiastic and good at making and maintaining relationships, and those who have been either a perpetrator or a victim of bullying and can now talk about their experiences in a constructive and reflective way.

The Training Program

A training program could be run at the beginning of the school year, on a recurrent basis, or as the need arises. I would suggest carrying out a training schedule over several weeks for two-hour periods out of class time. An optimum number for a training group is nine students (three groups of three), so that adequate time can be spent with each group and each individual.

The training program is designed to give the trainees the skills required for the job, to help them understand what the specific requirements are, to tell them what is expected and what is beyond the job, to familiarise them with the person supervising the scheme, and to introduce them to others who have been selected as peer mentors so that they can set up a support network.

Session one: introducing the scheme

When students have been selected for a scheme such as this, they tend to feel excited and a bit anxious. It is a good idea to provide tea/coffee and biscuits at the beginning of the first meeting to welcome them.

Introduction

The first session is an introduction to the program. The students should be welcomed and introduced to each other, using an exercise which helps to break the ice (see 'Ice-breakers' in Appendix IV).

The nature and extent of bullying

Most people have only a vague sense of what counts as bullying and often do not realise its extent. It is useful to ask students to brainstorm in pairs to provide a definition of bullying.

The group can be asked to guess at the percentage of bullying that gets reported, and to discuss non-reporting. The facilitator could explain that the mentoring scheme has been organised to combat bullying and to encourage its reporting.

The peer mentor's roles

There are three subroles a peer mentor must master:
- Getting to know the other person. In this role the mentor spends some time with the person being mentored, perhaps meeting them for a coffee or arranging to watch a video or movie together. They can simply meet at school and get to know each other.

- Talking things through in a general way. The mentor can ask how things are going and ask general questions to get to know the person: for instance, what he or she likes and does not like about the school, what he or she perceives the unwritten rules to be, how the person being mentored is coping, how the mentor coped. It is important to do active things together, such as going to a movie, playing video games at someone's home, mini-golf, or whatever else is popular after school hours. If the mentor has a regular sports activity, he or she could ask the mentored student along to watch or take part. Sometimes people being mentored are shy or cautious and it is important to establish a sense of trust before trying to deal with problems.
- Supporting the person to find a solution to their problem. When the person feels comfortable and safe with the mentor, he or she may want to discuss the bullying problem. It is important that the mentor knows how to discuss it, how to reflect back feelings, and what solutions and strategies to suggest.

At this point, it may be useful for the trainees to break up into three subgroups. Each group should be given a large sheet and assigned one role to talk about, e.g. getting to know the other person. The aim of this exercise is to find ways of effectively mentoring different types of people and problems. The exercise may be made very specific.

The groups can then reform as a class and share what they have discovered, commenting on each other's findings. As a way of consolidating this learning process, the trainer could take the three sheets, compile the findings and give them back to the students the following week for a brief review.

A way of recapitulating what has been learnt in this session is to ask the group the following questions:
- What do you know about bullying?
- How widely is bullying reported?
- What do you think students can do to help to stop bullying occurring?
- Name and describe the three elements of peer monitoring.

Session two: learning micro-counselling skills

At this session the trainees are given more concrete training through role play, small-group discussions, feedback, and the presentation of more detailed information.

Review of the last session

Everyone should be presented with a copy of a typed sheet that summarises the combined findings from the last session's brainstorming session about the three roles. There should be a brief discussion of the three roles and people's findings.

People's answers to the questionnaire should be returned and quickly reviewed (optional) (ten minutes).

Discussion of personal experiences
Students should be split up into groups of three and asked to discuss incidents of bullying in which they have been involved.

Teaching skills
Effective peer mentoring is essentially about having or acquiring active listening skills. In this session trainees will learn the following:
- active listening;
- providing useful feedback through paraphrasing;
- using 'I' statements, focusing on feelings, and avoiding blaming;
- supporting people in making their own decisions.

Students should be asked to role play as poor listeners. While this is acted out, they will recognise things they do when not paying attention to someone. (The facilitator can let a few people role play and ask the others to call out what they regard as bad listening. These suggestions can be written up on a board.)

Poor listeners can do any or all of the following:
- Look away, in the air, at their watch, or use body language that shows they are not listening, while murmuring agreement with the speaker or nodding. This gives a mixed message: 'Yes, I'm listening, no, I'm not'.
- They may interrupt what is being said when the speaker is halfway through, say something completely off the topic, or start telling the person about something similar that happened to them. They may change the subject.
- They may start to give advice about what the person should do.

The facilitator can now summarise what poor listeners do, including the above and any other suggestions that have been written on the blackboard.

Now the students should be asked, 'What do good listeners do?'
Good listeners:
- Give the other person their full attention. They look at the speaker and are fully engaged.
- May nod to indicate their understanding, or draw out the speaker with questions such as, 'How did you feel?' They do not take over the dialogue.
- Reflect back what they have heard. Reflecting is a passive activity in which the listener repeats what they understand has been said. The speaker can confirm that this understanding is right, correct any misunderstanding, and fill in any blanks.

Beyond being a good listener, a mentor also needs to help the mentored student re-establish their confidence and come to their own decisions. An effective mentor will do the following:
- He or she will provide useful feedback through paraphrasing. This means that when the mentored student has spoken, the mentor paraphrases what they have said and leads it back to them: 'So you felt really frightened and sad. That must have been very hard.'
- If the mentor wants to extend the feedback, he or she will avoid blame and focus on 'I' statements and on feelings. For instance, in relation to being physically bullied, a good listener could say, 'That would have been really scary. It

sounds frightening. The same thing happened to me. I felt really relieved I was still alive but I was angry I'd been so badly hurt.'

- He or she will not try to push their ideas but will draw out the thinking of the person they are mentoring so that they elaborate on their own feelings. It is important to give feedback on the speaker's experiences without any pressure that they should act as the mentor has done. In many cases, helping someone to make a decision may be a useful step towards retrieving self-esteem.
- It is important to support this process by asking open-ended and useful questions such as, 'What do you think you should do to sort things out?' rather than saying things that push the person into a corner and make them defensive, such as, 'Well, you've got a real problem here'.
- If the mentor is asked what they would do, they must answer honestly but avoid suggesting that theirs is the right answer. They must not 'rescue' the person by telling them what to do so that they become reliant on the mentor. A major element of the process is for the mentored person to learn to believe in themselves and to access their personal power.

Role playing to practise peer mentoring

It is helpful to develop the use of role playing even further, as it creates confidence in those taking the roles and graphically represents situations with which mentors need to be familiar.

Scenario: Peter has been bullied. After he reported this, the school intervened and stopped the bullying. Peter now feels that he will be beaten up for having narked. In the past he has stayed away from school to avoid being bullied and thinks that if things continue like this that he will drop out. What can be done to help Peter sort this out?

(NB: Other scenarios can be developed for role play purposes. These can be discussed with the trainer.)

Task: The group of three can take on the roles of mentor, mentored, and observer/recorder. The students switch roles so that they each have a turn at all roles. The recorder makes notes about the role play and provides feedback each time the scenario is played out, commenting on what they did well and what needs to be improved. The participants should be assertive and constructive in doing this.

Session three: reinforcing all that has been learnt

In this session, students practise what they have learnt, and identify difficult and important issues that may arise in peer mentoring.

Again the students should work in groups of three, but with different people from those they worked with the previous week. In the first exercise they again use role play to solve a particular bullying problem.

Each person should take a turn being the mentor, the mentored, and the recorder. After the scene has been played through, the recorder reports back to the other two, then the individuals change places until everyone has had a turn in each of these roles.

The group then discusses the scenario and what they think worked and did not work. Participants can each have another turn at playing the mentor.

Scenario: Joe is close to being excluded (expelled) from secondary school for repetitive physical bullying. Peer mentoring and an anger management course are being provided as a final opportunity for Joe. The mentor senses that Joe knows this is his last chance and really wants to succeed. If he finishes school, he will be eligible for entry to a chefs' course at the local polytechnic. His main problem is his short fuse. How can Joe be supported in working his way through this difficulty?

Comment: This scenario is presented as a way of practising the skills learnt in the last session. If one of the group wants to use an alternative scenario, this can be used instead if everyone agrees to it. It will need to be written down like the scenario above.

Other Issues

Ethics and confidentiality

In most counsellor/client relationships, confidentiality is sacrosanct. This situation is different in that peer mentoring involves two students, both of whom are the school's legal responsibility. If the person being mentored says something that suggests she is at risk, for instance, 'I feel so bad today that I want to end it. Don't tell anyone', what does the mentor do? Clearly the mentor is there to help but is neither a trained professional nor an adult. Mentors need to state at the beginning of a relationship that confidentiality will be kept *except* with their own supervisor and if a risk situation occurs. It is crucial that the mentor guarantees complete confidentiality as far as idle gossip and other students go.

The mentor, mentored, and supervisor will need to agree on their lines of communication. In a school that has an open and constructive attitude towards dealing with bullying, this should not be a problem. If it is a worry for the person being mentored, this will need to be talked through.

What are the limits of mentoring?

Mentoring is intended to provide a student with support and friendship, to give them someone to talk to, to support them through a difficult patch for a specified period of time, and to deal with bullying and bullying-related issues. If larger matters come up, such as suicidal feelings, having been badly beaten up, or having been sexually abused, then these are beyond the capabilities of the peer mentor and will need to be passed on to the guidance counsellor. This would also be the case if mentor and mentored do not get on. The counsellor makes a choice about pairing people. If this does not work, it is not a major problem, and another combination can be tried. If peer mentoring does not work for an individual, then another strategy will be needed.

Supervision

The supervisor (usually a guidance counsellor) should meet each mentor once every two weeks for half an hour to see how things are going. The person being mentored could be included at every second session.

Maintaining the program

It is important for the supervisor to meet all the peer mentors once a month to discuss the program and to check regularly on everyone involved, both mentors and mentored.

Period of mentoring

Six months is the optimum time for a mentoring relationship to last. Initially, it is important for the mentor and the mentored to agree to work together for three months, and then to review their relationship with the supervisor. It is important that a maximum time is set, and that at the end of that time the mentored student is helped through a satisfying closure process with the mentor.

As part of a monitoring system, the initial goals for each case should be noted and the outcomes recorded. The supervisor should attend both the initial and final sessions and should also go through a debriefing process with the mentor.

Peer mentoring will often need to be run in conjunction with other methods

If a student habitually bullies or is a victim, working with a peer mentor may be beneficial because the relationship accompanies them through a set period, giving them support while they try to change.

It would, however, be wrong to place too much responsibility on or to have too many expectations of a young, only minimally trained person. It may be beneficial to combine peer mentoring with other initiatives. For a person who bullies, an anger management program may be selected to be run in concert with peer mentoring. Similarly, peer mentoring for a victim of bullying may be used, along with an assertiveness training course or the taking up of a martial art or a self-defence course. When this is done, it is important that the supervisor, mentor, and mentored discuss the program as a whole to ensure that the individual components are not working at cross purposes. For instance, it may be more beneficial to do one program well rather than trying to do too much by adopting two strategies together.

Taking care of the mentors
The peer mentor must maintain their own academic and social life and should not mentor more than one person at a time. There should be a stand-down time between taking on students to mentor. It is important from the mentor's point of view that he or she does not become too involved in the personal life of the mentored person, and that some distance is retained. The supervisor is specifically the mentor's support person.

Letting people know about the program
It is important to let teachers, students, parents, and people in the community know about peer mentoring. This can be done through seminars, through eye-catching and informative notices posted around the school, and through constant reminders from classroom teachers and in school assemblies. This information should be readily available as part of a whole school/safe school approach.

Positive outcomes of mentoring approaches
If those being mentored are given the opportunity to voice their feelings about the upsetting aspects of their lives, this can be the first step towards feeling better about themselves. Mentors, on the other hand, benefit through acquiring problem-solving skills, developing leadership abilities, and learning about the dynamics of relationships. Students who take on these roles are largely seen as contributing positively towards the atmosphere of the school (see Cowie and Sharp, 1996, pp. 14-15).

Conclusion
From a guidance counsellor/deputy principal's point of view, a well-constructed peer support system has the potential to be logistically very useful because it means that teachers' loads can be lightened. In a school where most of the bullying is not reported, school staff end up fighting bush fires as they break out, and the school will only be dealing with the symptoms of bullying rather than solving the problem. That is one reason why it is important to consider strategies that use peer support. Encouraging these is like running an anti-virus program through a computer: it makes the system healthier and disinfects the problem areas.

11 Peer Strategies: Counselling and Mediation

Peer counselling and peer mediation are further examples of peer strategies. Like partnering and mentoring, peer counselling is based on a one-to-one relationship, but in this case it is a specifically advisory and supportive client-centred relationship. It is, therefore, a step further on from mentoring. Whereas peer partnering and peer mentoring are primarily preventative strategies that reinforce the introduction or maintenance of a safe school policy, peer counselling and peer mediation are action-based interventions.

Peer counselling is used to solve bullying problems by providing thoughtful listening and positive feedback. It is run by students with adult supervision. Its aim is to help individual students find their own solutions to bullying problems, and to sort them out immediately or after several counselling sessions. Because it is sometimes necessary to involve opposing sides in a bullying situation, peer counselling can also have a mediation dimension.

Peer mediation is another action-based strategy designed specifically to solve conflicts. It can be called upon when a conflict is observed or reported; or people in conflict can ask the mediators to deal with their dispute. The intention is to defuse a situation as quickly and as thoroughly as possible.

Peer Counselling[1]

Peer counselling is a form of active listening (Cowie and Sharp, 1996). As with peer mentoring, it is based on a process of careful listening, providing feedback, and helping people to find their own solutions. But, whereas the peer mentor plays a supporting role to one person over a negotiated period of time, the peer counsellor has a more formal counsellor-client relationship with several people and offers counselling by arrangement over a shorter period of time.

---

[1] In mapping out this section, I have been inspired largely by Cowie and Sharp (1996) and the Acland Burghley scheme (see references for this chapter).

Setting Up a Peer Counselling Scheme

The beginning of the school year is a good time to set up a peer counselling scheme. Everyone needs to be told what it involves, how it works, and what its purpose is. It may be useful to hold a meeting within the school community to discuss peer counselling, and to set up a display at a central location in the school to which students can come to register interest, either as potential counsellors or as clients.

An office should be allocated for the use of peer counsellors which has regular hours, displays photographs of the counsellors, and has a system for arranging appointments.

It is a good idea to have a range of students as peer counsellors, including those who have bullied and those who have been victims, and students who represent the ethnic, gender, and social class mix of the school. Only the youngest students need be excluded from volunteering.

It is important to decide how many volunteers are needed, and how many to train immediately.

The Effective Peer Counsellor

Figure 11.1 summarises the characteristics and skills that make an effective peer counsellor. Some are innate and are reasons why the student was asked or volunteered to become a peer counsellor (for example, awareness of others, empathy, good listening and relationship skills, social conscience). Others can be learnt through a training program and extended through experience (for example, active listening, being supportive, focusing on feelings, reflecting back). In all cases, training with an experienced adult counsellor is a prerequisite for a successful peer counselling scheme.

The training program is designed to give trainees the skills and confidence they need, to pass on useful information about bullying, and to define the boundaries of the job. Training is done via group work, so the trainees are given an opportunity to get to know the person supervising the scheme as well as their fellow peer counsellors. This is essential in building up a support network for the counsellors.

Training should provide the counsellor trainee with the basic skills of:

- having good listening skills (giving full attention, being quietly encouraging, not interrupting, not taking over);
- having good observation skills (the emotional climate of a meeting can change, and being able to mirror someone's posture to help them relax or to emphasise the feelings being expressed is very useful);
- being able to give good feedback (paraphrasing);
- responding to emotion (clients are often angry, distressed, or sad, and these feelings need to be met by the counsellor);
- helping clients find their own solution (by providing feedback and quietly pointing out the next logical step from the information they have provided,

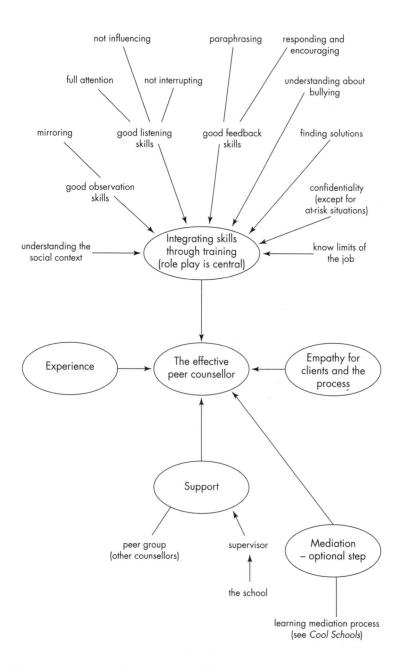

11.1 Becoming an Effective Peer Counsellor

i.e. paraphrasing what they have said and asking, 'What do you think you should do now?');

- creating a sense of trust in their client (through providing supportive feedback and indicating that confidentiality will be kept if there is no fear of risk situations occurring);
- knowing the limits of the job, that is, that the purpose of peer counselling is to deal only with bullying (other issues that arise should be referred on); and
- being creative in their thinking.

It is crucial that peer counsellors are able to empathise. Training exercises will help to harness and give shape to students' empathy. Being empathic also means treating peers as equals during counselling and, within reason, respecting their right to confidentiality.

When students learn to be peer counsellors, they start with little, if any, experience of counselling. Besides training, one of the most important components of a peer counselling scheme is its network of support. Peer counsellors are regularly supervised by an adult counsellor, who is often the person who trained them. Supervision can occur in pairs, between the supervisor and the counsellor; or in groups, where several cases are discussed together with the supervisor.

For instance, in the video about the Acland Burghley peer counselling scheme (see references), a male peer counsellor felt unable to come up with a solution in a bullying case and sent his clients (two boys) off to see a teacher. With honest feedback and support from the group and the supervisor, he took the case up again and arranged an interview that included those responsible for the bullying (two girls). One of these girls was on the verge of being excluded from the school, and another peer counsellor (a slightly older but more mature girl) was assigned to counsel her and help sort things out. This worked well, with the outcome that the girl was seen more sympathetically (she had a hearing disability that had not been taken into account) and her antisocial behaviour was turned around. Under the guidance and control of the deputy principal, the joint supervision sessions were able not only to find constructive solutions for the bullying problem itself but also to help the peer counsellor to extend his skills.

Joint supervisions provide an internship period, giving support and validation to trainees and to counsellors as they explore all the different situations that are likely to confront them.

As peer counsellors gain experience, they can handle situations with more confidence and knowledge. Their own counselling experiences, their reflections on these, and the insights and role modelling that occur in the supervision sessions, are all helpful. Students who have either been bullies or who have survived being bullied can call on their first-hand knowledge to help bullies to stop or can empathise fully with the painful feelings of victims.

The Peer Counselling Training Course

Trainees need to understand what the specific job requirements are, what is expected of a peer counsellor, and what the boundaries are (that is, what is no longer peer counselling). The purpose of anti-bullying peer counselling is to learn how to be an effective listener and to deal only with bullying and then only with cases that can be handled.

Rather than providing a complete training package, the following sections suggest a template for training peer counsellors and focus on aspects of peer counselling training that are specific to the method. Previous chapters provide guidance on developing and using role play (Chapter 8), and how to become an effective and supportive listener (Chapter 10). Appendix IV gives a selection of ice-breakers to help people relax and work together in groups, and the next section on peer mediation gives an outline of a fuller training course that can also be adapted for training peer counsellors. What follows can be used as presented, or modified to meet specific needs.

The training workshops can be held at lunchtime, after school, or in the weekend.

The first session: introductory

When a training course begins, roughly 90 per cent of the time is spent settling people in and subtly creating a safe environment. By the last session, this trend should have been reversed so that 90 per cent of the time is spent on intense activity and 10 per cent on warming down.

Cowie and Sharp (1996, pp. 52-3) suggest a good way to start that emphasises the nature of peer counselling and also opens people up to the training process. Everyone sits in a circle and thinks about something very personal that they have never told anyone (they are not required to say what it is). The students are then asked to imagine confiding in someone about this issue and to think about the sort of person that would be. Descriptions include 'caring', 'respects confidence', and 'solid and reliable'. The trainer then points out that these are the qualities needed in a peer counsellor.

The students should then split into groups of three or four, each provided with a large sheet to record their findings. They should think about the following:
· the purpose of peer counselling;
· the skills that are required;
· the limits of the role;
· the sorts of cases they will deal with; and
· the resolutions they would hope to achieve.

After this has been done, the groups should present their findings. The supervisor's job is to applaud the efforts and fill in the gaps.

As a final exercise, the students should be asked individually to answer the following questions on paper:
· What do you know about bullying?
· How widely is bullying reported?
· Name and describe the purpose and elements of peer counselling.
· How do you think peer counselling can help to stop school bullying?

Their answers can be written down and collected, compiled, and photocopied, and returned at the next session. The purpose is not to mark the answers but to use them as a basis for discussion at the beginning of the next session.

The second session: learning micro-counselling skills

Review of the last session
Everyone should be presented with a copy of the typed sheets containing the combined findings from the last session. The trainer can give a summary of the findings.

Discussion of personal experiences
Students should split up into groups of three and discuss incidents of bullying in which they have been involved as bullies or victims, what they did, and how they were affected.

Teaching the skills through role play to practise peer counselling
Role play for peer counselling has a specific purpose. It is not intended to instil empathy in children who have never learnt to empathise, as is suggested in Chapter 8. Nor is it used to help someone in a befriending situation understand what it is like to need support. The peer counsellor is called on to resolve a specific difficult situation. Role play is used to give them a vehicle for refining and tuning their counselling skills, and for practising and becoming familiar with the useful responses of active listening, finding good solutions, providing their full attention to the client, giving good feedback, mirroring, and paraphrasing what they are hearing.

> **Scenario:** A third form girl named Mary is being made fun of by a group of girls in her class. They have started to follow her wherever she goes, to comment on her clothes, and to ridicule and draw attention to her in front of other children in the playground. She has not told her parents because she is afraid they will tell the school and that the girls will really hurt her. Besides, she feels too ashamed to tell. She is desperate and, as a last resort, has come to the peer counsellors. She is afraid the girls will find out and wants to keep her visit confidential.

(NB: A range of other scenarios can be used for role play purposes. If another is preferred, it should be discussed with the trainer.)

The trainees can first take on the roles played out in the bullying scenario, and change roles so they all become familiar with being a bully, a victim, and a bystander. They can then transform it into a peer counselling session and take turns in the three roles of counsellor, Mary, and recorder. The counsellor and client (Mary) should play out the scenario when Mary first comes to the peer counselling room. The recorder comments on the role play, and then people switch roles and the recorder plays out the peer counsellor role, with modifications based on what was recorded. Each person says what he or she thinks the others did well and what needs to be improved. It is important that they are assertive and honest in doing this. Feedback will help trainees to explore and develop the skills they need to be good listeners and observers in this setting. After this has been done, each group chooses two people to role play the counselling scenario before the entire group.

Subsequent training sessions can explore scenarios that arise in the school or in the past personal experience of the trainees. The main point of peer counselling training is to give trainees practice in handling counselling sessions, and strengthening their interpersonal and listening skills.

The Extra Step—Mediation

Acland Burghley School, a comprehensive secondary school in Camden, North London, set up a peer counselling scheme in 1994. The peer counsellors responded creatively when they found that, in certain cases, active listening to a victimised person was not sufficient to solve the bullying problem. They added a mediation step to deal more effectively with these particular cases.

In such situations, peer counsellors (with the permission of the bullying victim) arranged interviews between themselves and those accused of bullying. If the counsellor felt that a further meeting between the two parties could resolve the problem (and both parties agreed), then a conciliation meeting was arranged and an agreed settlement sought. This is not only beneficial for the victim but also gives the bully a clear message that the students of the school will not tolerate bullying. In the Acland Burghley case, it also gave children who were on the verge of being excluded a way to sort things out.

If a school decides to expand the repertoire of its peer counsellors to include mediation/conflict resolution, then some extra skills will need to be learnt. The process of peer mediation is as follows:

1. A set of ground rules is agreed upon. Both sides must agree not to interrupt or be abusive in any way, to be honest and open, and to try to find a solution.
2. Each side in the dispute tells their story. The peer counsellor listens carefully.
3. The peer counsellor needs to paraphrase what has been said and repeat it to the disputants to allow any elaborations and corrections to be made. Both sides are given this opportunity. This can go back and forth a few times and interruptions should not occur. Once a person has spoken, the other can seek clarification.
4. The disputants are each asked what they would like to come out of this process, and how they would like the matter resolved. This is discussed until an agreement is reached.

If, at any point, the disputants break the rules they have agreed upon, the peer counsellor will need to point this out. If this continues, then the meetings should be stopped. The peer counsellor can then decide whether it is best to bring in an adult or to have a twenty-four-hour cooling off period.

For a more complete overview of mediation, refer to the next section on peer mediation.

Other Issues

Ethics and confidentiality

In most cases, it is important to offer clients confidentiality so that they can talk freely about their situation, but it is also important for the peer counsellor to be free to tell an adult if a situation of risk arises. When a counsellor recounts a case during supervision, this can be done without providing names, but confidentiality cannot be guaranteed as schools are usually small enough for people to know who is being discussed. Participants must agree, however, that no personal information gained during counselling sessions will be revealed outside.

Involvement of adults

Above and beyond issues of confidentiality, some cases are very difficult. A student can decide to call a halt to proceedings at any time and can either continue the case after having talked things through with the supervisor, a peer, or another adult, or can pass the case on to another counsellor or to an adult.

Counsellor/client relationships

It must be made clear (and a way to make this possible must be developed) that, when a counselling session ends, people do not carry their counselling role out into the school community. Peer counsellors must learn to leave the role behind in the counselling room, so they will not take worries home with them and will neither patronise nor favour people who have been their clients.

What are the limits of peer counselling?

The purpose of peer counselling is to help sort out individual bullying problems. If it is done well, however, it is likely that clients may want to talk about other things (such as problems with family or sexual abuse). Such problems are outside the anti-bullying peer counsellor's brief, but he or she can act as a first port of call and take the client to an adult who can help them (or refer them on).

Supervision

It is important to have a supervision session once a week at a set time, convened by the staff member in charge of the scheme. This is an opportunity for peer counsellors to talk about their cases and to get feedback from peers, the supervisor, and any other trained person present. It is a chance for supervisors to model counsellor behaviour, and it gives members of the peer group the opportunity to learn from the experiences of their peers.

Supervision also has the effect of affirming the work the peer counsellors are doing and the scheme generally.

Maintaining the program

The guidance counsellor or the person in charge of the program should meet all the peer counsellors once a month to check on them, the students they are seeing, and how the program is working generally.

Evaluating the program

An important feature of any program is regular evaluation to make sure it is doing what it was set up to do, and to remind people what its purpose is. Evaluation can be done in several ways:

- A survey. A brief and straightforward questionnaire about the effectiveness of the scheme is a good way of gathering information.
- Speaking with children. A less formal way of evaluating the program's effectiveness is to talk with pupils who have been clients and to find out what has

happened for them in both the short and long term. For instance, was the service useful in finding a solution? Have things returned to the way they were before the intervention? Has there been a permanent and easily visible change in the atmosphere of the whole school?

- Speaking with the counsellors. It is important for the guidance counsellor to monitor the counsellors. Has the job been satisfying? Should people do it only for a limited time because it tends to cause burn-out? Are there known instances where people have taken advantage of their peer counselling position? Are there enough representatives from ethnic minority groups? What has been learnt over the last year about what is required to be an effective peer counsellor?

Peer Mediation: The *Cool Schools Programme*

The *Cool Schools Programme* is a type of peer mediation in which student mediators act as intermediaries to find solutions for specific conflicts, such as bullying, which occur at school. The *Cool Schools Peer Mediation Programme* (usually referred to just as *Cool Schools*) was developed in Auckland by Yvonne Duncan, Marion Hancock, and Alyn Ware of the Foundation for Peace Studies Aotearoa/New Zealand. *Cool Schools* was designed initially for primary (including intermediate) schools (five- to twelve-year-olds) to teach both classroom and playground mediation to students. It has been used extensively in schools in New Zealand since it was introduced in late 1991. Owing to its success, it has been expanded to include a separate program for secondary schools and for parents.

Cool Schools addresses bullying both by having processes for dealing with bullying, and by creating an atmosphere in which a mobilised and empowered group of students finds bullying unacceptable.

As Yvonne Duncan explains, central to the *Cool Schools* approach is 'the belief that if you raise children's awareness and understanding of what conflict is about and teach them skills they can implement themselves, it is the most effective way of changing behaviour' (Duncan, pers. comm., 5 December 1996).

Cool Schools has been very successful, for several reasons:
- It is very accessible, easy for teachers, pupils, and parents to understand and use, and it is practical and down-to-earth.
- Separate programs have been developed for the primary and secondary sectors and for parents. This recognises that the dynamics, needs, and stages of development are different for the two sectors and for parents.
- Dealing with major school issues such as bullying often falls on one individual. If that person leaves or burns out because of the demands of an often massive task, then their efforts can die away. *Cool Schools* is overseen by adults but relies on the participation and enthusiasm of students. In other words, it aims to alter the system of the school.
- Children often feel uncomfortable talking to adults but think people their own age will be more understanding. Evidence collected by the deputy principal of a New Zealand primary school supports this. He ran a survey to determine

the effectiveness of peer mediators' abilities to resolve conflict in the playground in his school. Over 80 per cent of the children surveyed felt they could approach a peer mediator and preferred doing this to discussing problems with the teacher on duty.

The developers of *Cool Schools* argue that their program makes sense not only in terms of resolving conflicts but also reflects some of the aims that have been identified within the New Zealand National Curriculum as essential learning areas, particularly in relation to health and well-being, and social studies. The teaching and learning experienced through *Cool Schools* is said to contribute to communication skills, problem-solving skills, social and cooperative skills, and self-management and competitive skills in particular.

They say that schools report the following benefits:
- Students develop an appreciation of conflict as something that can be handled positively and learnt from.
- In many schools, disputes between students are permanently settled in 80-85 per cent of cases.
- Students become equipped with valuable skills for handling conflicts both within and outside the school.
- A much improved and more cooperative school atmosphere develops.
- There are fewer incidents of students involved in troublesome behaviour beyond the school gates and a general increase in students' self-esteem.
- Teachers are more able to leave students to find suitable solutions to their problems, thus freeing teachers from a good deal of time-consuming dispute settlement and disciplinary action.
- Students are provided with an excellent resource for dealing with future conflicts in life (Duncan and Stanners, 1999, pp. 4-5).

Philosophically, the *Cool Schools* program is based on a belief that mediation is preferable to discipline. Discipline involves a person in authority either dishing out a punishment or deciding on a solution, whereas, in mediation, the disputants themselves try to find a facilitated solution within a non-threatening structure. Because the disputants are in charge of their actions rather than being forced to act by an authority figure, they are empowered. It is also argued that, with an effective mediation system, the need for discipline is reduced.

The *Cool Schools* program intends to complement the aims of a whole school approach. Its proponents argue that it works best within an environment and school philosophy which aims to handle conflicts constructively; works hard to enhance self-esteem; promotes cooperation and communication skills; acknowledges the diverse cultural, social, and psychological backgrounds of pupils; involves pupils, where possible, in decision-making; supports teachers and pupils under stress; encourages the expression of feelings; and negotiates its way through problems rather than imposing a decision from the top down (Duncan and Stanners, 1999, p. 11).

Cool Schools is designed for use both in the classroom and the playground. If the program is to be used in schools that are not completely supportive, the trainers suggest it should focus first on the smaller unit of the classroom and, if this proves successful, to apply it throughout the school. In schools that are completely supportive of the program, it can be run throughout the school from the start.

Classroom Mediation

For classroom mediation, it is important to train all pupils in mediation skills. This means that, although not everyone may choose to be a mediator, they all know how the process works and will have some ownership of the scheme. So that mediation can be used when needed, it is suggested that a corner of the classroom be set aside for dealing with conflict if it occurs.

If a dispute arises in the classroom, there are three choices for resolving it:

- a class member can offer to mediate;
- one of the disputants can suggest that they approach a class member to mediate; or
- the teacher can refer students to a mediator.

A by-product of the training is that students may be able to solve the problem without resorting to a mediator.

School-based Mediation

I will now examine the six-step process that has been developed for peer mediation outside the classroom (for primary schools).

Step one: securing support from school administration and from parents

Principals' support

Cool Schools very sensibly suggests gaining the support of the principal, providing general information about how the program works, what benefits it could bring to the school socially and possibly academically, what financial and time commitments are required, and what else the school may need to provide.

School commitment

In terms of reducing discipline problems and improving relationships between pupils, any time expended should be regained several times over. In order for the program to work, the school will need to commit itself in several ways:

- one teacher will need to be in charge overall and for the day-to-day running of the program;
- teachers (and administrative staff preferably) will need to be available for one full day's training;
- whole classes should be given training, using time slots from the health or social studies curriculum;
- senior children will be playground monitors but some skills should be taught to junior children;
- the school will need to purchase or make identifiers for mediators (badges, T-shirts, or caps).

Staff support

Staff need to learn how the process works, its intentions, and its structure. Although a teacher will be administering the process, it is important to establish a *Cool School* 'culture' in the school. This means, for example, that staff will not invoke their own solutions to a dispute that has been settled by pupils.

The approach suggests various ways of enlisting teachers' support, such as providing a selection of key chapters from the handbook for them to read, having a general discussion about conflict resolution and discipline strategies, providing a survey on conflict resolution strategies (available as Appendix 1c in the program handbook), and discussing the benefits after the classroom approach has been implemented.

Parent support

Parent support is essential. It is important to inform parents about peer mediation by sending a letter home, holding a meeting to explain what is happening, and showing them how *Cool Schools* works (through children role playing a theoretical situation). It is also important to liaise with local cultural committees (in New Zealand this would include, for Maori, local marae committees) and with the board of trustees/school governors.

If parents see that their children can help to solve conflict or have their difficulties dealt with, they tend to be supportive. It is also helpful to encourage the use of the process at home.

It is particularly important to explain *Cool Schools* to the parents of mediators so that they can appreciate and value their children's contribution.

Comment: Without proper support, the program will be undermined. Peer mediation challenges traditional, hierarchical ways of dealing with conflict and discipline issues, in which the pupils usually have no input. With *Cool Schools*, responsibility is given to selected children. Some parents who are traditional or authoritarian (and this is a cultural issue as well) do not think children should have this amount of responsibility.

Step two: teacher preparation/training

When a school chooses to adopt *Cool Schools*, it is important to decide who will put the program in place and oversee its development and running. If this person has not been trained in peer mediation, he or she will need to be.

The training of teachers in peer mediation has several spin-offs. It gives them the skills to intervene when conflicts get out of hand, and can also provide help in resolving teacher/pupil, teacher/teacher, and teacher/parent conflicts.

Comment: Once it has been decided to introduce *Cool Schools*, it is important that one person takes responsibility but that the rest of the staff participate in the training provided by the Federation for Peace Studies so that they understand and support the program.

Step three: selection of student mediators

Students selected as peer mediators should have these qualities:
- leadership skills or potential;
- respect of peers or ability to gain this respect;
- good verbal skills;
- initiative;
- willingness to be innovative; and
- ability to maintain commitment.

The selection of mediators should reflect the school make-up in terms of ethnicity, gender, and social group, and there should be a combination of older and younger students (though in the case of primary schools none below Standard 2 age). A wide age range means that there will be mediators to whom any school child can relate, and younger trained pupils will be able to take the place of older students as they leave school. Those students who are cast as rebellious or antisocial can bring their understanding of difficult situations into play, so it is essential to include them as well.

Step four: conducting the training

At each training session, one or two essential skills are taught (see 'The Training of Peer Mediators', below).

Step five: publicising and implementing the scheme

Once the scheme is set up, it must be publicised. It is best to introduce peer mediators to the school and to have them, rather than adults, address the students about the program. It is also important to place notices around the school. Mediators should work in pairs. In co-educational schools, a boy and girl team works best. If there is an ethnic minority population and there is an ethnic conflict, then those chosen as mediators should reflect this. Clear procedures should be developed for all eventualities, for instance, how to deal with serious disputes that are beyond the mediators' ability.

Step six: ongoing evaluation and improvement

The mediators need adult support and should check in daily with supervisors to debrief and discuss any concerns. The role can be boring if there are no mediations to deal with, depressing if a situation is not effectively solved, or frightening if an aggressive situation is encountered. Mediators require report forms to provide details of cases they have handled. Regular feedback and evaluations of their performance are important parts of the process.

The Training of Peer Mediators

Peer mediators are trained through seven sessions of forty-five to sixty minutes. Each session is conducted in the school, and a gap of a week between is recommended so that children have time to integrate the one or two skills they have learnt each time. All sessions are structured in the same way:

- the session starts with a welcome and a warming up activity; followed by
- a review of what was learnt in the previous session in order to reinforce this before moving on to new skills;
- new skills are then taught and students are given a chance to practise them;
- a cooperative task is undertaken; followed by
- an evaluation of the session when students state what they learned and what they found difficult; and
- the session finishes with a practice task.

The seven sessions are devoted to active listening, using 'I' statements and affirmations, recognising types of responses to conflict, open and closed questions, the role of the mediator, mediation processes, and handling difficult situations. I will describe the sessions to give a sense of the structure in action and an overview of the themes developed. The sessions give useful basic training that is reinforced regularly through meetings with adult supervisors.

Session one: skill—active listening

In this session, students are taught about how to listen effectively. Using role play, poor listening skills are demonstrated. Three of these are identified:

- Busy listening. The person says he or she is listening but keeps doing something else or looks at other people or things while the other person is talking.
- Me too! Instead of listening properly, the person talks about his or her own similar experiences.
- Advice is given or the person changes the subject.

It is useful, first of all, to talk about these types of poor listening and to role play them.

Next, it is important to show how good listening works. Three characteristics are given here too:

- Full attention is given to the speaker. Neutral or warm eye contact is maintained which does not make the other person feel uncomfortable.
- The person can be drawn out with such questions as: 'What happened next?' 'How did you feel?'
- It is important to provide feedback and mirroring of the feelings that are expressed, e.g. 'So you felt you were not listened to and became frustrated'.

In the evaluation, it is important to get feedback about what students learnt, what they enjoyed, and what they felt could be improved.

The participants are asked to go away and practise passive listening with a friend or family member, recording the details in a folder.

Session two: skill—using 'I' statements and affirmations

Using 'I' statements makes the listener focus on what they are feeling in response to what is happening. It means that the listener does not tell the disputants what to do and what they are like. It helps to create a safe foundation upon which to build a settlement to a dispute.

Session three: skill—recognising three different kinds of responses to conflicts

In a conflict, people sometimes respond by denying that they are upset even though they are extremely annoyed. They send out mixed messages, which can be confusing for the person receiving them. If a person responds aggressively, either physically or verbally, the conflict is likely to escalate and there will be little basis for finding an answer. Responding in a problem-solving way provides the basis for finding a fair and agreeable solution. This session teaches how to recognise these strategies and how to deal with them.

Session four: skill—open and closed questions

Open questions do not elicit a 'correct' answer, but give people room to move. They allow people to find their own solutions. Closed questions require yes/no answers or other limited responses and are not useful in peer mediation processes. An example of a closed question is, 'Do you think this program is stupid?' The open version is, 'What do you think about the program?'

Session five: skill—role of the mediator

This session clarifies the role of the mediators. Their job is to provide the skills and processes for others to arrive at good solutions, not to provide advice and hold the power. The disputants are responsible for finding solutions.

Session six: skill—reviewing the process

The skill being practised here is recognising how the process works. The students are told that the process will be reviewed. Students form into groups of four: two disputants, one mediator, and one evaluator.

A scenario is provided.

Step 1: The mediator introduces herself.

Step 2: She asks if the disputants want to solve their problem with her.

Step 3: If they agree, they need to move to an appropriate spot to do this. (If they do not agree, the process is stopped, and they are told it can be started again later if they decide to solve the problem.)

Step 4: The mediator explains the four rules of the process:
- do not interrupt—all participants will get a chance to talk
- no put-downs of the other person or name-calling
- be honest
- agree to find a solution to the problem.

Step 5: The mediator suggests that one person starts off, usually the angriest.

Step 6. An open question should be asked, e.g. 'What happened?' 'Was there anything else?' 'How did you feel?' The mediator should reflect back what the disputants say.

Step 7: The same process should be repeated with the second person.

Steps 6 and 7 will need to be repeated until all of the information is gathered ('What else happened?' 'Was there anything else you need to say?'), and before they can proceed to a solution.

Step 8:   Each person is asked to say what they need to happen in order for an agreement or solution to be arrived at. This should be expressed in 'I' statements.

Step 9:   An agreement is reached and participants are asked if there is anything they would do differently next time.

Step 10:   This step, an affirmation of each other, is optional.

Step 11:   A meeting is arranged for the next day at a specified time to see if the resolution worked.

Session seven: skill—handling difficult situations

- When lying occurs, several strategies are suggested so that disputants are encouraged to take responsibility for the situation and pave the way to a solution. The disputants could be told, 'Unless we know what really happened, the problem can't be solved'. Mediators could talk to the disputants separately, or the session could be halted and the disputants told to come back if they really want to solve the problem.
- Where there is a lack of cooperation, it is suggested that the mediators are encouraging to disputants, and model 'I' statements such as, 'When you don't answer any of my questions, I think that you don't want to solve the problem'. The mediator should try to find out if there are underlying reasons for the behaviour, such as confusion about the process. Mediators are asked to confirm that the disputants want to continue with the mediation.
- When control of the situation could be lost there are strategies for retaining it, such as being assertive and reinforcing the ground rules. If disputants become abusive, they should be separated and asked if they want to continue, and told that the rules can be reviewed or a cooling-off period can be introduced. If the mediators are unable to find a solution, then they can suggest that the disputants go to a teacher.

Conclusion

The *Cool Schools* program has been used widely in New Zealand and is starting to be picked up by schools in Australia. It is a useful and down-to-earth approach to mediation among school-age students that has the potential to be used by schools internationally.

Is Peer Support a Good Thing?

There are a number of advantages in developing a peer support system that could include any of the approaches described, either individually or in a combined form.

- Through peer support, students cease to be helpless onlookers to events of bullying, i.e. rather than having no strategies, they are provided with a vehicle to use either individually or as a group.

- The school has the means to deal with a greater number of problems as they arise because there is a cohort of students on which to call.
- When students take on a supportive role in a peer support system, they learn about the characteristics and dynamics of bullying in a new way. This means that those who have been bullies are less likely to bully in the future, and their leadership potential can be turned towards prosocial ends. And those who are survivors of bullying can empathise and share real experiences and solutions with victims in a safe environment.
- Although students are not professionally trained as certificated counsellors or therapists are, they know from personal experience how their peer group works and can 'talk the talk' in a way that adults cannot. They also experience similar emotions to their 'clients', and may have recently experienced the same events and can therefore empathise fully.
- The underlying philosophy of peer conflict resolution is to find solutions in a non-confrontational way so that all parties feel that a fair resolution has been achieved. Not only do participants resolve problems, but they also acquire useful skills for life.
- Introducing a peer support initiative has the added, vitally important effect of raising the level of awareness about bullying in the school. By involving students, a culture is encouraged that does not tolerate bullying and contributes to the creation of a safe school.
- Because peer mentoring or counselling can also be used in other areas besides bullying, such as academic planning for the future, drug abuse, and truancy, it can contribute to the general health and well-being of the school.
- By being available and well established in a school, peer support can prevent bullying from escalating and even stop it from happening. It is also reactive because, when bullying does occur, peer support can be called on to help to find a solution.

12 The *No Blame Approach*

The *No Blame Approach* to bullying was created by Barbara Maines and George Robinson in 1991 in Bristol, England, in response to a bullying crisis that needed a quick and effective solution. Their development and use of this anti-bullying strategy has been very well received. The program comprises a video and a booklet. The video focuses on a typical bullying situation to demonstrate how the approach works. The booklet complements this and provides a clear and well-constructed, step-by-step guide to using the method. In the UK, Maines and Robinson are available to provide training days for teachers around the country.

The Underlying Philosophy

- The *No Blame Approach* is a feelings approach to bullying. It starts with the understanding that it is more important to solve the problem of bullying than to punish the bully.
- It aims to get pupils to empathise with the victim of bullying rather than to get to the root of the problem, i.e. although it is clear who the bullies are, there is no intention of punishing them.
- The structure is logical, easy to use, very workable, and practical.
- The approach encourages and supports the peer group, including the bullies, in providing solutions and taking responsibility for putting them in place.

How It Works

Step One: The Victim is Interviewed

What happens

Once it has been established that a child has been the victim of bullying, either through self-reporting, through a teacher noticing, or through somebody else informing a staff member, the child is interviewed. He or she is asked if they want to pursue the issue and, if so, is asked to draw a picture or write a poem to describe the effect the bullying has had on them.

> **Comment:** In this step, the child who has been bullied is encouraged but not pressured to take part in the *No Blame* program. The process is intended to empower the child who is being bullied, so the adult makes the case in a way that is supportive and encouraging but lets him or her make the final decision.

Step Two: A Meeting is Convened With the People Involved

What happens

A small group of students is asked to meet with the teacher or the person who is handling the incident. This will include those doing the bullying, others who have witnessed it but have not taken part, and other members of the peer group who may not have been involved at all but who could make a positive contribution to the process.

> **Comment:** The purpose behind this meeting is to invite the whole group to take responsibility for the bullying. Instead of blaming the child who has done the bullying, the adult facilitating the session talks about how the person who is being victimised is feeling. The facilitator will not say to the bully, 'You are bad to bully this child', or to those may have supported the bullying or observed but not intervened, 'How could you be so gutless as to support it or just stand there and watch?'. Instead, the adult describes how the bullied child feels unhappy and cannot sleep and feels bad about coming to school. Surprisingly, the children typically respond that they did not realise how awful the victim felt. This allows the uneasy observers and those frightened to intervene to make positive suggestions and to help find a solution. It is important that children with clear prosocial behaviour traits are part of this process.

Step Three: The Problem is Explained to the Group

What happens

The bullying is explained to the children and it is emphasised that the bullying makes the victim feel really bad. The others are read the child's poem or shown the picture; either is used as the basis for discussion. No one is blamed for the bullying but solutions are sought.

Comment: This is where the scheme comes into its own. If children have no experience of the *No Blame Approach* and they expect to be blamed, their body language and prepared stance will probably be defensive and passive-aggressive. They know they have been caught and think that the person questioning them will blame them and punish them for what they have done. Their one satisfaction may be that they will retaliate later and intimidate their victims so they dare not tell again. Once it is clear that the bullies will not be blamed, however, they cease to feel threatened. This allows them to respond objectively to the act of bullying and be part of finding a solution. Often, those who are leaders in the act of bullying can use the skills that bring them to the fore to find and endorse a more prosocial way of behaving. In this meeting everyone, including the convenor, sits in a circle, an arrangement that creates a sense of equal power among the participants.

Step Four: The Responsibility is Shared

What happens

The responsibility for the bullying is shared by the group. Although blame is not attributed and punishments are not meted out, the act of bullying has to be acknowledged (rather than glossed over) so that the group can move on to the next stage.

Comment: In taking responsibility for the act of bullying and feeling remorse rather than the humiliation of punishment, bullies can acknowledge what they have done, and those who are observers can see that, in doing nothing, they were condoning the bullying and must therefore also accept responsibility.

Step Five: The Group is Asked For Their Ideas

What happens

The group is asked what they feel should be done. After brainstorming, individuals suggest solutions, how they feel they can help, and what they will do. Good positive suggestions for making things better are sought.

Comment: In the *No Blame* video, each child offers to do various things with or for the child who has been bullied. These are helpful and small things that, done in a concerted fashion, create a sense of the children working together positively.

This is a practical problem-solving session. The solutions sought are intended to support the reintegration of the victim into the class, not to 'rescue' her—that is, they are assertive and empowering, not patronising, solutions.

Step Six: It is Left Up to the Group

What happens

The responsibility for carrying out their suggestions is left up to the group. They go away feeling they will do something positive that is supported by the teacher who has conducted the session and in conjunction with the efforts of their peers.

Comment: With the understanding that they will meet again at a specified time, the individuals are then free to carry out their solutions or suggestions. When a girl has been isolated, for instance, a child may offer to play with her during lunchtimes. Another may offer to walk to and from school with her to make sure no bullying occurs. Step six is useful because it turns theory to practice, stops the bullying for the victimised child, and gives a constructive focus for the group's energy.

One of the important outcomes of this method is that, even if a perpetrator of bullying remains intransigent, he or she will probably have lost the support of the peer group, which means either that there is no audience to applaud and encourage and therefore no reward for doing the bullying, or that observers may now intervene and stop it because they realise how they would feel in this situation. Mark Cleary, the principal of a New Zealand secondary school, told me of one case where he used the *No Blame Approach*. He experienced a lot of resistance from the group of students involved and came away feeling he had failed, yet soon after this meeting the bullying stopped. There was clearly some further processing among the students after the formal process had finished.

Step Seven: Meet the Group Again

What happens

A week or so later (at an agreed time), the group meets again to discuss what they have done and what effect they have had.

Comment: This meeting allows the group to get together and discuss what they have done to provide relief for the one being bullied. Each student describes what they have done and the positive effects that have been accomplished. This gives them a sense of success, both as individuals and in their peer group. They have created a safe place for the victimised child and for themselves. This also provides reinforcement for the concept that it is better to be supportive and positive than to bully, and that students acting as a group have the power to stop the bullying.

Applicability

Robinson and Maines consider that the *No Blame Approach* can be used throughout the school years. Smith and Sharp (1994) and Rigby (1996) suggest that, whereas it works well with primary and intermediate students, the Pikas Method (see Chapter 16) works better with secondary pupils. On the other hand, Mark Cleary (pers. comm., 18 March 1999) indicates that he has used it on a number of occasions with secondary students and found it appropriate for them. Cleary also reports that Tom Hales, a Rotorua secondary school principal, has extended the *No Blame* groups to meet on a regular basis to discuss bullying problems. As a result, former bullies are now the staunchest defenders of the school's anti-bullying stance.

Young (1998) carried out a study of the Kingston-upon-Hull's Special Educational Needs Support Services' use of the *No Blame Approach*. She is critical of Smith and Sharp's cautious approach to the method, and in her study over a two-year period the *No Blame Approach* was used in fifty-five cases (fifty-one primary, four secondary). In three cases the child concerned left the immediate situation, but in all other cases there was a degree of success (80 per cent immediate success, 14 per cent success delayed, 6 per cent limited success).

It is important to be aware that a child who has been bullied and has been restored to the safety of a healthier peer group via the *No Blame Approach* may need further support and monitoring. This could be the next step that a school counsellor takes.

13 A Circle of Friends

A Circle of Friends is an approach developed originally in Canada to help include children with disabilities in mainstream schools and to support adults with disabilities in the community (see Snow and Forrest, 1987; Perske, 1988; and Pearpoint et al., 1992). In the UK, it has been used with students whose behaviour has hurt or upset others.

Gill Taylor's 1996 case study of the use of the Circle of Friends method is excellent. Inspired by the research of Tina Axup at the University of the West of England, Barbara Maines and George Robinson (who developed the *No Blame Approach*) have created a video and accompanying booklet to teach this very accessible strategy.

Like the *No Blame Approach*, *All for Alex: A Circle of Friends* is straightforward, well considered, and effective. The thinking behind the program is that children with emotional and behavioural problems need teaching and support rather than punishment and isolation (which their behaviour often brings). I recommend this program as a useful tool, particularly for children in the primary and intermediate sectors.

Barbara Maines is employed by Bristol City Council as a support teacher for young people with emotional and behavioural difficulties. *All for Alex: A Circle of Friends* is a retelling of a case with which Maines was working. At the time, the student involved, Alex, was an eleven-year-old, Class 6 boy at a Bristol school. He had been identified as having behavioural problems and these seemed to be getting worse. Maines found out that his mother had been diagnosed with a life-threatening illness and that he was very worried about her. Maines felt that the Circle of Friends would be a useful strategy for supporting Alex through her illness, and that it might also help to solve some of his emotional and behavioural problems.

Part One: Arranging the Circle of Friends
Step One: Permission From the Young Person

In step one Maines discussed Circle of Friends with Alex and explained how it worked. She and Alex decided that she would talk to the class about his sadness, without him present. A group of volunteers would be asked for and chosen as his circle of friends. It was important to negotiate this with Alex so that it was clear he agreed and felt safe to go ahead.

> **Comment:** In this step Maines makes sure that Alex wants to go ahead and that he knows he has the power to say no and that he can negotiate the terms. He is also warmed up to the process.

Step Two: Planning with Staff, Agreement From Parents

The next step was to speak with Alex's teacher and to get his agreement to create a circle of friends for Alex. An important and sensitive consideration was that, in providing the class with information, Alex's mother's illness would be discussed publicly.

> **Comment:** If a program like the Circle of Friends is to be successful, the teacher's role is central. He or she must first understand both the intentions and processes of the initiative, provide advice and monitor it on a day-to-day basis, and support the efforts of the circle. By implication, if the teacher supports the program the circle can be widened to include the rest of the class as secondary participants.

Step Three: Talking to the Whole Class About Circle of Friends

In step three, Maines talked to the class, without Alex present, about his mother and about how he had been feeling. Maines's intentions were to reframe Alex's behaviour as sad and troubled rather than as difficult and naughty, and to encourage the group to feel empathy towards him. She asked the children to volunteer to be members of the circle of friends by writing their names on pieces of paper and placing them in the box provided.

> **Comment:** In this step, Maines presents not only the process but also lays the groundwork for a better and less punitive response to Alex and for his acceptance by the class. The aim is also to create a positive atmosphere and to encourage more prosocial behaviour from Alex.

Step Four: Taking Questions About Circle of Friends

In step four, Maines answered questions about the process from Alex's classmates. She closed by thanking the children for their time and attention.

Comment: This is a useful exercise in clarification. The questions the pupils ask are: 'What does the circle of friends do?' 'Can I drop out?' 'How do you choose the circle of friends?' 'Will Alex get to know what the circle is doing?' In her answers, Maines is able both to provide specific details and give a sense of the intentions and philosophy. Such explanations also allow children to feel closer to the aims of the program because they understand it better, even if they do not volunteer or are not chosen as members of the circle.

Step Five: Choosing the Circle Members

After meeting with the class, Maines went through the names of the volunteers with the teacher. They chose some children whom they knew to be reliable and also chose two students who were known to have conflicts with Alex.

Seventeen children volunteered and six were chosen. Wanting to encourage a sense of support in the class generally and to acknowledge those who put themselves forward but were not chosen, Maines wrote a note of thanks to each of them.

Comment: The circle of friends is balanced by including both boys and girls, and supportive as well as challenging children. Two girls are chosen because they are close friends and in their friendship have excluded Alex (they have written on their piece of paper, 'Take both of us or neither'). It is particularly important to choose people who are at odds with Alex because, if their attitudes towards him can be turned around, this will affect the way others treat him. The remaining children are known to be reliable and stable. Their presence gives a sense of legitimacy to what the circle children do in their contacts with Alex.

Part Two: The Meetings

Maines had half a term (the remainder of the school year) to arrange meetings and to implement the program. She decided to arrange four meetings but to avoid the daily follow-up that some facilitators use. She planned that Alex would not be at the first three meetings but would be at the final meeting.

Meeting 1. Forming the Group, Planning the Action

The purpose of this meeting was to welcome and thank those who had volunteered, to validate them for the special gesture they had made, to revisit the purpose of the group, to set ground rules in place, and to help all members of the group come up with a positive intention towards Alex. Maines closed the session by thanking the participants again.

CIRCLE OF
FRIENDS

Comment: In the video, Maines is able to elicit a positive commitment from each member of the circle of friends to do something constructive to acknowledge or help Alex. Any of the children are allowed to pass the first time around but the next time round they are asked for a contribution. Now that they have seen other people's suggestions, they have a sense of what is needed.

The process of helping the students decide what to do is interesting. Maines reflected their suggestions back to the children. This helped to clarify what they would do and also made it possible for them to each do something different but along similar lines. Here are two examples:

Dialogue number one

Nicky (a girl): Well, you could give him special attention when he's in quite a good mood, and when he's sort of in a bad mood, you could just keep out of his way.

Maines: That would be like focusing on the good things rather than paying attention to the bad. That's really good.

Dialogue number two

Matthew: I would tell him not to take any notice of people that crack jokes about him.

Maines: Right. Can you explain that a bit to me, what happens when somebody cracks a joke?

Matthew: Normally he just goes after them and starts pushing and punching.

Maines: Right. He sometimes takes things that are not meant to be serious too seriously and too personally.

Matthew: Yes.

Maines: So how would you remind him or help him not worry about that too much?

Matthew: Just to put it away and tell them to think about things that have happened to them in the past.

Matthew's last statement is slightly unclear, but it is supportive of Alex, and the intention is to try to find a solution rather than meeting him head on (which is probably what has happened in the past).

Meeting 2. Monitoring Progress—Praise and Encouragement

The purpose of this meeting was to carry out a maintenance check: to get feedback from circle members, to help them modify their plans if they did not seem to be working, or to give reassurance or encouragement. A major purpose in touching base was to keep the momentum going.

> **Comment:** Maintaining the program, giving pats on the back, reassuring students that what they are doing is good even if they do not see the results immediately are all part of the hidden but essential work in setting up such a program.

Meeting 3. Reflecting on the Work, Planning the Final Meeting

The group had been working for three weeks at this point. Maines expressed amazement at the pupils' insights and their commitment towards Alex. Two themes emerged from the meeting:
* the group members stated they had a different view of Alex and they felt they now understood him better;
* they felt that he might be blaming himself for his mother's illness.

The meeting closed with a decision to invite Alex to the next and final meeting.

> **Comment:** The group has obviously learnt through their experiences. As their efforts have met with a positive response from Alex, they have seen, first, that they have the power to change things and, second, that it is better not to make quick, angry responses to all situations but to learn to reserve judgment and give others a chance.

Meeting 4. Talking with Alex, Planning the Celebration, Closing the Circle of Friends

During this final meeting, Maines acted as facilitator and allowed the individuals from the circle to express what they had done to help or support Alex. They decided (at Maines's instigation) to celebrate their achievements by giving certificates to those who had participated and (at their own instigation) that these should be presented by Alex.

> **Comment:** This last meeting is very important because it both values the children's contributions and reinforces the positive behaviour the circle has been exhibiting. (Remember that some of these children had been meeting Alex's aggression head on with their own.) It also gives Alex the opportunity to see that he has truly been supported, and it acknowledges that his peers think he is worth it. The facilitator must bring things to a close when the goals have been achieved, rather than letting the program drift on and peter out.

I particularly liked the understated way, throughout this and other meetings, in which Maines was able to encourage change while allowing the participants to retain their personal power. Alex was never patronised or demeaned.

Step Six: A Parallel Step—Keeping in Touch with Alex

During the period in which the circle was meeting, Maines arranged short meetings with Alex so that she could be sure things were going well for him, and so that, if any problems arose, she could support him and incorporate these difficulties into the meetings.

Part Three: The Follow-up

The final meeting coincided with the breakup of this class before its move to secondary school. Consequently, no follow-up was done. Maines suggests that, if circumstances were different, if it were a younger class, or this had happened at an earlier point in the year, then they might have continued for longer, changed some of the group members, and followed up at a later date.

Step Seven: Celebrating with the Whole Class

The final step acknowledged the circle's efforts and achievements. The principal of the school was invited to say a few words and to call out the names of the children in the circle so that Alex could present their certificates. They chose to have the celebration in the classroom to reinvolve the whole class who had been part of setting up the circle, and to include any who had felt left out. The occasion turned into a party, with drinks and biscuits. Maines felt that this had a very positive effect and that the whole class took ownership of the circle process.

Step Eight: Evaluating the Whole Process

Maines's evaluation is a reflection of Alex's circumstances and the effect of the Circle of Friends method.

Maines points out, first, that Alex was a pupil who had been referred because of difficult behaviour before his mother's health worries arose and, second, that his anxiety caused his behaviour to deteriorate and made it harder for him to be at school.

Maines observed that the Circle of Friends initiative brought about an improvement in Alex's behaviour for two reasons:

- Alex was clearly and genuinely supported by his circle of friends;
- the circle's expectations changed: they wished for, looked for, and reinforced improvement as they felt a sense of ownership towards the Circle of Friends and all it entailed.

14 The *P.E.A.C.E. Pack* and *Bullying in Schools*

This chapter examines two complementary bullying resources that have been produced by Australia's leading anti-bullying researchers. Phillip Slee of Flinders University has created the *P.E.A.C.E. Pack*, which is a useful resource for examining bullying in general and for devising strategies to deal effectively with it. The second resource is a video about bullying produced by Ken Rigby of the University of South Australia, and Slee.

The *P.E.A.C.E. Pack*

The *P.E.A.C.E. Pack* has been generated from at least ten years of research into bullying carried out in Australia by Slee (often in partnership with Ken Rigby). It is now in its second edition (1997), is attractively presented, and is inexpensive to purchase.

The acronym P.E.A.C.E. stands for the following:

- **P** stands for preparation. In the preparatory stage of an anti-bullying initiative, information about bullying is provided as the initial basis for informed policy development and selection of interventions, and so that parents and students will become involved in the process.
- **E** stands for education. The next step entails the gathering of information upon which to develop interventions. The author suggests (a) reviewing the school's policies and procedures for dealing with bullying, (b) observing in the school to get a sense of the type of bullying that is occurring, (c) interviewing students, teachers, and parents, and (d) carrying out a survey of bullying in the school in question.
- **A** stands for action. The purpose of the third step is to identify what can be done and to find ways of accessing the systems in the school that can be adapted for doing so, and involving students, teachers, and parents.
- **C** stands for coping. This step deals with the author's ABC of intervening in the school. A stands for attitudes (and ethos), which means both creating an

open and reflective attitude in the school and having this reflected in the vision and policies of the school; B stands for behaviours, which means creating a set of behavioural strategies for dealing with bullying; and C stands for curriculum developments, which focus on bullying and enhance the students' understanding of it.

- E stands for evaluation. This final process is intended to see if things are working as planned. The processes of surveys, interviews, and observation are suggested as a means of verification. An additional element in this step is the celebration of success.

The Booklet

A twenty-four-page booklet provides a clear and well-written overview of recent statistics and information about bullying. The *P.E.A.C.E. Pack* defines bullying as 'physically harmful, psychologically damaging, and socially isolating' (p. 4).

It aims to give a fresh look at children, families, and schools when they are in crisis. The intervention works well in conjunction with other initiatives such as behaviour management and pastoral care. It is based on the philosophy that, when bullying occurs, it is part of a system, and the system itself must change in order for behaviour to change.

Slee explains the intentions of the program, and the constructivist philosophy on which it is based. In other words, it is concerned to examine and change the dynamics of bullying and the system in which it takes place, rather than being focused only on the individual participants:

> A child's mis-conduct in school (e.g. bullying or being victimised) is understood to serve some purpose within the system or reflects something about the system itself. The behaviour is not simply the result of some inner psychic disturbance or carried out for some reward. The students' behaviour is in a sense, a window, through which we can look, to understand the student's place in the system, and provides important insight into the various roles and relationships within the system (p. 4).

A first-order change occurs when the school attempts to change the behaviour of a bully. A second-order change occurs when the system itself changes. The second type of change is clearly preferable to the first but, at the same time, the program recognises that, when a crisis— in the form of an act of bullying — occurs, then this is the immediate concern. Another major theme of the program is that each situation needs to be handled in its own right and should not be manipulated to meet a predetermined set of behavioural outcomes.

In schools that adopt only the first-order type of change, the bully is seen as a 'bad' student who needs to be controlled and changed. In this sort of school, the bullying is located solely in the person doing the bullying. Slee argues that, although this may provide some short-term solutions, in the long run, and in a safe school, it is much more important that the school examines and changes its system where appropriate:

In shifting the focus and thinking in more systemic terms, change will resonate throughout the school system. Instead of focusing on changing the 'bad' behaviour of the bully and on 'helping' the victim, consideration might be given to roles, relationships and interactions and communication within the system which encourage or discourage bullying. When the system itself begins to change or re-align 'second-order' change has occurred (p. 5).

The booklet also contains information on the details of successful intervention programs implemented in schools, and a list of useful anti-bullying resources available in Australia, including reference to books, chapters in books, and articles that have been written and can be easily accessed through libraries.

Phillip Slee and Ken Rigby have developed an excellent questionnaire that can be obtained from Rigby at the University of South Australia. In Australia, the ACER (Australian Council for Educational Research) in Melbourne, for a reasonable price, will administer this questionnaire and then analyse the responses and provide a report.

Videos available are also listed as well as organisations and individuals (including reference to an innovative theatre group that focuses on educational issues in personal development). There is a section on special interest publications relating to bullying involving peer mediation and peer counselling, school counselling for bullying, and special needs children.

Fourteen Practical Worksheets

The pack includes seven double-sided cards containing information to complement the introductory information in the booklet. These worksheets provide ideas for policy development, lesson planning, and details of interventions with bullies and victims.

Each side of a card provides full details for a workshop. The first two workshops (card one) deal with how to prepare (P) a school for developing an anti-bullying initiative, and how to educate (E) students, teachers, and parents about bullying. Card two deals with action for staff, and action for students (A).

Cards three and four (workshops 5 to 8) focus on what is loosely termed coping (C). Workshop 5 deals with examining the ethos of and attitudes in the school, and ways of examining the school's vision and the development of an anti-bullying policy. Workshop 6 covers behavioural strategies for dealing with bullying (such as the development of a clear set of procedures for taking a grievance), and for addressing specific bullying issues in the school, for instance, how to make the playground a safe place. Workshops 7 and 8 deal with the introduction of relevant material into the curriculum to reinforce a strong anti-bullying message in the school; and the development of processes to involve parents in the reconciliation process that accompanies the handling of bullying.

Workshop 9 is entitled 'Evaluating and celebrating' (E), and workshop 10 provides six examples of successful interventions.

Workshops 11 and 12 deal with special interest topics, that is, important areas that are outside the general brief. This extra material focuses on bullying and young children, bullying and special needs children, bullying and the playground, and peer mediation. These special topics all have two parts. Part one provides a description of the issues in the area, and part two, interventions or, in the case of peer mediation, how to set up a program.

The final two workshops (13 and 14) provide comparative perspectives on bullying from other countries: Canada, England, Japan, the Netherlands, New Zealand, Norway, and the USA.

Presentation Overheads

The pack includes eight pages that are designed to be used as overheads or in conjunction with workshops or lectures. They cover a definition of bullying, profiles of bullies and victims, frequency of bullying, a schematic representation of how the *P.E.A.C.E.* program works, graphs of students' opinions about actions to stop bullying, and students' perceptions of teachers. The well-prepared, accessible overheads are accompanied by useful discussion questions. These sheets can also be photocopied and handed out.

This is a compact and well-presented package that could be used creatively in its own right or in conjunction with other resources.

Bullying in Schools

Ken Rigby and Phillip Slee produced a video and accompanying booklet called *Bullying in Schools* which, although made in the early 1990s, provides a very useful introduction to bullying and some of the forms it takes. It discusses physical bullying (as portrayed by a group of boys) and more subtle bullying (through staring and intimidation), done by one girl against two others. It also usefully discusses some of the myths commonly held about bullies and victims and the attitudes that boys and girls have towards victims of bullying.

There is a useful interview with a school principal who talks about the effects of introducing an anti-bullying policy in the school, particularly in assuring students that it is all right to tell. He also discusses the importance of including students in the process and tells how the student council played a very important role in disseminating information.

The video has been thoughtfully prepared and professionally produced. It would be a useful addition to any library.

15 *Kia Kaha* and *Stop Bullying*

This chapter examines two anti-bullying resources developed by the New Zealand Police. *Kia Kaha* is a kit designed for use by schools ('kia kaha' means 'be strong'), and *Stop Bullying* is a video about bullying that provides information for parents.

Kia Kaha

In New Zealand, the police's Youth Education Service has developed a series of initiatives designed to help schools identify and prevent physical and sexual abuse, drug dependency, and bullying (*Keeping Ourselves Safe, The D.A.R.E. Programme*, and *Kia Kaha*, respectively). The anti-bullying initiative, *Kia Kaha: A Resource Kit about Bullying for Students, Teachers and Parents*, was initially developed with support from Commercial Union Insurance and later from Telecom New Zealand. The kit is lent to schools free of charge. Although an exact figure is not available, I have been told that more than 3000 kits have been distributed since the program was initiated in 1992.

If a school has a bullying problem, it can contact the local police. They will then put the school in touch with a police education officer who will talk about *Kia Kaha* and help the school introduce the program if it chooses to do so. In addition to this, police education officers make periodic contact with schools in their catchment areas to inform them about police initiatives and interventions. If a school decides to implement *Kia Kaha*, these officers provide regular 'maintenance' programs once every two years so that new cohorts of students and new teachers can be introduced to the program.

When a police education officer first visits a school, he or she discusses the need for the school to think about its organisational structure, and may ask such questions as 'Is there a person (a guidance counsellor, for instance) to whom pupils can go if they are being bullied?' and 'Does the school have a whole school anti-bullying policy in place?' If the school does not have these resources, the officer will provide advice. He or she may then arrange to meet with teachers from the school to discuss introducing the program. Education officers often spend eight to ten hours either helping schools to establish *Kia Kaha*, or helping to solve a particular bullying problem. The program is both comprehensive in covering a range of important issues and also flexible in being adaptable to the needs of individual schools.

The program is designed to be used with children from year 5 to year 10 (approximately from nine until fifteen years of age). It consists of an attractive boxed set containing a soft-cover booklet (the teaching guide), which provides an overview of the program, and instructions for planning and implementation, as well as a video, and an explanatory leaflet for parents and caregivers.

Although *Kia Kaha*'s primary purpose is to provide an anti-bullying resource for schools, it also meets the requirements of two essential learning areas within New Zealand's curriculum framework: health and physical well-being, and social sciences. Consequently, it has also been used in some schools primarily as a curriculum resource rather than as an anti-bullying program.

The Kit

The two main components of the kit are the teaching guide, which provides a comprehensive overview of how the program works, and the video, which presents five bullying scenarios. A pamphlet included with the kit is a useful addition because it gives information for parents/caregivers and also suggests how to involve the community in the program.

The teaching guide

The introduction to the teaching guide clearly explains the rationale, aims, and objectives of *Kia Kaha*, the level the kit is aimed at, its place in the curriculum, and how best to use the video and the variety of other classroom activities.

In Section One, eight logical steps for the implementation of *Kia Kaha* are suggested:

Step one: checking the prerequisites

The first step is intended to check the awareness and readiness of school staff for an anti-bullying program. For instance, do staff need training in listening skills, facilitating discussions, sharing decision-making with students, and facilitating role play? It is suggested that some of the health education resource units from the national curriculum can be used as preliminary steps before introducing the program, specifically the units for junior, middle, and senior primary students that are concerned with building self-esteem and relating to others.

Step two: holding the first staff meeting: overview and introduction

In the second step, the school holds a forty-minute meeting for staff designed to give an introduction and overview of *Kia Kaha*. Participants are encouraged to discuss what bullying is and to talk about their own experiences of bullying. After a personal context has been established, staff watch the *Kia Kaha* video and discuss it. The suggested structure for the implementation of the program is then outlined. Also discussed is the issue of how best to involve the parents of students.

Step three: holding second staff meeting: planning and preparation

At the second meeting, participants are divided into six groups. For the first twenty minutes, each group brainstorms about one of six important areas of concern:

- What steps can we take to support the victim involved in specific incidents of bullying?
- What steps can we take to handle the bully involved in specific incidents of bullying?
- How can we model positive interactions for students?
- How might we improve our existing physical environment to make our school a safer place where bullying cannot flourish?
- How might we improve our existing organisational procedures to make our school a place safe from bullying?
- What further strategies could we develop to handle bullying in the school?

Each of these groups can produce a number of creative responses. The second half of the meeting is used for the groups to report back their findings, and for the meeting as a whole to come up with a series of recommendations for staff comment.

Step four: involving parents and caregivers

Strategies to involve parents will have been decided at the first meeting, e.g. sending a letter home in whatever language is most appropriate for the recipient group (in New Zealand, for example, letters in Maori, Samoan, or Tongan could be sent). The suggested format for the parent meeting is: welcoming the parents, introducing the *Kia Kaha* program and the topic of bullying, and explaining how it is important to deal with bullying in the classroom, the whole school, and at home. The video is shown and parents are told that students will be bringing home work that relates to the program. They are given suggestions about how they can help with this process. The action plan strategy of *Kia Kaha* is explained, and parents get the opportunity to ask questions and are given the explanatory pamphlet. Parents are then encouraged to talk about ways in which they can have useful long-term involvement in the program.

Step five: planning the teaching sessions

This meeting is intended to select classroom activities from those provided and to discuss how best to introduce students to the video and its concepts. Police education officers or visiting teachers could assist with this process. A planning chart is provided in the teaching guide. Teachers need to decide how best to use the resources and activities provided in the teaching guide so that they are appropriate for the age and the particular class they are dealing with, and to do this so that the activities complement the showing of the video. The central mechanism of the program is the video. Activities should be selected from the three categories of feelings, coping strategies, and practising coping strategies.

Step six: teaching the program

The teacher (with help from the police education officer if requested) teaches the program to students, with parent involvement at home to provide reinforcement.

Step seven: evaluating the program

The purpose of this step is to evaluate the program and to see how effective it has been in changing student behaviour, how useful the school's guidelines and strategies have been, and what impact parents/caregivers had on helping children develop positive interactions. A number of suggestions for doing this are provided.

Step eight: reinforcing learning

This step focuses on reinforcing what has been learnt through *Kia Kaha* by carrying out a variety of interesting tasks, which include:

- holding regular class discussions about how students are handling bullying;
- choosing some of the activities to do as extensions;
- getting the class to review the guidelines they have set up for keeping their classroom safe;
- setting up role plays to explore incidents of bullying that may arise (p. 9).

Other activities

The final section of the booklet provides practical guidance on some of the activities available in the program. It consists of three copysheets, a note on how to use role play appropriately, and a list of relevant school journal articles.

Copysheet 1: plan of action for bullies and victims

This is a five-step plan intended to defuse a situation.

- Stop (try to keep calm. Take some deep breaths).
- Think (convince yourself that you can do something about the situation).
- Consider the options (either decide what you can do to stop being a bully or decide what you can do to avoid being bullied).
- Act (choose the option you feel most comfortable with).
- Follow up (decide if this was a good choice for you. Consider how you feel about the way you handled the incident. Talk to someone you trust about how you got on).

Copysheet 2: situation cards provide bullying scenarios that are intended to get pupils to brainstorm and come up with workable solutions to bullying

Copysheet 3: *Billy the Bully* is a song in which a young person is initially frightened by a bully, but then befriends the bully

The video

A thirteen-minute video is part of the kit. In the video, five different well-presented bullying scenarios are portrayed. These provide the basis for discussing both what is happening and how these situations can be resolved. A number of useful ideas come out of the video:

- that students can discuss the problem with a parent, another trusted relative, or a school friend;
- that those who are bullied or who feel uncomfortable about bullying can help each other to solve the problem, i.e. motivating the peer group to work together;
- people who bully are often unhappy individuals who are victims of bullying in their own homes.

Here is an example of one of the scenarios:

Scenario three: Lucy's exclusion of Karen

Lucy is critical of Karen and often mean to her. Lucy invites Karen to her birthday party at five o'clock on Saturday but it actually started at two o'clock and when Karen arrives the others have all left to go to a movie.

After the scenario has been presented, the video asks, 'If you were Karen, what would you have done?'

Karen, who is Maori, seeks advice from her grandfather, who tells her: 'Well girl, kia kaha, kia toa, kia manawanui. Kia kaha is to stand strong. Kia toa is to be a warrior. Kia manawanui is to be brave.'

'You mean I should fight Lucy?' Karen asks her grandfather.

'Kaore! Kaore! [No! No!] What it means is to stand up for yourself. Don't let people push you down and make you feel that there's something wrong with you. Do you deserve to be treated like this?'

'No.'

'Well then, girl, stand up for yourself.'

After her talk with her grandfather, Karen is assertive when she sees Lucy and Gemma at school on Monday by the bike stand.

Lucy: Where were you on Saturday?

Karen: That was a really mean trick, Lucy.

Lucy: You're so dumb you fell for it, eh, Gemma.

Karen: You're always going on at me about being dumb, Lucy. Just because it takes me longer to finish my work than you, that doesn't mean you can treat me like I'm not a real person.

Lucy: What's the matter, can't you take a joke!

Gemma: Karen's right. We have been really mean to her.

Lucy: You stick up for her then, Gemma. See if I care. But you're never coming to another birthday party of mine. (She goes.)

Gemma: I'm sorry, Karen. I didn't really want to do it. I guess I was glad that Lucy was giving you a hard time instead of me. Still friends?

Karen: As long as you promise to treat me like a proper friend.

Gemma: I will. I promise.

In this scenario Karen is purposely left out and cruelly tricked by being given the wrong time for the party. She seeks her grandfather's advice and confronts her tormentor in an assertive fashion. She focuses on 'I' statements and is calm and clear. She not only makes her point and regains some of her personal power, but also gets support from a friend who had gone along with the bullying but obviously felt bad about what happened. It is a very good example of standing up for oneself in a situation that is unlikely to escalate into physical violence.

Conclusion

Although a formal longitudinal study has not been carried out,[1] feedback from many schools has been positive and the Education Review Office recently reported very favourably on *Kia Kaha*.

The police are rethinking their focus and are intending to develop curriculum materials to fit into the health syllabus area of building healthy relationships. They also wish to devise a series of curriculum units which are aimed at all levels of the school from year 1 to 13. They intend to do this by working with Special Education Services to ensure that a revised *Kia Kaha* program and SES's successful Eliminating Violence strategy (see Appendix II) are complementary.

Stop Bullying

Further to the *Kia Kaha* kit, the police have produced a video entitled *Stop Bullying: Helpful Information for Caregivers and Young People from the Police and Telecom*, and an accompanying booklet, *Stop Bullying: A Collection of Children's Short Stories*. This kit is intended to provide information for parents and can be obtained free of charge at video hire outlets throughout New Zealand. The video features Michael Jones, a popular rugby player who was a New Zealand All Black for a number of years. It shows him discussing bullying with a group of high school students, and also features individual interviews with another group of students. The video focuses on answering a number of key questions, first of all about the nature of bullying: 'What is bullying?' 'Why is bullying wrong?' 'Why do people bully?' and 'Who gets bullied?' It then concentrates on what to do about it: 'What should children do?' 'What should parents do?' and 'What should teachers do?' Michael Jones finishes with this statement:

> We all need to share responsibility for making our communities safe places for everybody. People who are bullied should keep four simple things in mind:
> 1. Firstly, admit to yourself that there is a problem. You are being bullied!
> 2. Secondly, tell someone you can trust who can help you, and keep communicating until the problem is fixed.
> 3. Thirdly, realise that it's not your fault. It could happen to anyone. You are not the problem.
> 4. Finally, remember you are a really special person and you will get through this.

I found this video to be very well-presented, realistic, and optimistic in its approach. The pupils featured represent a cross-section of typical New Zealand secondary school students, and the responses they provide are considered and intelligent, giving an overview of the nature of school bullying. The booklet accompanying the video contains twenty-one short stories about bullying that were selected by popular children's writer Joy Cowley and edited by Rob Lee of the New Zealand Police.

---

1 Sullivan (1998) carried out a small evaluation for the police which applauded the police's efforts and made a number of recommendations for updating the program.

16 The Pikas Method of Shared Concern

When I visited the Tayside Anti-Bullying Initiative late in 1995, I was impressed by the seriousness with which the anti-bullying team attacked the problem of bullying in local schools. In the UK during the early and mid-1990s, as well as a major commitment from the Scottish Council for Research in Education, various local authorities spent money developing resource kits to deal with bullying. Walsall, Islington, Strathclyde, and Cardiff are notable for their efforts. None, however, had created a full-time team to combat bullying (comprising teachers, social workers, and psychologists) as was the case with the Dundee-based Tayside initiative.

In setting up anti-bullying initiatives to meet the varying needs of schools in their catchment area, the team had examined a number of schemes and chose to use the Pikas Method of Shared Concern. As with the *No Blame Approach*, this program tries to find practical solutions to break dysfunctional patterns, and provides an opportunity for those committing antisocial acts to come up with prosocial alternatives. The most hard-nosed opponents of such feelings approaches think that it is important to make people see the error of their ways by giving programs a consequences or punishment base; they believe that, particularly with tough cases, a 'touchy-feely' approach will not work. But members of the Tayside team whom I interviewed in December 1995, and Alison Duncan (1994) in her report of the use of the Pikas Method of Shared Concern in Dundee, argue that this method was very successful, even with very difficult cases. The method has also been used successfully by schools in the Sheffield project (Smith and Sharp, 1994), in Australia (Rigby, 1996), and in Scandinavia (Björkqvist and Österman, 1999), among other places.

The Foundations of the Method of Shared Concern

Anatol Pikas's Method of Shared Concern has been widely applauded as an effective way of dealing with bullying behaviour. Several anti-bullying scholars have written about it. Pikas (1989), Sharp and Smith (1994), Duncan (1994), Fuller and King (1995), and Rigby (1996) have provided useful information about how it works and what its strengths and weaknesses are, and I have distilled this information to give an overview of the method.

Professor Pikas, a psychologist in the Education Department of Uppsala University, Sweden, devised this method to deal with the bullying of one or more children by a group of children (a type of bullying referred to in Scandinavia as mobbing). According to Pikas (1989, p. 93), the concept of 'a mob' is important in finding a solution, because the thoughts and feelings of the group are simpler than those of any of its individual members, and the members of a group strive towards what he calls a 'common psychological denominator', or a collective mind.

This means that the actions of the group are predictable so, when bullying is involved, it is possible to handle the situation and to find a solution.

When a case of group bullying is suspected, it can be dealt with by a teacher or a counsellor (Pikas calls this person a therapist, I will use the term 'counsellor') using the Pikas Method of Shared Concern.

The Procedure
Step One: The First Meetings

The procedure
When a decision has been made to address bullying (either through self-reporting or referral), then it is important to initiate the procedure straightaway. Pikas insists that his procedures be followed strictly because he has created a clearly mapped-out series of interrelated steps which cause subtle changes, creating an emotional climate designed to produce results.

During the first step, the counsellor speaks with the ringleader and then with each of the other suspected mobbers (three to six is usual) for ten to twenty minutes each. These meetings should be held consecutively and all at the same time so that the individuals involved cannot converse with each other. It is important not to interview the victim(s) before all the bullies have been interviewed so they cannot assume that the victim has told tales.

The counsellor should be non-threatening and make it clear that there is no intention of attributing blame. He or she should stress that the victim is being made miserable by the bullying. Each of the bullies is asked how things could be made better for the victim. The counsellor sits opposite the child being interviewed so that their eyes are at the same level and they are communicating on equal terms, and always makes sure that eye contact is maintained.

The process
The counsellor or teacher doing the interviewing starts.
1. 'I would like to talk to you because I've heard you've been mean to Justin/Julia.'

This is an assertive statement of fact. It is not accusatory and is intended to get to the bottom of things. It is not said angrily, but neutrally. It is important that the counsellor shows empathy towards the victim and that this is made clear without being threatening.

2. 'What do you know about it?'

The second question is intended to get the bully to talk about the bullying. Most people will freely talk about it. If, after several attempts to initiate the process, there is no movement, then the counsellor should finish the session.

Comment: This is the most important part of the proceedings. It aims to help the bully take responsibility without feeling shame or resentment towards the victim. Pikas says that it is vital at this point to reinforce the person's answers, and to ask further questions so that the process moves towards a predetermined goal of shared concern.

This sharing underlies the interaction: a problem of bullying has been identified and it should be solved together. The counsellor must proceed with an expectation that the two of them can construct a solution. In doing this, the counsellor models empathy and support but is not too friendly (or patronising).

At this stage, barriers to success may appear that will need to be removed to hasten the process. Sharp and Smith (1994) suggest that the following may occur:
- The child has no idea of any solutions. If a child genuinely cannot come up with solutions, the adult can suggest some. It is important not to hurry the child.
- The child is uncooperative. It is best not to try to force a child, but to be silent and wait. If there is no response after a reasonable time, the counsellor could say, 'We don't seem to have anything to discuss today. You can go back to class.' This usually makes the child want to talk.
- An impractical or impossible solution is provided. If this happens, the counsellor should not respond negatively but ask, 'Do you think that would stop the bullying?' and then move towards other solutions.
- Involving others in the solution. If it is suggested that the solution lies with another person, e.g. the ringleader, then it is important to emphasise that the person being interviewed must provide the solution. The counsellor could say, 'I was thinking more about something you could do'.
- There is a complaint about the provocative behaviour of the victim. Pikas suggests that any discussion of the bullying at this stage is helpful so it is important to encourage talking and to listen patiently. Some of the information that emerges may help in the process of finding a solution for provocative and passive victims. It is then essential to return to the fact that the pupil being bullied is having a hard time and that this is the issue which must be resolved. The counsellor could say, 'Thank you for this extra information. Julia is feeling very sad and miserable because of being bullied. What can you do to change this?'

There is no need either to blame or to get the absolute truth but to rebuild the situation constructively so that the bullying problem is solved.

3. 'All right, we've talked long enough. Let's move on.'

When the counsellor has enough information it is important to move things along pleasantly and clearly. If the discussion has been difficult and there is no sense that any progress has been made, this can be a crucial point in the proceedings. This statement underlines the fact that the point of the intervention is to find a solution, not to blame or punish.

> **Comment:** By now, there is enough information about the bullying to move towards a solution. There is a sense of relief and a reduction of tension as the focus is clearly turned to a positive outcome. No hidden blame or punishment waits around the corner.

4. 'What can you do? What do you suggest?'

It is at this stage that the discussion culminates in the bullying child making a clear suggestion about how to proceed. This may take the form of a solution or a promise to stop bullying.

5. 'That's good. We'll meet again in a week, then you can tell me how you've been getting on.'

The final statement by the counsellor is meant to reinforce the relationship that has been established between the counsellor and the student, that they are working together to find a solution to the bullying. The counsellor says goodbye and the student returns to class. The counsellor then sees the other members of the bullying group one by one.

> **Comment:** The last stage of the first meeting emphasises the gravity of the effects of the bullying on the victim, rather than focusing on blaming or punishing. The perpetrator(s) and supporter(s) of bullying are given the opportunity to act positively, to speak as individuals, and to reclaim their personal power. In this way, the power of the 'mob' is broken and the 'common psychological denominator' of the group is undermined. Although it has not been stated, the fact that the ringleader has been taken out of the class will have indicated that something is afoot. That person's return to class gives two messages: to their fellow mobbers, 'It's OK, I've had to deal with this and so will you'; and to the victim of bullying, 'I'm going to be nicer to you'. The removal of punishment takes away the likelihood of retaliation, and tension and aggression are defused.

Step Two: Meeting with the Victim

Immediately after the first series of meetings the person who has been bullied is interviewed and encouraged to talk about the bullying. Pikas states that, in his experience, victims are not afraid to speak. This meeting allows the counsellor to establish whether the person being victimised is a passive or a provocative victim, as solving the problem differs with the type of victim, as well as with each individual.

> **Comment:** If someone provokes the bullying, this does not mean that the bullying is excusable, but it does mean that their behaviour is a contributory factor and this needs to be acknowledged assertively, and without the counsellor attributing blame or judgment. The provocative victim can make suggestions about how they can improve things. For a passive victim, the counsellor proceeds in a more fully supportive fashion.

Step Three: Meeting with the Individuals Again

A series of further meetings is held to meet individually with students to see how things are going. Often, the student has not done exactly what was agreed to in the first meeting but he or she has usually left the victim alone. If this is not the case, then the counsellor will need to go through the procedure again in order to come up with workable solutions and a commitment from the student to do what was agreed on. The counsellor and the student should decide to meet again to see what progress has been made. About a week later, the talks are repeated, either with the individuals involved in the bullying, or with the group as a whole.

> **Comment:** Because this method relies on follow-through, the school must be committed to dealing with bullying. The students can process what is happening, to think, and to realign how they will act over a period of time. They are also given an opportunity to correct their behaviour without being punished.

Step Four: The Group Meeting

When it is clear that the bullying group has changed their behaviour, they must meet the counsellor and consolidate their changed behaviour. It is critical for them to discuss the person being bullied and to make positive comments about him or her. When it feels safe, the victim(s) should be invited to enter. The chairs should be in a circle and the victimised child must be able to enter and sit down without having to run the gauntlet (it is probably best that the victim(s) sit(s) next to the counsellor).

The group should be praised for having created a positive situation out of a negative one. If positive statements have been made about the victim(s), the students who made them should be asked to repeat them.

> **Comment:** Even if there has been a successful resolution, this meeting is necessary, for several reasons. It rounds things off, and tries to reintegrate

those who have been bullied safely into the group. It is also important to acknowledge that a bullying situation has been turned around. The counsellor can ask what can be done to make the new dynamic a long-term one, and enlist both ideas and commitment from the group, with the victim(s) being equally involved in this venture.

Two Case Studies

The following two case studies of the Pikas Method of Shared Concern are taken from the experiences of two teachers from Tayside, Scotland, after they had been trained in the method by Professor Pikas (Duncan, 1994). These examples show how the method works in practice and indicate that it is effective when accompanied by the creative and practical problem-solving skills of experienced teachers and counsellors.

A Primary School Case Study

A P4 pupil (seven to eight years old) named Nicola was brought into the school by her mother one morning because of a series of bullying incidents to which she had been subjected. These included physical aggression and name-calling, both at school and outside by a group of similar-age children consisting of three boys and a girl (the ringleader). Nicola's mother thought her daughter was being victimised because she was different from the other children—she was well dressed, well cared for, and regularly went on outings and on holiday with her family. Nicola could be described as a passive victim.

Her teacher said that, as a result of hearing about the bullying, she followed the Shared Concern Approach by:

- talking individually with those doing the bullying;
- talking with Nicola, the victim of bullying;
- talking with those doing the bullying in a group; and
- talking with those doing the bullying and the victim of the bullying together.

She was surprised how quickly the children's responses changed afterwards. Although they were young and had difficulty saying why they had bullied, they established empathy with the victim very easily. Apparently, a reason for the bullying was their envy of Nicola's more stable home background.

At the meeting between the bullies and Nicola, she was understandably apprehensive, but those who had bullied put forward their suggestions for solving the problem and were very pleased to be part of the solution. The meeting finished amicably. The teacher thought that, because the children were so young, this made them open to changing their ways; she felt older children might be more cynical. Of the method, the teacher says:

Professor Pikas' Shared Concern Method has much to offer primary schools. The non-authoritarian, patient approach of the therapist pays dividends in offering bullies shared responsibility in resolving problems and my limited experience of this method to date has been positive and rewarding (Duncan, 1994, p. 8).

A Secondary School Case Study

Caroline went to the assistant head teacher (AHT) of her secondary school to complain about being bullied by a group of former friends. She related a recent scene in the canteen where she was kicked, punched, and whispered about, and had a label placed on her back with an insulting name written on it, which she wore for a long time before realising it was there. When Caroline was picked on, she received support from her friend Pauline.

Both girls then became the target of the bullies, and were victimised: they were called names, cold-shouldered, ignored, and in the public areas of the school—the corridors, the canteen, the playground—were jostled and pushed. Both girls were so distressed they told their parents what was happening.

Caroline's parents wanted the situation handled. She had a history of bladder problems and had been teased at primary school about this. A group of the bullying girls had brought this weapon with them to the secondary situation and had been using it intermittently to tease Caroline (others had also picked up on it). Pauline's parents asked her older sister, a pupil at the school, to defend her; and they threatened to remove Pauline from the school if the bullying was not handled.

The AHT listened to Caroline and comforted her, then called a meeting of all the girls to attempt a conciliation. Caroline's mother arrived uninvited as she did not want her daughter to be unsupported amid her tormentors. The result was an unproductive meeting that ended with bad feeling. Caroline's parents were angry with the school and wanted the bullies punished.

On the following Monday and between classes, Caroline was kicked and punched by a member of the bullying group. As a result, the AHT asked an outside counsellor who had been trained in the Pikas Method to try to sort things out.

The counsellor felt her first task was to get the girls' parents to agree to the use of the method. She explained to them that the purpose was to get the girls to work things out between themselves. The parents of the victims reluctantly gave their permission for the intervention to go ahead.

Step one: individual interviews with bullies and victims

The bullies and victims were interviewed. Jenny was identified as the primary bully. When she arrived to be interviewed, she appeared nervous, was uncommunicative, and said that everything was OK, there was no problem. With the counsellor's gentle probing, she admitted that recently Caroline had been having a hard time and was feeling hurt. She avoided saying why. (The counsellor says she suggested to Jenny at this point that it might be because Caroline was being left out. She says in retrospect that she probably should have followed Pikas's script and not prompted Jenny.)

Jenny took this suggestion up and said that Caroline was feeling left out because she had recently moved to a different part of town and was being given much less freedom than her peers.

At this point the counsellor decided to have a group meeting the following day rather than waiting a week, as is suggested by Pikas. She did this for two reasons: she was responding to the sense of urgency surrounding the case, and she came away sensing that Jenny would 'crow' to her friends about pulling the wool over the counsellor's eyes. The counsellor says in retrospect that missing out this 'stand-down' period was a mistake.

Step two: the group meeting

As she anticipated that a lot of mediation would be required, the counsellor went straight to the group meeting rather than meeting the bullying group first (she says this shortcut was another mistake). If she had met with the bullying group, she could have reinforced and consolidated the positive sense of shared concern. Instead, it was immediately apparent that there was an oppositional feeling in the meeting, with a lot of giggling and sneering.

The bullying group, with Emma (rather than Jenny) as their articulate spokesperson, told of the group's keenness to move towards a solution. Caroline and Pauline, however, were distrustful and repeatedly referred to the hurt the bullies had caused them. In response, Emma defended the group and provided counter-arguments against the alliance of Caroline, Pauline, and Pauline's older sister. As the arguing continued and it was clear that Pauline and Caroline were becoming angry, distressed, distrustful, fearful, and hurt, it was decided to call a halt.

Trying to salvage the situation, the counsellor suggested that they would all meet again soon when they felt fresher and keener. She suggested optimistically that this meeting had not been a failure, but had given everyone the opportunity to say how they felt. She also told the group that they could meet as many times as required to come to a resolution.

When the bullying group departed, the counsellor spent an hour comforting Caroline and Pauline and told them that when they were feeling ready she would arrange another meeting with the bullying girls to try to find a solution. A major issue that emerged from the post-meeting discussion was the prominence in Caroline and Pauline's thinking of their parents' anger, which was acting as a barrier to progress.

An unusual thing then occurred. Led by Emma, those who had done the bullying asked for a meeting with the counsellor. They met for ten to fifteen minutes and she reassured the group that her original intention of finding a resolution remained intact, that it was not her intention to get revenge for Pauline and Caroline but to work out a way for them all at least to coexist.

The process was marred by messages from both Caroline and Pauline that their parents would not allow them to meet with the bullies again. After ten days of gentle persuasion and a letter home to their parents, Caroline and Pauline agreed to attend a further meeting with the girls who had bullied them. (The counsellor noted that it was good to listen to parents' advice but it was Caroline and Pauline who had to live with those girls every day at school.)

This meeting was very productive and provided a resolution to the bullying problem. The mood was generally positive, although Pauline and Caroline were distrustful. The counsellor made it clear that they did not have to be friendly with their former tormentors, merely to agree to be tolerant and to develop a working relationship. Fine details were discussed, such as how to greet and reply to each other. The group agreed to meet a week later.

Step three: the follow-up meeting

The whole group met the following week. The meeting was brief but positive, with progress reported by all. Another group meeting was arranged after the impending holidays. In the meantime, the counsellor met Pauline and Caroline. Caroline was positive but Pauline was still wary about trusting the group and about making friends with them. The physical bullying, sneering, and teasing had all stopped after the first meeting had taken place. The counsellor met Caroline and Pauline twice more and both reported that everything was OK.

The counsellor stated that she knew this case would be hard and complex, that she had spent approximately five hours spread over several weeks on it, and that six months after the intervention the girls were getting along fine.

Comment on case study 2

We learn by our mistakes, and I applaud Alison Duncan's honest description of this case study. What Pikas says in his description of the Method of Shared Concern is that the person applying the method must be calm, clear, and in charge. In this case, the sense of urgency meant that the procedures were changed. The counsellor felt she could not wait a week before calling a follow-up meeting because she did not want Jenny to think she had got away with anything. She also felt pressured by the school and the parents to take this matter in hand. She did not, therefore, follow Pikas's procedure and allow her initial meeting with bullies and victims to take effect over the following week.

Although there were alterations to the prescribed formula and problems with the various stages, the counsellor persevered. Eventually, the bullying stopped and an unhealthy interaction pattern between this group of girls was halted. The counsellor describes the former situation as follows:

> The pattern of their social relationships before was one of smooth patches followed by conflicts. This was so noticeable that one guidance teacher had completely lost patience with them and ordered them to go away and grow up! I would like to think that the experience of SCM [Shared Concern Method] has helped them a little to do that (Duncan, 1994, p. 21).

17 Follow-up Strategies for Students

As an adjunct to anti-bullying programs, schools can promote strategies for those identified as chronic bullies or victims. I will deal here with some of those strategies: assertiveness training, anger management, and self-defence and martial arts training.

Assertiveness Training

People tend to respond to conflict in three ways: they are passive, aggressive, or assertive. With bullying, however, the likelihood of an aggressive response from a victim is very slim, and another type of response is likely to occur in which the victim is 'rescued' by a third party.

As stated earlier, it is useful to think of bullying as a dynamic rather than as a static process. Rather than there being bullies, victims, and bystanders trapped in their roles, a dynamic event occurs in which the roles are assumed and are fluid. Assertiveness training is based on an assumption that the dynamics in relationships can be changed by developing strategies that will empower the protagonists and change the nature of the relationships. A passive or aggressive individual can learn how to be assertive. And someone who likes to rescue others can learn to be supportive, which allows the relationships to remain equal.

The Three Triangles

The scenario: Jasmine, Andrea, and Melanie. It is a rainy lunchtime. The pupils have been let into their class after eating. The teacher is marking assignments at the front of the classroom. At the back of the class, Jasmine, who enjoys reading, has picked up and is looking through the new illustrated storybook the teacher has put on display. Andrea leaves her group of friends, who are chatting, comes up quietly behind Jasmine and snatches the book away. 'Give that to me,' says Andrea. 'Let someone who has a brain have a look.' She walks away and adds as she does, 'My God, your shoes are ugly. They are so uncool!' The teacher does not seem to notice.

A bullying triangle response

Embarrassed and unsure what to do, Jasmine stares ahead. She looks as if she might cry but just manages not to. Melanie, who has been standing close by and watching, smiles smugly. Jasmine is such a wimp, she thinks to herself. The class has gone quiet as this scene is acted out. Others have stopped to see what will happen. Nothing does, so people go back to what they are doing, and the sound level in the class returns to normal. The teacher looks up because there has been a lull in class activity but as he does not detect anything out of the ordinary and the noise level is returning to normal, he goes back to his marking.

Comment: In the bullying triangle, it is clear that Andrea has all the power. She pushes Jasmine around and neither the peer group nor the class in general appear prepared to take Jasmine's side. What is more, Andrea manages to hide what she is doing in the general mêlée so the teacher is unaware that any bullying is going on. Jasmine has no support, but Andrea has the support of her friends and, by their non-participation, of the rest of the class. Melanie probably has mixed feelings. She thinks Jasmine is a wimp but probably also feels guilty that she does nothing to intervene. The message to the rest of the class is that Andrea and her friends could also pick on them so it is best to keep quiet.

A rescuing triangle response

Embarrassed and unsure about what to do, Jasmine stares ahead. She looks as if she might cry but just manages not to. Melanie has been standing close by, watching. Jasmine is such a wimp, she thinks, but nobody deserves to be treated like this. 'Give the book back to Jasmine,' she says loudly. Andrea looks to her mates, who snigger in support. 'Give the book back,' Melanie repeats more force-fully. The teacher has become aware of the situation and knows that Andrea has a tendency to push people around. He interjects, 'Yes, Andrea, you give that book back to Jasmine, right now'. Andrea grudgingly shoves the book at Jasmine. 'What's the matter, can't you stand up for yourself?', she mutters as she pushes past her roughly and returns to her mates. 'That's enough, Andrea!' says the teacher.

The class has gone quiet as this scene is acted out. Others around have stopped to see what will happen. The noise level in the class returns to normal. Jasmine smiles sheepishly at Melanie who shrugs her shoulders without smiling.

Comment: In this scenario, Jasmine is pushed around by Andrea but is rescued by Melanie, who becomes a sort of hero. She has stood up to the bully and, as the situation has been brought to the teacher's attention, an adult also supports her. Although the bullying is stopped, there is no sense

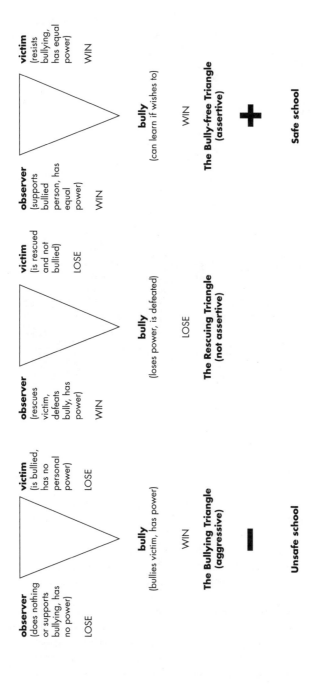

17.1 An Assertive Approach to Bullying – The Three Bullying Triangles

The Bullying Triangle (aggressive)

observer (does nothing or supports bullying, has no power) — LOSE

victim (is bullied, has no personal power) — LOSE

bully (bullies victim, has power) — WIN

Unsafe school

The Rescuing Triangle (not assertive)

observer (rescues victim, defeats bully, has power) — WIN

victim (is rescued and not bullied) — LOSE

bully (loses power, is defeated) — LOSE

The Bully-free Triangle (assertive)

observer (supports bullied person, has equal power) — WIN

victim (resists bullying, has equal power) — WIN

bully (can learn if wishes to) — WIN

Safe school

of follow-through. Rescuing Jasmine puts Melanie in a powerful position. Although it is good that Melanie has supported Jasmine, the feeling is of a duel, and Jasmine knows that if Melanie is not around she will be a target for bullying by Andrea and possibly by others.

An assertive triangle response

At a louder volume than the noise in the class and with a sense of determination (but not aggressively), Jasmine says, 'Give me back that book. I haven't finished reading it.' Melanie has been standing close by and watches as things unfold. Seeing what Andrea is doing and in support of Jasmine, she says, 'Yes, give the book back, Andrea. Jasmine hasn't finished looking at it.' Andrea stares at Jasmine and then at Melanie and looks to her friends for their support. Their faces are blank. They are not smirking or laughing. She gives the book back without expression and walks away. The class has gone quiet as this scene is acted out, watching to see what will happen. As the situation is resolved, people go back to what they are doing and the noise level returns to normal.

The teacher has looked up and become aware of the situation, having been alerted to it by Jasmine's loud but reasonable request. He is ready to intervene if Andrea does not return the book, but sees that Jasmine, with Melanie's support, has handled it so intervention is not necessary. The teacher returns to his marking. Jasmine thanks Melanie for her support. Melanie smiles and says, 'You'd do the same for me.'

> **Comment:** In this situation, Jasmine is assertive. She has been treated like this by Andrea in the past, but knows her rights and has decided not to allow it to happen any more. When she responds, she is not aggressive, and although she has every right to be rude to Andrea, she chooses not to. She acts with dignity and wins the day, probably also gaining the respect of the class. What is more, in being assertive, she has got the teacher's attention and, because of her reasonable stance, has got him on side. Melanie has provided support to Jasmine as an equal, knowing Jasmine would support her if the tables were turned.

The message to the rest of the class is that bullying is not acceptable. There is a good chance that they will support Jasmine if a similar situation occurs again. It is in their best interests to do so because it means that, in a safe culture, such things are less likely to happen to them.

Setting Up an Assertiveness Training Program

Assertiveness training that goes hand in hand with attempts to change a school from an unsafe to a safe place is worthwhile, but if it occurs in a bullying culture it will have very little chance of any real success.

It is important, therefore, to adopt a two-pronged assertiveness training program:
- Teaching victims of bullying to be assertive.
- Establishing an assertive culture in the school for everyone.

For those who are bullied

An assertive response is better than a passive or aggressive one. For many children, being assertive is a new and useful experience that allows them to claim or reclaim their personal power and self-esteem. But, the onus for change should not fall on the victims alone. Being assertive is not a secret weapon to be given only to those in trouble. It is a way for everyone to learn to be honest, clear, and fair in sorting out conflict.

For those who bully

Research indicates that, in social situations, bullies often make mistakes, and identify aggression or ill-intent when none is intended. They fall back on aggression because it comes easily, and this antisocial behaviour is reinforced because of the power inherent in the bullying role. If they are taught, through assertiveness training, that there are benefits to responding in prosocial and assertive ways, that they will be better liked, and that bad behaviour will not be accepted, then they may have no choice but to stop their aggression.

For those who observe bullying

In an assertive school structure that stands up to bullying, there is the potential to harness the goodwill of a majority of students. If this attitude is clearly stated in school policy, and the concept of assertiveness is explained and demonstrated in the school, most students will gratefully accept it.

Implementing a Program

The purpose of an assertiveness training program is to teach about the dynamics of power in school bullying, and how to respond assertively to being bullied. I have developed the following program.

Setting up a group

If a whole school program is being developed, it is a good idea to bring together mixed groups of students to work on assertiveness training. Some should lack assertive skills, some should be very assertive, and some should be in the middle. I would suggest two trainers: one to facilitate and gauge what is going on with the group, and one to direct role playing.

In the first session, it is important to state that the group will be closed, that is, once it has started, people will not be permitted to enter or leave, as this will upset the dynamics of the group. This also requires individuals to make a commitment to being a member of the group. Second, in order for people to feel safe in the group, ground rules will be needed that focus on confidentiality and mutual respect (no interrupting, making constructive responses, etc.).

Length of time

The course should run once a week for about an hour (or less for young children) over a six- to eight-week period (as suggested by Sharp et al., 1994).

A number of components can be learnt

Each session should focus on a specific skill the students can then practise.

- Learning to use 'I' statements and to focus on feelings. The children should learn to be in touch with their feelings and how to express them under stress (such as when bullying starts to occur). It is important that they state their case clearly and focus on how the act of bullying makes them feel. They should avoid being insulting, attributing blame, or being drawn into an argument.
- Learning to relax. In a tense situation, it is important that children try to control their body's natural inclination to fight or retreat— either attacking the other person or running away. There is nothing wrong with calmly leaving the situation or learning to find the weakest link in a mob and pushing through it. Children can be taught to breathe in deeply and exhale slowly to the count of ten as a way to keep their pulse rate down and prevent panic.
- The broken record technique. Children can be taught that if someone does not hear them, or ignores their reasonable request, they should repeat this request over and over, calmly and quietly, until they get a response.

- Masking out the noise. When children bully, they often use a lot of insults and name-calling to make the victim feel bad or provoke him or her into an attack. Children must be taught to block out insults and not to react to them; this takes away their power. The bullies then usually give up or respond by becoming angry and aggressive. In a situation like this there is no point in staying around. Moving away with certainty (without panic) is the best thing to do. Rehearsing such a situation with a group of people is a good way of practising how to deal with it.
- Focusing on body language. Body language is a good indicator of a person's strength, weakness, or resilience. If children are trained to stand and look assertive, this will help them to avoid difficult situations. This can be done through role play. It is useful to show the body language of an unassertive and an aggressive person. An assertive person stands with their back straight without being stiff, looks their opposite number in the eye without being aggressive, and is pleasant but not obsequious.
- Agreeing with criticism. When someone sets themselves up as judge and jury and lists all the things that are wrong with another person, a good strategy is to agree with one of the statements and to ignore the others. This is called fogging.
- Putting it all together. Over the course of several weeks children will have learnt a series of skills to help them respond to an aggressive situation assertively and to change the nature of the encounter. Towards the end of the course, a series of scenarios can be provided to allow the students to try out all the learned strategies. For instance, they should practise using 'I' statements and saying how they feel. They will be better able to identify which sorts of stance and reaction are helpful, and what alternatives are available to them in any situation.

Use of role play

Role plays can be developed to allow children to re-experience being unassertive and then to help them develop more assertive strategies through reflection and suggestion, finally trying them out in preparation for handling the next bullying incident (see 'Role Play', and 'Four Bullying Scenarios' in Chapter 8).

Allow students to try out easy situations they can handle in order to gain confidence. Each week the scenarios should get harder so that, during the last sessions, the students are dealing with really difficult situations. Students should also be encouraged to learn to be assertive in non-bullying situations, and can be given assignments to be assertive in their own lives, reporting back to the group each week about what happened.

Structure of the sessions

For sessions to run well, they need a clear structure, for example:
- Greet people. Use an ice-breaker to get people relaxed (see Appendix IV).
- Recapitulate what the focus of the previous week was. Briefly summarise. Ask people if they have any questions.

- Explain what the focus for the week is. The instructors/helpers provide a role play that illustrates the technique being taught.
- Get people to divide into groups and practise using several theoretical scenarios to try out different responses and roles.
- Call people back together and summarise what has been learnt.

Conclusion

The first and the last sessions are important. The first establishes the group and sets the tone; the last ties up the loose ends, sends the individuals back into the school with their new skills, and allows them to celebrate their accomplishments.

During the first session, it is important to clarify what a person's rights are. Students need to know what is reasonable and unreasonable behaviour, and when someone is being unfair or disrespectful. Sometimes people know within themselves when they are being treated disrespectfully, but either do not think it is really happening (they are misreading what is going on), or do not think they have any right to object. People often give themselves mixed messages. They tell themselves, 'I don't like this. I'm being treated disrespectfully', but, on the other hand, 'They're probably just messing around. If I let it go they'll probably like me.'

Bullying often thrives on this lack of clarity and the resulting indecision to act. Bullying is harmful behaviour, and must be recognised for what it is. If people are disrespectful of others and nothing happens to stop this, their behaviour will only get worse. Being assertive is the best choice in this situation.

In the first part of this section, I provided a bullying scenario that showed three different responses: passive, rescuing or being rescued, and being assertive. In the first session, it may be useful if one of the group leaders plays out the various responses and gets others in the group to participate. She can say how she felt in each of the roles and she can ask other people what they felt. The group can discuss each of the scenes.

During the final session, it is important to sum up what people have learnt and to have a small celebration; if it seems appropriate, certificates can be given to those who have finished the course. Consider, too, a range of complementary options that can be run for bullied individuals in conjunction with assertiveness training to help build or rebuild a person's self-esteem (such as peer support, peer mentoring, and self-defence).

Anger Management

Anger is a natural human emotion. It is not bad in itself, but it can be used in negative ways. Anger management is a process whereby anger is accepted as a feeling but managed constructively. Various organisations and practitioners offer anger management courses, and schools can use the approach by hiring a skilled practitioner, or by referral to an outside agency. It is also possible for teachers to learn some anger management skills and use them, when appropriate, in the classroom.

If an angry child is told to stop being angry, the anger will either go underground or erupt into more anger and possibly violence. Children often need to be taught acceptable ways of expressing their feelings. A strong feeling like anger cannot be ignored; it should be recognised and met. But if it is destructive it must be controlled and redirected.

Anger is sometimes a defence to avoid painful feelings, or it may be a reaction to anxiety. Anger sometimes comes from sadness and depression, sometimes from shame. It is important to look at the causes of anger, not in order to excuse the behaviour but so that it can be understood.

Anger and aggression are separate things. They may sometimes go hand in hand, but they should not automatically be assumed to do so. Anger is often a completely rational response to a situation; at other times it erupts out of underlying feelings. Aggression may occur because of anger, because of another problem, or because of deep disturbance.

Children who are habitually angry usually lack basic skills. They do not know how to get along with other people. They retaliate rather than compromise, they see only their own point of view, they blame others when things go wrong, and they often misinterpret what others say to them.

Such children often come from homes in which they are not loved and cared for, where their dependency needs are not met, and where they are angrily and aggressively treated. They do not grow up with a sense of self-worth or a feeling that the world is a just and safe place.

For these children, vulnerability, sadness, and despair are the horrors that loom in the darkness. In order to keep these at bay, they hit out and mask their true feelings. In their cases, anger management awareness in the classroom and the school will help, but outside intervention from therapists or anger management professionals may be essential.

Anger Management in the Classroom

Teachers have developed various strategies for dealing with anger. Many use a 'cool-down area' where children can go when they feel stressed and on the verge of losing their tempers. Some teachers have objects like stress balls for the children to use when they need to. Others institute special social skills programs which they teach themselves or hire an outside expert to teach. These can cover such areas as anger management, empathy training, and impulse control.

At the intermediate and secondary school levels, anger management strategies comprise the recognition of anger cues and triggers, the use of positive self-statements and relaxation techniques to prevent the onset of angry feelings, and reflection on the anger-provoking incident. For younger children it involves the recognition of anger followed by relaxation techniques, such as deep breathing and counting, and the use of self-statements such as 'calm down'. While younger children may require adult assistance in using these techniques, older children can use the techniques by themselves once they are trained, and this knowledge will be invaluable to them throughout their lives.

Some teachers develop, with their students, immediate and often preventative strategies for use in the classroom. These can include the children using a prearranged signal to indicate they are upset (e.g. a red card that is put into a desk pocket, or a physical gesture such as a child putting her head down on the desk); learning some calming techniques (such as deep breathing and visualising something peaceful); and being able to draw, talk, or write out their feelings.

Teachers can use role play to show their students some strategies for dealing with anger. In these role plays, children can identify the triggers for anger, and the best ways for dealing with their own and others' anger. They can learn such things as:

- recognising triggers and deciding to signal that a trigger has been tripped;
- working out the anger with calm words, not fists;
- stopping to think before acting;
- owning their feelings and not blaming someone else for how they feel;
- thinking how the other person might feel;
- separating big issues from small issues, and talking out the big issues and letting the small issues go.

In a classroom where everyone is working together to deal with anger, there is a chance that healthy support and change will develop.

An Anger Management Program

A school may decide to develop its own anger management program, with the help of the counselling staff and/or outside practitioners. Alternatively, it may choose to refer specific students to outside agencies or therapists. In New Zealand, Men for Non-Violence is an excellent resource for adolescent boys with anger management problems.

The following suggestions for an anger management program are taken (with permission) from the Dean of Students Office, St Francis Xavier University, Antigonish, Nova Scotia, Canada, and were devised by the previous dean, Rick Benson.

Introduction

If students are referred to an anger management course, they are likely to be in denial. Therefore, the process must be explained fully at the beginning with time for questions, and ground rules must be set, which must include:
- no name-calling;
- no violent outbursts;
- respect for others (including facilitators) and self;
- confidentiality among students and facilitators.

The students should be told that the goal of anger management is to reduce the feelings and physiological arousal that anger causes. Although the things that cause anger cannot be got rid of, people can learn to control their feelings.

It may also be useful to discuss with the students a contract that has been drawn up for those attending the course, and to ask each one of them to sign it.

Anger Management Course Contract

1. I will attend the course which is being held at _____ from _____ to _____.
2. I will arrive on time.
3. I will participate in all group activities.
4. I will keep confidential everything that happens in this room.
5. I will respect everyone in the room. I will not harass or intimidate anyone.
6. If I get physically or verbally aggressive towards anyone on the course, I will apologise.

I agree to abide by these rules for the course.

Name: _____

Date: _____

Witness: _____

Date: _____

Why they are there

Without providing details of any specific incidents, it is important to say why everyone was referred to the course. If students have been referred to the group because of bullying behaviour, they may not want to talk about it. They should be encouraged to discuss what triggered it and how they felt. They could also talk about how other people reacted to the incident, and how they would like it to have turned out.

What is anger?

Anger itself needs to be discussed. The students should be assured that anger is completely normal, but that it can also be very destructive. Some people are more easily angered than others, and there are different ways of being angry: aggressively, passive-aggressively, and assertively.

Aggressive anger is expressed by someone overtly trying to hurt someone else, physically, emotionally, or psychologically, e.g. hits and kicks, harassment, put-downs, threats. Aggressive people blame everyone else and act out.

Passive-aggressive anger is expressed circuitously. The anger is repressed by internalising and denying it, and the passive aggressor gives the cold shoulder, spreads rumours, purposely snubs someone, or accidentally-on-purpose harms someone (physically, by bumping into someone—'Oh, I'm so sorry', or psychologically, by pretending not to see them—'Oh, I was off on another planet'). The passive-aggressive person denies and devalues his or her own feelings, and the anger escapes in an indirect way.

Assertive anger is expressed clearly in a straightforward, non-threatening manner. The only issue at stake is what caused the anger.

Anger management strategies

It is now time to go through some of the proven anger management strategies. Some will work better than others for different people. They include:
- recognising angry feelings;
- relaxation techniques, e.g. deep breathing, repeating a calming word or phrase, use of imagery, non-strenuous exercise;
- changing thoughts, e.g. choosing rational words rather than angry words, making 'I' statements, not blaming;
- checking the facts, not taking offence;
- using humour;
- changing small things that cause frequent frustration;
- thinking about what happens after an angry outburst and imagining something better and preferable;
- accepting the anger as natural, but deciding that no one else has to pay for it.

In groups, the students can talk about alternatives to their behaviour. Role play is useful in this setting. And further discussion should encourage participation from all present, and openness and honesty. If students watch others act out an angry scene, it becomes easier for them to think of alternative ways of behaving, and to see how closed the anger system is.

Closure

Such a course may be insufficient to make some people change their behaviour, but follow-up sessions should help because they will allow students to monitor angry situations in which they find themselves and give them support to change their behaviour. This will reinforce what they learn, and provide opportunities to put it into practice. If they do not succeed the first time, they may the second or third.

Self-Defence and Martial Arts Training

Much of the focus of contemporary anti-bullying programs is on finding non-confrontational, non-violent solutions to physical bullying, rather than advocating the more old-fashioned approach of standing up to the bully. It is a myth that, if bullies are confronted or spoken to sharply, they will run away. This may be a little like the commonly held belief that if you speak sternly to a shark or tap it on the nose, it will swim away. Confrontation with a violent bully is more likely to end in an escalation of violence.

I have a black belt in karate and have taught Kyokushin karate, which includes a self-defence component, for six years. Since I took up karate, I have had to defend myself only once when I was attacked in the street by an angry and deluded man. He was a similar height to me but weighed less. He grabbed me around the neck and tried to strangle me. I quickly removed his hands and could very easily have knocked him to the ground. Instead, I chose to move away from the situation. Knowing that I could call on karate techniques allowed me to act rationally, to be calm, and to cause the least amount of damage. Having managed to avoid conflict, I felt that my martial arts training had served me well.

For children who have been the victims of bullying, a course in self-defence techniques or taking up a martial art may be helpful. But this is because the knowledge gained will give confidence, not because it will encourage them to try to inflict damage on anyone who attacks them.

Self-Defence

Self-defence may be taught within any martial art, or separately as a specific program. Self-defence programs are usually taught by taking people through dangerous scenarios in which they might find themselves, and teaching techniques that they can use to get out of those situations. Good self-defence courses develop people's natural skills and confidence so that, if threatened, they can react spontaneously and assertively.

Self-defence skills are usually based on the use of excellent natural weapons such as elbows, hands, knees, the forehead, the side of the head, and feet to good effect, with fast escape as the ultimate defence. Basic martial arts techniques, such as some easy-to-use kicks and punches, are also taught.

But 95 per cent of self-defence is more about attitude than fighting ability, so that although specific techniques may not be remembered some time after the course, the person is able to stand more confidently and know that there is a way out. Self-defence also arms each person with the ability to identify potentially dangerous situations. For instance, if a girl on the way to school sees a group of girls ahead who have been tormenting her, then it will be sensible for her to stay close to nearby children or adults, remain far behind her potential tormentors, or take another route to school (as long as this does not put her in more danger).

Children who are victimised often lack the self-assertiveness or anticipatory skills to assess potential danger. A good self-defence course can start to reverse years of poor avoidance techniques.

Recently, there has been a lot of emphasis on teaching women self-defence and a number of excellent courses specifically for girls and women have been devised (Sue Lytollis's course is an excellent New Zealand example).

Taking Up a Martial Art

Aikido, judo, karate, kick boxing, kung fu, and tae kwon do are all forms of martial arts. Martial arts teach sets of techniques for self-defence and attack that are learned individually, practised thoroughly, and put together as combinations. They are also grounded in well-established philosophies, and learning a martial art also means becoming familiar with this philosophy and becoming a member of a large extended family. When martial arts skills are used in competition, this is the sports dimension.

Taking up a martial art requires much more commitment than doing a self-defence course. When people watch martial arts films, they see very dexterous opponents executing a series of difficult and impressive techniques. These are the outward manifestations of a process of physical and psychological growth and development. People with some degree of accomplishment in martial arts tend to be calm and confident, which are good body language signals to give to potential bullies.

It is true that some people who study martial arts lack self-discipline and want to use their skills to show off. Such attitudes are, however, antithetical to the discipline of all martial arts, and such people have neither the staying power to train to a good standard nor the personal qualities to allow them to grow within the art. Bullies are not tolerated in martial arts.

If it is taught well, a martial arts training does several things:

- It encourages physical fitness.
- It teaches a series of skills, such as hand locks, kicking, punching, rolling, throwing, and various disabling techniques that can be used either in competitive tournaments or in defence.
- Through repetition of basic techniques it teaches the ability to respond without thinking in a challenging situation.
- It develops physical stamina through hard training.
- When people master a martial art through consistent and hard training, they build both their physical skills and a sense of self-esteem and confidence.
- Martial arts teachers discourage people who show off or bully as a result of learning martial skills.

Which Martial Art Should I Choose?

When choosing a martial art there are several factors to consider. There are various basic differences in technique and approach.

- Grappling. Judo concentrates on learning various techniques for disabling an opponent, essentially by throwing.
- Redirecting others' energy. Aikido anticipates the opponent's moves and uses the person's weight and direction to disable the attacker.
- Punching and kicking. Karate focuses on learning a variety of kicks, hand techniques, and blocks, often in quick succession and in combination.

Some martial arts, such as jujitsu, combine aspects of these three approaches.

Martial arts also work on building body strength, stamina, and flexibility, and include various loosening up and strengthening exercises. Within the various martial arts there are a number of individual styles.

Before choosing a martial art, it is a good idea to observe training sessions, talk to the instructors, and choose a martial art and style that feels suitable.

For a person who has been bullied, perhaps quite seriously, there are no miracle cures. A comparison can be made with someone who is overweight and wants to get into shape. First, the person will have to change what they eat, will have to exercise regularly, and will have to change their lifestyle. If this is done with self-discipline, then a year later real change may be achieved. Similarly, taking up a martial art or doing self-defence must be done with consistency and dedication, and perhaps in conjunction with other initiatives, such as assertiveness training. A change will come about after realistic amounts of time and energy have been expended.

Conclusion

Although bullying is a difficult problem, we increasingly understand how it works and have developed a range of excellent strategies for stopping it. A strong and resourceful global anti-bullying movement has emerged with three complementary perspectives that are personified in the researchers, the program developers, and the practitioners. There are crossovers between these roles, but most of us gravitate towards one of them.

- The researchers have developed anti-bullying research projects and gathered information about the extent and nature of the problem. They have initiated schemes in which various approaches and programs have been tried out and evaluated for their effectiveness.
- The program developers have responded to bullying, sometimes using the information provided by researchers, sometimes instinctively, and have produced programs to deal with bullying, and to improve the safety of individual students and schools.
- The practitioners include teachers, deputy principals, and guidance counsellors. They take note of research and deal with the problem of school bullying on a day-to-day basis, selecting particular programs they think will work.

The informal partnership that has developed between these three groups has nurtured the development and improvement of our understanding and ways of dealing with bullying. Although a lot of money and energy has been spent on these processes, a concerted effort supported by modern technology has ensured that the excellent anti-bullying resource base now available is inexpensive and readily accessible by telephone, fax, email or the World Wide Web.

This book has provided an overview of what I think is the best of what is available and has made suggestions for developing workable anti-bullying processes and programmes. However, every situation is unique, and creative thinking and energy are needed to develop effective and long-lasting solutions.

Appendix I: Two Examples of School Anti-Bullying Policies

Colenso High School Bullying Policy, Hawke's Bay, New Zealand

Rationale

Colenso High School actively seeks to provide a learning environment that is safe from intimidation.

Purpose

- To outline strategies for staff to help students to combat social, emotional, and physical intimidation.

Guidelines

- Staff should treat any report of bullying seriously.
- Staff should first listen to the student or students, and make such enquiries as may be necessary to clarify exactly what has been happening.
- The student(s) should be assured that they have acted correctly in reporting the bullying.
- The staff member should make a written summary of the information and pass it on to the form teacher, dean, or deputy principal as appropriate.
- The staff member should attempt to give advice on how to deal with any repeat incidents that may happen before the intimidation can be dealt with.
- Follow-up should be discussed with the student. It is important that the staff member checks a week or so later with both the student and the person to whom the information was sent.
- In cases of serious intimidation parents of both (all) students are to be contacted.
- An anti-bullying program will be run with each year 9 class each year.

Camdean Primary School Anti-Bullying Policy, Fifeshire, Scotland

Rationale

The purpose of this policy is to promote consistency of approach and to create a climate in which all types of bullying are regarded as unacceptable.

Attitudes and practices can contribute to bullying, to lower levels of confidence, self-esteem, and lack of achievement.

The Camdean policy endorses the views of Fife Council, promotes the aims of the Kidscape organisation, and takes account of the requirements of the 1995 Children (Scotland) Act.

Aims

- To promote a secure and happy environment free from threat, harassment, and any type of bullying behaviour.
- To take positive action to prevent bullying from occurring through a clear school policy on personal and social development.
- To show commitment to overcoming bullying by practising zero tolerance.
- To inform pupils and parents of the school's expectations and to foster a productive partnership, which helps maintain a bully-free environment.
- To make staff aware of their role in fostering the knowledge and attitudes which will be required to achieve the above aims.

Achieving Aims

All action relating to curricular issues underpins the belief in valuing people as individuals and their right to a bully-free environment.

The stated aims will be further achieved through the school's policies and programs already in practice.

Staff Responsibilities

- To implement procedures to confront bullying in any form.
- To listen to all parties involved in incidents.
- To investigate as fully as possible.
- To take appropriate action, or to refer the matter to a member of the management team for further action.
- To record and inform parents of bullying incidents.
- To promote the use of a range of teaching and learning styles and strategies which challenge bullying behaviour.
- To promote open management styles which facilitate communication and consultation throughout the education service.
- To foster by example the values we as a school believe in.
- To promote the use of interventions which are least intrusive and most effective.

- To monitor the extent to which the above are being carried out by:
  Regular discussions between management, staff, pupils and parents.
  Recording incidents of bullying in a discipline file.
  To retain records for monitoring purposes.

As head teacher, I accept the responsibility to ensure that this policy is adhered to as fully as is practicably possible. I am therefore the named person in this context.

This and other school policies will be reviewed regularly and revised as necessary, in the ongoing process of school development planning.

January 1998

Comments to: camdean@itasdarc.demon.co.uk

Appendix II: Other Anti-Bullying Programs

Introduction

This book has focused on a useful cross-section of approaches from which schools can select in support of an anti-bullying initiative. Space does not permit me to deal with all available anti-bullying programs at length, but it is important to describe as many as possible since each school must find an approach that fits its policies and philosophy. This appendix gives a brief account of more resources that are useful either as programs or for the information or supplementary material they provide.

Bully No More and *To Bully No More— The Pupil Pack*

Kevin Brown of Penicuik near Edinburgh has developed two interconnected packages, entitled *Bully No More* and *To Bully No More—The Pupil Pack*. Both contain a video and an instruction booklet.

Bully No More provides an overview of how one school in the Edinburgh area went about setting up a non-punitive anti-bullying program using two of Barbara Maines's and George Robinson's programs, the *No Blame Approach* as a bullying intervention, and *Stamp Out Bullying* as a preventative measure. The school teachers worked with local agencies and went through a step-by-step process that fully developed their initiative.

To Bully No More—The Pupil Pack is a very good program. It contains a video just over twenty minutes long, accompanied by a well-written booklet. The program consists of seven interrelated steps which, with the worksheets, are designed to assist students in both understanding and discussing bullying in all of its forms.

The basic premise of the program is that bullying consists of a variety of roles —the bully, the victim, and the watcher (who can be a bystander, a rescuer, a punisher, or indifferent)—and that everyone knows the scripts for these roles and can take any of them on (although individuals may be inclined more towards one than another).

It assumes that the way to deal with bullying is to be assertive and to change the dynamics of a group so that bullying is resisted within the school culture. The program provides the basis for learning through discussion about bullying, through role play (often in a triangle where people change from role to role, with the three corners being bully, victim, and watcher), and through worksheets. From a learning point of view, providing three different ways of finding out about and experiencing bullying roles is very powerful.

The seven sections are entitled: What is Bullying?, Who is Involved?, Role Swapping, How Do We Feel?, The Rescuing-Indifferent-Punishing Syndrome, Assertiveness—Breaking the Bullying Cycle, and Supporting People. This is a very down-to-earth and useable package.

These two programs are complementary as they deal with the macro (the larger issues to do with school organisation) and the micro (the experiences of pupils) dimensions of bullying. The tape in the first package has some technical faults but other than this I fully recommend this set.

Contact

Further information about these programs can be obtained from:

Kevin Brown, Mainstream Relationships in Education and Business, Uttershill House, Penicuik, near Edinburgh EH26 8LT, Scotland, telephone 00 44 1968 678985

e-mail Kevin.Brown@virgin.net

Kevin Brown has also written a book entitled *Bullying: What Can Parents Do?*, Monarch Books, Crowborough, 1997.

Bullying: Don't Suffer in Silence. An Anti-bullying Pack For Schools

The most thorough and far-reaching study of bullying to date is the British Sheffield study, which was funded by the Department for Education (DFE), and produced the excellent books by Sharp and Smith (1994) and Smith and Sharp (1994). Another product of this research is this pack for schools (including a 141-page document and a video). The video is an excellent resource for examining how to use the playground creatively, and the written material is a well-organised, very readable resource which communicates in a practical way the lessons learnt from the research (Smith, 1999, states that 19 000 schools had requested copies of it).

The book consists of eleven parts. Part One tells how to develop, implement, and monitor a whole school policy, and the other parts provide examples, details, and information about strategies suggested in Part One. The advice given is based on the experiences of the twenty-three schools in the Sheffield study (sixteen primary and seven secondary schools) and supplements this information with findings from a Calouste Gulbenkian Foundation-funded research project on playgrounds.

The information in this book is well explained, to the point, and very useable. It is an excellent resource.

Contact

DFE 1994, *Bullying: Don't Suffer in Silence. An Anti-bullying Pack for Schools*, HMSO, London.

General References

Sharp, S. & P.K. Smith (eds) 1994, *Tackling Bullying in Your School: A Practical Handbook for Teachers*, Routledge, London & New York.

Smith, P.K. and S. Sharp (eds) 1994, *School Bullying: Insights and Perspectives*, Routledge, London & New York.

Smith, P.K. 1999, 'England and Wales', in P.K. Smith et al. (eds), *The Nature of School Bullying: A Cross-National Perspective*, Routledge, London & New York.

Bullyproofing Our School. Promoting Positive Relationships

This program was developed by Alan McLean, Principal Psychologist, Glasgow North End, for the Department of Education of Scotland's Strathclyde Regional Council. It is usually referred to as the Strathclyde program.

The Strathclyde program consists of a video and ten accompanying booklets. These cover three workshops (for teachers, parents, and senior pupils), some background readings, a set of master copies that can be made into transparencies for use at workshops or elsewhere, a pupil advice leaflet, a parents' advice leaflet, and a user's guide to explain how these link together. The underlying philosophy is to embed approaches to managing bullying in school policies in order to promote positive relationships through a caring school ethos. The program is founded on an understanding that the extent of bullying is underestimated and schools need to develop strategies to deal with it more effectively.

An important focus of this particular package is the power of the peer group. Three particular issues are identified:

- the importance of harnessing the support of those pupils with leadership potential in order to develop an anti-bullying ethos in the school;
- encouraging the natural tendency of the peer group to stand up against bullying, which in any case they do not agree with or feel comfortable about;
- recognising that students are the real experts and that their knowledge and ideas should be used to build a program.

The underlying perspective is dynamic and constructive, and does not approach bullying in terms of fixed personalities and relationships. The bully is not blamed and the victim is not expected to find a solution. Instead, there is an attempt to create a healthier social relationship within the whole peer group.

Two videos accompany this package, one designed for use in primary schools and the other in secondary schools. I found the secondary school video, *Sticks and Stones*, particularly useful.

The strength of this program lies in its dynamic approach to bullying, which it regards as grounded in social interactions that are not static and can be changed. The workshops are designed to raise the awareness of all participants.

Reference

McLean, A. 1994, *Bullyproofing Our School. Promoting Positive Relationships*, Strathclyde Regional Council, Glasgow.

Eliminating Violence—Managing Anger Program

The *Eliminating Violence* program has been praised in many quarters as being New Zealand's most effective and extensive anti-bullying initiative. It was developed in 1992 by the Special Education Services group at Manukau North in Auckland and is funded by the Ministry of Education. Its intention is to deal with violence and anger in schools through the examination of school culture, and its aim is to modify practices, structures, systems, and values that encourage or support such behaviours, and to encourage and develop a pro-social ethos in schools.

The program consists of fours steps. Step one includes a presentation to staff, the establishment of a steering group, and data collection. Step two is a two-day workshop covering a series of topics, including a presentation of the findings about violence in the school. Step three draws together a core group from the school to take responsibility for staff training, student dissemination, parental community involvement and participation, school policy development, and maintaining enthusiasm. Step four is intended as a feedback, follow-up, and maintenance step. The program requires a twelve-month commitment from schools.

Over eighteen months, Moore et al. (1997) conducted an evaluation of the program in three schools. They found that there was a reduction in both the level and severity of violence, and lower tolerance to violent behaviour in all three schools. In all cases, this created a safer and more welcoming environment, and better staff relations. The major criticisms were that the program was less successful in teaching students specific skills to manage their own and others' anger, and in developing prosocial alternatives to violent behaviour, and that there was insufficient community involvement. Since this evaluation, the *Eliminating Violence* team has taken heed of the criticisms and made major modifications, e.g. the involvement of the Pacific Island community in the program.

Contact and Web Site

In New Zealand, contact the local Special Education Services Manager for details, or the *Eliminating Violence* team, telephone 09 279 6600.
http://www.ses.org.nz

General Reference

Moore, D. et al. 1997, *Eliminating Violence from Schools Evaluation Project, Final Report—April 1997*, Auckland UniServices, University of Auckland, Auckland.

Tackling Bullying in Primary Schools

This resource book was prepared by Jim Tuthill and Fay Howe as a collaboration between Powys Area Child Protection Committee and the NSPCC (National Society for the Prevention of Cruelty to Children) Cymru/Wales. It is a forty-seven-page, well-presented resource book that has been written specifically for primary age pupils. It offers practical ideas that teachers can use on a day-to-day basis and that can be easily linked into curriculum activities. The book provides a brief but accurate overview of all key issues about bullying. It also suggests how to address bullying through the curriculum and through several interventions. Its steps for setting up a whole school anti-bullying policy are particularly useful.

Contact and Web Site

The book can be purchased from the NSPCC Publications Department, 42 Curtain Road, London, EC2A 3NH, England, telephone 00 44 171 8252775, or 00 44 171 8252597.
http://www.nspcc.org.uk/info/publication/

Teaching Prosocial Behaviour to Adolescents

Kate Prescott has produced an excellent spiral-bound book (254 pages) that gives an overview of programs used to support and develop prosocial behaviour in adolescents in Australian schools. It is the outcome of an eighteen-month research program that was supported by the Australian federal government and was run in three Australian states (New South Wales, South Australia, and Victoria).

The project documented and evaluated the implementation of programs designed to teach and develop prosocial behaviour, and compiled a directory of practices and programs in use or available for Australian schools.

Seventeen schools were selected and their initiatives examined. These schools attempted an array of approaches, focusing on such themes as assertiveness training, initiating a bullying policy, peer counselling/mediation, and sexual harassment, to name a few. The overview of individual schools' efforts are illuminating in that they provide, in a straightforward fashion, what the school's intentions were, how they were put into place, and how successful they were. They give much food for thought for schools planning an anti-bullying initiative.

Also included are one-page summaries of forty commercially available programs (from Australia and overseas) and of fifty-one school-developed programs, as well as information about related resources and useful books, videos, and posters. The introductory part of the book also gives some basic and accessible theoretical information.

Although this is an Australian-based resource, it is also valuable for schools in New Zealand and further afield. Many of the commercial programs are from overseas and the problems and solutions that are generated and solved in the Australian setting are universal.

Contact and Reference

The book is available from the Australian Guidance and Counselling Association Ltd, c/o Ministerial Advisory Committee, GPO Box 2370, Adelaide, South Australia 5001, Australia.

Prescott, K. 1995, *Teaching Prosocial Behaviour to Adolescents: A Directory of Processes and Programs Used in Australian Schools*, Australian Guidance and Counselling Association, Adelaide.

The *S.A.F.E. Program*

S.A.F.E., which is an acronym for Safety and Assurance for Furthering Equality, was developed in England by the Walsall Education Committee's Equal Education Support Unit. It is an inexpensive kit that provides a program generated after working with six junior schools. The program is intended to give junior schools a series of issues for discussion and writing about bullying. Included in the kit are ten situation cards that are used to get children to think about and suggest solutions to bullying. This is meant to develop children's awareness of bullying and to increase their ability to identify it. The kit, which is designed to empower children and to increase their assertiveness, provides ideas for posters, slogans, and a good behaviour guide for classes. The kit also includes a useful draft anti-bullying policy and background materials.

Contact

Further information can be obtained from the Equal Opportunities Unit, Walsall Education Committee, EDC, Field Road, Bloxwich, Walsall WS3 3JF, West Midlands, Birmingham, England, telephone 00 44 1922 685812.

The Scottish Council for Research in Education Anti-Bullying Packs

The Scottish Council for Research in Education (SCRE) developed an excellent anti-bullying pack, *Action Against Bullying: A Support Pack for Schools* (Johnston et al., 1991), which was distributed to schools throughout the UK. Two years later, a second anti-bullying pack entitled *Supporting Schools Against Bullying: The Second SCRE Anti-Bullying Pack* (Munn and Mellor, 1993) was produced. The first pack was aimed at teachers, and the second pack built on the themes of the first but focused on involving parents, non-teaching staff, and head teachers in anti-bullying initiatives. These materials are excellent.

The main message of *Action Against Bullying: A Support Pack for Schools* is that the single most important thing a school can do is to have a clear policy to which staff, pupils, and parents are committed. The kit is very well written, concise, easy to follow, and probing. It has the right tone for teachers, providing useful information but also being questioning. The booklet has three sections entitled 'Introduction', 'What is Bullying?', and 'Anti-Bullying Action'.

The additional materials consist of four 'Action on Policy' one-page synopses, six bullying scenarios, and two information sheets. The 'Action on Policy' pages cover 'A School Policy on Bullying', 'Publicising Your Policy in the School', 'Publicising Your Policy to Parents and the Wider Community', and 'What Happens in Your School'. Together they provide a useful basis for forming and disseminating policy. The information sheets make suggestions about in-service training for teachers and provide curriculum materials.

This kit is well compiled. It provides an overview of important information without being either dogmatic, repetitive, or overly academic. Although much work has been done in the eight years since it was developed, it is still a very useful tool. It has a constructivist approach similar to Phillip Slee's 1997 *P.E.A.C.E. Pack*.

The second SCRE kit consists of two booklets entitled *School Action Against Bullying: Involving Parents and Non-Teaching Staff* (by Pamela Munn) and *Bullying and How to Fight It: A Guide for Families*. It also contains support materials taken from the first booklet which can be used as individual handouts.

This material is presented in a very straightforward and useable fashion. It provides information and practical suggestions and its focus is on involving parents and non-teaching staff, and raising awareness about the seriousness of bullying in schools. It suggests what a good anti-bullying policy should contain and how to develop this and evaluate the current policy. The booklet emphasises the need for active commitment from parents, trustees, and non-teaching staff, and provides suggestions for how to obtain this.

A set of support materials is included. Six realistic and diverse bullying incidents are provided on a single page each so that they can be photocopied and used in workshops. Useful open-ended questions are listed, and a seventh worksheet is included to enable schools to create their own scenarios.

Three information sheets, entitled 1. Does bullying exist in your school? 2. Two case studies of school action, and 3. How well is your policy working? provide valuable materials for investigating the level of bullying in a school, two examples of successful anti-bullying initiatives, and a series of checks for investigating whether or not a school's anti-bullying policy is working. Sheet one suggests how to improve and develop the playground so that it is both stimulating and safe for children. Sheet two lists information about books, articles, and workshop materials (mostly out of date now), and sheet three gives information about anti-bullying programs in the UK.

Although there have been many developments since these kits were released and the resources to which they refer have been superseded, they are still very useful for raising awareness, changing attitudes, and getting people involved. In particular, the action plan suggestions are straightforward, easy to use, and practical. The variety of bullying scenarios presented by the two kits is a powerful tool in making the problem generally accessible. Both kits are inexpensive.

References and Web Site

Johnstone, M. et al. 1991, *Action Against Bullying: A Support Pack for Schools*, SCRE, Edinburgh.

Mellor, A. 1997, *Bullying at School. Advice for Families*, SCRE, Edinburgh.

Munn, P. & A. Mellor 1993, *Supporting Schools Against Bullying: The Second SCRE Anti-Bullying Pack*, SCRE, Edinburgh.

http://www.scre.ac.uk/bully/links.html

We Don't Have Bullying Here

This is an accessible one-day, in-service, anti-bullying training program designed by Val Besag to complement her book, *Bullies and Victims in Schools*.

The program introduces the topic of bullying by providing a range of useful and down-to-earth processes and tools. In very understandable language, the program is described, focusing on the important issues and goals. Besag advises that a special interest group takes responsibility for organisation, and suggests a timetable consisting of five sessions spread through the day which are designed to inform participants about the issues, to discuss specific case studies, and to come up with whole school solutions appropriate for the school in question. The kit provides a variety of useful materials to give substance to these steps.

The program is very friendly, full (127 pages), and accessible. It has been designed to provide, in just one day's intensive work, a good grasp of the issues and an introduction to some possible solutions.

Contact and Reference

This program can be ordered from Val Besag, 3 Jesmond Dene Terrace, Jesmond, Newcastle upon Tyne, NE2 2ET, England.

Besag, V. 1989, *Bullies and Victims in Schools: A Guide to Understanding and Management*, Open University Press, Milton Keynes.

Appendix III: The Strathclyde Relationship Maps

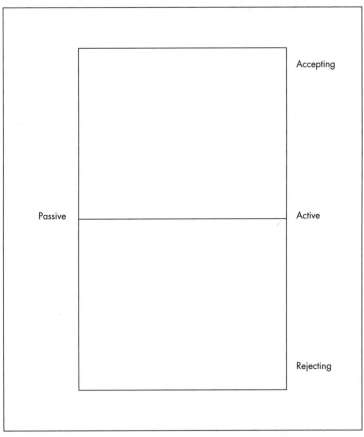

AIII.a The Strathclyde Relationship Maps—diagram A—The social map
Source: McLean, 1994.

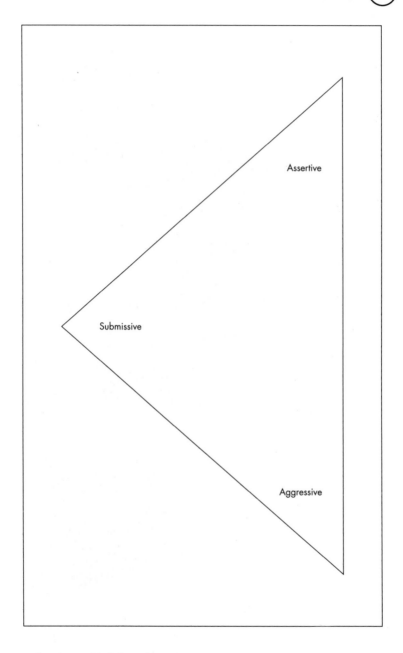

AIII.b The Strathclyde Relationship Maps—diagram B—The assertiveness
map
Source: McLean, 1994.

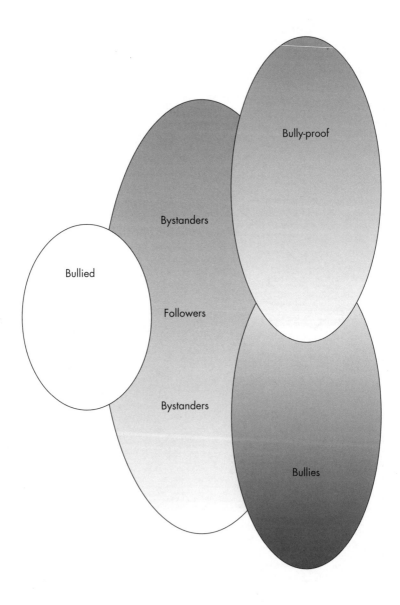

AIII.c The Strathclyde Relationship Maps—diagram C—The bullying map
Source: McLean, 1994.

Appendix IV: Ice-Breakers

Coming up with activities that break the ice is a good way to cut down on the time needed to establish trust and openness in interactive meetings. It is human nature to build walls and facades, to show people only what we want them to see. Ice-breakers are a means to break through those walls, and to help people relax and loosen up.

Various approaches can be used. Here are some that work well with children. They are arranged in order, with the first ones being suitable for younger children and the later ones for teenagers.

M&Ms

Pass around a big bag of M&Ms (or any other sweets) and tell everyone to take as many as they like but to make sure that they do not eat them. Then they are allowed to eat one M&M for every piece of information they tell about themselves.

Ball Game

Each group is given a ball, which is thrown from one person to another. The person's name is said as the ball is thrown to them. The aim is to get the ball to everyone without repeating anyone as quickly as possible.

Balloon Game

Everyone must write one piece of information about themselves on a small piece of paper that is then rolled into a ball and put into a balloon which is blown up and tied. All the balloons are thrown into the middle of the circle and popped one by one. As each balloon is popped the students must guess who the piece of information is about.

Spelling Bee

In a group of twenty-six children, put one letter of the alphabet on each person's back. Then one person from the group should say their name and try to organise the group to spell their name. If they need to use a letter more than once, then that person should rush from place to place in the line. If the group is bigger than twenty-six, extra vowels can be assigned.

Storytelling

- The children are asked to make up a story. The first must make up a sentence that begins with 'fortunately', and the second follows with a sentence beginning 'unfortunately', and so on, e.g. the first person says, 'Fortunately, we won the lottery', and the second says, 'Unfortunately, we couldn't find the ticket', and the third person says, 'Fortunately ...'.
- A story is told in a round. Each student is only allowed a certain number of words, e.g. five. If a student runs out of words before finishing a sentence, the next person simply continues where they left off, and so on.

If You Love Me, Baby—Smile

This game is for small co-ed groups. One person is chosen to say to anyone in the circle, 'If you love me baby—smile'. The person to whom this is said must respond without smiling, 'I love you baby, but I just can't smile'. As long as no one smiles this process continues. Once someone smiles, they take the place of the person who says 'If you ...'.

Name Game

Each student should introduce themselves by saying their name and something they did in the holidays that starts with the same letter, e.g. 'Hi, I'm Hannah and I hitchhiked to Auckland'. The next person in the line or circle does the same but must introduce the students who went before them and their holiday activities.

Dyads

The group should be divided up into pairs, preferably of students who are not particular friends. They should be sent off into different areas of the room for ten minutes to get acquainted. They should 'interview' each other (perhaps using a prepared set of questions) so that they gain some knowledge and understanding of each other. When the ten minutes are up, they should come together as one group, and each partner introduces the other and tells a little about him or her.

Appendix V: Anti-Bullying Resources on the Internet

Much of the information in this book has been generated from local experiences, but it is applicable worldwide. And much that has been learnt globally can be applied locally. This is doubly the case with information on the Internet, as information can be downloaded instantly, and materials can also be purchased almost as quickly internationally as they can locally.

Over the last few years, a number of useful anti-bullying sites have been developed for the Internet. A quick visit to a selection of sites will provide useful and largely up-to-date information about bullying, materials to download, addresses of other anti-bullying links, and information about anti-bullying products. As with other resources, the quality is variable. I have chosen a number of the most useful sites, which also meet a variety of needs. I have provided a description of each site, some of which are more detailed than others. This tends to reflect the amount and diversity of information at that site, as some cover one topic briefly, whereas others cover a range of subjects and have links to a number of other interesting sites.

This section on anti-bullying web sites is by no means exhaustive.

Australia

Ken Rigby's Site at the University of South Australia, Adelaide

http://www.indigenet.unisa.edu.au/bullying/

The art of building effective web sites is new and many websites can appear attractive but are superficial and move in circles. Ken Rigby's anti-bullying site is an excellent example of how to do it correctly. His information is well written, accessible, diverse, and up-to-date, and I would recommend it as an excellent place to start travelling around the anti-bullying sites. Within Rigby's site are a number of pages that I found to be particularly useful.

'An Introduction to Bullying'

http://www.indigenet.unisa.edu.au/bullying/intro.html

This provides a succinct one-page overview of bullying and also gives access to two specific subtopics: 'Does bullying really do children any harm?' and 'What children tell us about bullying in schools', both of which provide relevant and up-to-date information.

'The Bullying Questionnaire Page'

http://www.indigenet.unisa.edu.au/bullying/questdescrip.htm

An important initial procedure for setting up an anti-bullying program is getting a sense of the extent of bullying in a school. With Phillip Slee, Ken Rigby developed an extensive and useful questionnaire for schools. This proved to be useful for research purposes, but a bit unwieldy for schools themselves to use without some form of backup for carrying out statistical analysis. A question-naire that better meets the immediate needs of schools has been developed and information about it and how to obtain it is provided at this page.

'A Brief Guide to Bullying on the Internet'

http://www.indigenet.unisa.edu.au/bullying/guide.html

Rigby has also provided access to other useful international anti-bullying sites, and to anti-bullying articles of interest. These are organised under three head-ings: students attending school, parents and family members, and educators.

The Internet page for 'Students' gives access to nine sites and is meant to provide information for those who are being victimised, those who may wish to stop bullying, and for those bystanders who wish to become more involved. Among the selections, Coosje Griffith's (from Western Australia) 'Knowledge of Power' site is potentially useful. It has been designed to provide strategies for young people who are victims of bullying. The address of Griffith's site is: http://www.dotu.wa.gov.au/know/bully.html

The 'Parents and Families' section provides access to information (eleven sites) to enable parents and families to support their children or siblings in dealing with bullying.

The largest selection of bullying sites—twenty-three—is for 'Educators, Teachers, Counsellors and Administrators'.

An example from this section is 'Teachers' Notes, Bullying', address: http://www.its-online.com/archive/bully.html This web page focuses on the use of a package of teaching materials entitled 'Feedback', which was designed to develop discussion and debate about bullying between students.

Child and Adolescent Psychological and Educational Resources (CAPER), Flinders University, Adelaide

http://www.caper.com.au/peacepack.htm

This website gives a description of Phillip Slee's anti-bullying *P.E.A.C.E. Pack* program, and links to other useful resources and information from CAPER.

Behaviour Management Unit, Queensland Education Department

http://www.qed.qld.gov.au/tal/bmu/program.htm

The above address is the home page of the Behaviour Management Unit of the Queensland Education Department. This gives access to all the programs they run, each of which has its own address. The unit has developed an anti-bullying program entitled *Bullying—No Way!* and it gives two web pages that deal with bullying.

Bullying—No Way! A Professional Development Resource for School Communities

http://www.qed.qld.gov.au/tal/bmu/bullying.htm

Bullying—No Way! is a whole-school anti-bullying program that focuses on defining and understanding bullying and harassment and identifying approaches to achieve positive change. Part One identifies a range of bullying behaviours, the role of power, and the need for schools to address bullying. The focus then shifts to ways of understanding and explaining bullying and the implications for subsequent action within the school community.

Part Two deals with key considerations for a whole school approach. Included are checklists for mapping structures and programs already in place, and for planning further positive change. Resource lists and additional readings are provided.

'A Facilitator's Guide and Resources' assembles workshop materials including activity sheets, overhead transparency templates, and bullying scenarios with key questions and notes to support discussion. A videotape to accompany the written material provides scenarios of incidents of bullying and harassment among primary and secondary students and is intended as a prompt for discussion about underlying power issues.

The address for *Bullying—No Way! Workable Solutions to Bullying* is: http://www.qed.qld.gov.au/tal/bmu/antibull/worksol.htm This web page provides case studies of twenty-five Queensland schools (twenty-one primary and four secondary school) that have developed anti-bullying initiatives. For example, a report from one case study school, Sunshine Beach State School, describes how the main strategy developed was to train the school community in choice theory and reality therapy so that individuals, bullies, and victims would take responsibility for their actions.

Canada

Taking Action Against Bullying, **Bully B'Ware**

http://www.bullybeware.com/

Bully B'Ware is an initiative from Coquitlam, British Columbia, on Canada's West Coast, a company that has produced materials for an anti-bullying program. This web site provides an overview of foundational information and the philosophical underpinnings of the Bully B'ware approach. It discusses what bullying is, kinds of bullies, and what contributes to making bullies and victims. It also discusses what is likely to happen to those who both bully or are the victims of bullying and why action must be taken to stop bullying. The philosophical crux of the approach is the proposition that students are largely responsible for the success or otherwise of an anti-bullying campaign. The kit consists of a book, a video, and posters entitled *Taking Action Against Bullying*. Bully B'ware's contact details are:

Bully B'ware Productions, 1421 King Albert Avenue, Coquitlam, British Columbia, Canada V3J 1Y3, telephone/fax 604 936-8000 or 1 888 552 8559.

Bullying and Victimization: The Problems and Solutions for School-aged Children

http://www.crime-prevention.org/ncpc/

This is an initiative of the National Crime Prevention Council of Canada. It is a very useful site providing a summary of up-to-date research on the nature and components of school bullying, and strategies for dealing with it. It profiles typical bullies, victims, and onlookers, and looks at solutions that can be found in the school community—teachers, peers, other staff— and also in the family and broader social context.

Bullying: Information for Parents and Teachers, London Family Court Clinic (London, Canada)

http://www.lfcc.on.ca/bully.htm

The London Family Court Clinic has developed an extensive and well-considered anti-bullying program entitled *A School-based Anti-Violence Program (ASAP)*.

ASAP is a complete resource package to get schools started on violence prevention with support from teachers, students, parents, trustees, and administrators. It is designed to begin with small steps, such as awareness sessions for students and teachers, and to move into a more comprehensive program that includes policy and curriculum integration, and the use of age-appropriate video, theatre, and curriculum resources to develop understanding and solutions.

65 Friendly Lessons on Violence Prevention, A Curricular Resource, London Board of Education, London, Ontario

http://www.lfcc.on.ca/friendly.htm

65 Friendly Lessons on Violence Prevention is a curricular resource document that has been developed to accompany the *ASAP* program with practical cross-curricular ideas for all teachers to use within the junior secondary school years (Grades 7-9/10). Although designed for older children, the lessons are also adaptable for use with younger children.

ASAP is available from the London Family Court Clinic. Prices vary depending on which components are required. It can be ordered from:

London Family Court Clinic, 254 Pall Mall Street, Suite 200, London, Ontario, Canada N6A 5P6, telephone 519 679-7250, fax 519 675-7772.

e-mail: info@lfcc.on.ca

England

The *No Blame Approach*, Lucky Duck Publishing

http://www.luckyduck.co.uk

George Robinson and Barbara Maines have produced a number of useful books and videos that focus on a feelings approach to dealing with bullying. Their materials are well regarded and they are best known for the *No Blame Approach*.

The following web page also provides an overview of the *No Blame Approach*: http://www.globalideasbank.org/BI/BI-9.HTML

Kidscape

http://www.educate.co.uk/bull2.htm#top

Michelle Elliott and the Kidscape employees are well known for their anti-bullying efforts in London. Elliott has written widely on school bullying and other forms of child abuse and has done extensive work with schools in London.

The web site for Kidscape gives useful information about signs that may indicate a child is being bullied, details the Kidscape Keep Safe Code, and provides contact information.

Bullying, What Can Parents Do?, Childline

http://www.childline.org.uk/bullying/index.html

This very useful site has a selection of topics for helping parents to deal with bullying. These are: What is bullying? The effects of bullying, Racist bullying, Recognising the signs of bullying, Helping children who are being bullied, Is your child bullying others? Is your school tackling bullying? What to read, and Who to contact.

Its-online Bullying

http://www.its-online.com/archive/bully.html

This is a basic site but the information is well organised and helpful. It also gives access to an archive of materials and to other anti-bullying Internet sites.

Bullying, A Survival Guide, The BBC Anti-Bullying Site

http://www.bbc.co.uk/education/bully/index.htm

Bullying, A Survival Guide contains guidelines for dealing with all aspects of bullying, from school to work. Advice is given for dealing with bullying in general, for victims of bullying, for friends and family of people being bullied, as well as for those in positions of authority and perpetrators of bullying. A page entitled 'Help and Resources' gives information about a range of helpful organisations. There is also a section with quotations from celebrities who have been bullied.

Tom Field's Bullying Pages on Workplace Bullying

Although the main emphasis in this very useful site is on bullying in the workplace, Field has several pages that are very useful in relation to school bullying and bullying in general. I have listed these with some background information.

Those Who Can, Do. Those Who Can't, Bully. Abuse Explained

http://www.successunlimited.co.uk/abuse.htm

This web page discusses bullying within the wider framework of abuse. A definition of bullying is provided, issues of anxiety discussed, and the relationship between upbringing and serial bullying examined. Seven types of abuse are identified, and corporal punishment, sexual assault, pornography, and the reporting of abuse are also covered.

Those Who Can, Do. Those Who Can't, Bully. The Serial Bully

http://www.successunlimited.co.uk/serial.htm

This web page deals specifically with profiling the serial bully. It maps the serial bully's behaviour onto the DSM-IV diagnostic criteria for Antisocial Personality Disorder (APD), and Narcissistic and Paranoid Personality Disorders. The site producers argue that this is essential information for those who have experienced bullying, harassment, or physical or psychological violence, and it is essential reading if legal action is being taken or if someone is coming to terms with a violent experience.

Those Who Can, Do. Those Who Can't, Bully. Child Bullying and School Bullying

http://www.successunlimited.co.uk/child.htm

This gives ideas for how to select a safe school and information on child bullying.

Europe

European Conference on Initiatives to Combat School Bullying

http://www.gold.ac.uk/euconf/index.html

This conference was sponsored by the European Commission (DG XXII) under its Violence in Schools initiative, and the Department for Education and Employment, London. It was organised from Goldsmiths College, University of London, with co-ordinators from PMVO (Safe School Project), Den Haag, The Netherlands, and the Anti-Bullying Centre, Dublin, Ireland. The web site gives details about the conference program, summaries of the keynote addresses of a range of prominent anti-bullying researchers in Europe (and contact details if the full reports are required), workshop summaries, and posters. The keynote speakers were:

Helen Cowie (School of Psychology and Counselling, Roehampton Institute London, West Hill, London SW15 3SN, UK) 'From Bystanding to Standing By— The Role of Peer Support Against School Bullying'.

Jacques Pain (Département des Sciences de L'Education, Université Paris X, 200, Avenue de la République, 92001 Nanterre Cedex, France) 'Classroom Initiatives to Reduce Violence in School'.

Rob Limper (Vereniging Openbaar Onderwijs, Blekerstraat 20, Postbus 10241, 1301 AE Almere, Netherlands) 'The Only Way to Combat Bullying is a Cooperation Between All Those Involved in School: Good Practice in the Netherlands Initiated by Parents'.

Mona O'Moore (Anti-Bullying Research and Resource Centre, School of Education, Trinity College, Dublin, Ireland) 'Critical Issues for Teacher Training to Counter Bullying and Victimisation'. This paper is available in full at the following address: http://www.gold.ac.uk/euconf/keynotes/omoore.html

Rosario Ortega Ruiz (Departamento de Psicologia Evolutiva y de la Educacion, San Francisco Javier s/n, 41005 Sevilla, Spain) 'The Seville School Anti-Bullying Project (SAVE): An Educational Model to Prevent Violence At School'.

Erling Roland (Centre for Atferdsforskning, Postboks 2557, Ullandhaug, 4004 Stavanger, Norway) 'The 1996 Norwegian Program of Preventing and Managing Bullying in Schools'.

New Zealand

No Bully

http://www.nobully.org.nz/default.htm

The *No Bully* web site is part of the Telecom/Police Stop Bullying Campaign. The police's Law in Education programs are designed to help young New Zealanders to avoid becoming offenders or victims of crime. The programs encourage children and young people to act safely and confidently to protect themselves and their property, and avoid drug abuse. The site provides useful anti-bullying information.

There are a number of interesting and useful pages in this web site. Of particular use are the links to other sites and the listing of all organisations in New Zealand that have something to do with anti-bullying initiatives. The police's *Kia Kaha* program is also described here.

This web site is very user-friendly, with items aimed at both children and adults. In my opinion, the best individual item at this site is Mark Cleary's comprehensive 'Guidelines for Schools', a very sensibly written piece that would be useful for teachers, school administrators, and parents, not only in New Zealand but also elsewhere.

Scotland

'Bullying at School Links', Scottish Council for Research in Education

http://www.scre.ac.uk/bully/links.html

The SCRE was a forerunner in the development of anti-bullying work in the UK. They appointed an Anti-Bullying Development Officer from April 1993 to December 1995 (Andrew Mellor), whose job was to address the area of bullying in Scottish schools. The SCRE home page reflects the council's anticipatory and professional approach. The page provides some basic but useful information that has been published by SCRE (*Let's Stop Bullying: Advice for Young People, Let's Stop Bullying: Advice for Parents*), but other than this it acts as a broker for other sites and provides links to a selection of useful international sites.

There are links to five anti-bullying organisations, three from the UK and one each from Canada and New Zealand. These are: Childline, Kidscape, the National Society for the Prevention of Cruelty to Children (NSPCC), Bully B'ware (Canada), and *No Bully* (New Zealand).

The site lists thirteen further addresses. Included in the list is the site of a Scottish primary school that has published its anti-bullying policy. Its Internet address is: http://www.rmplc.co.uk/eduweb/sites/camdean/bully.htm

This policy may be of interest to schools going through the process of developing anti-bullying policies, as it could be used as a template. The school is also happy to receive comments about it. Their e-mail address is: camdean@itas-darc.demon.co.uk (see Appendix I).

United States

Brave Enough to be Kind, Maine Project Against Bullying

http://lincoln.midcoast.com/~wps/against/bullying.html

The Maine Project Against Bullying (MPAB) is funded through the Maine Department of Education through a Carl D. Perkins Grant. The membership consists of educators from a variety of statewide disciplines and positions. This Maine-based anti-bullying web site has been set up to disseminate information about bullying. It gives a useful overview of bullying in American schools and also provides links with other similar web sites in the United States.

Another useful American bullying web site that can be accessed via this Maine Project Against Bullying web page is the Bullying Program (below).

The Bullying Program

http://www.cary-memorial.lib.me.us/bullyweb

This site gives a description of the bullying program affiliated with the Maine Project Against Bullying. It lists different approaches that do not work with bullying, and gives information about bullying, comprehensive interventions, interventions with bullies, and support for victims. It outlines its own strategies, and provides useful sources. The e-mail address is: stan@magicwithmeaning.com

Act Against Violence Outreach Campaign

http://www.krma.org/aav/bully.html#bibliography

This Colorado-based program is closely linked to Peace Studies in Education, and links through to such sites. It gives a useful overview of the state of bullying in American schools and some useful ideas for introducing anti-bullying themes into the curriculum.

Angries Out

http://members.aol.com/AngriesOut/bullyb.htm

This useful site for children, parents, and teachers deals not only with bullying, but also with other topics such as abuse, anger, assertiveness, and stress. It is a colourful and interactive site that is especially useful for younger children.

It has been developed by Lynne Namka, who is a psychologist, therapist, and trainer in Arizona. Her contact details are:

Lynne Namka, Talk, Trust and Feel, 5398 Golder Ranch Rd, Tucson, Arizona 85739, USA

e-mail address: lnamka@rtd.com

References

Chapter 1

Lind, J. & G. Maxwell 1996, *Children's Experiences of Violence at School*, Office of the Commissioner for Children, Wellington.

Chapter 2

Adair, V. 1999, 'No Bullies at this School: Creating Safe Schools', *ChildreNZ Issues, Journal of the Children's Issues Centre*, Vol. 3, No. 1, pp. 32-7.

Adair, V. et al. 1999, '"Ask Your Mother Not to Make Yummy Sandwiches": Bullying in New Zealand Secondary Schools', *New Zealand Journal of Educational Studies* (under review).

Almeida, A.M. 1999, 'Portugal', in P.K. Smith et al., *The Nature of School Bullying*, Routledge, London and New York.

Alsaker, F. & A. Brunner, 1999, 'Switzerland', in Smith et al., *The Nature of School Bullying*

Batsche, G.M. & H.M. Knoff 1994, 'Bullies and Their Victims: Understanding a Pervasive Problem in the Schools', *School Psychology Review*, Vol. 23, No. 2, pp. 165-74.

Besag, V. 1989, *Bullies and Victims in Schools: A Guide to Understanding and Management*, Open University Press, Milton Keynes/Oxford University Press, Bristol.

Björkqvist, K. 1994, 'Sex Differences in Physical, Verbal, and Indirect Aggression: A Review of Recent Research', *Sex Roles*, Vol. 30, pp. 177-88.

Björkqvist, K. et al. 1992, 'Do Girls Manipulate and Boys Fight? Developmental Trends in Regard to Direct and Indirect Aggression', *Aggressive Behavior*, Vol. 18, pp. 117-27.

Bowers, L. et al. 1992, 'Cohesion and Power in the Families of Children Involved in Bully/Victim Problems at School', *Journal of Family Therapy*, Vol. 14, pp. 371-87.

Bowers, L. et al. 1994, 'Perceived Family Relationships of Bullies, Victims and Bully/Victims in Middle Childhood', *Journal of Social and Personal Relationships*, Vol. 11, pp. 215-32.

Byrne, B. 1999, 'Ireland', in Smith et al., *The Nature of School Bullying*.

Charach, A. et al. 1995, 'Bullying at School: A Canadian Perspective', *Education Canada*, Vol. 35, No. 1, pp. 12-18.

Craig, W.M. & D.J. Pepler 1995, 'Peer Processes in Bullying and Victimisation: An Observational Study', *Exceptional Education Canada*, Vol. 5, pp. 81-95.

Cullingford, C. & J. Morrison 1995, 'Bullying as a Formative Influence: The Relationship Between the Experience of School and Criminality', *British Educational Research Journal*, Vol. 21, No. 5, pp. 547-60.

DFE 1994, *Bullying: Don't Suffer in Silence. An Anti-bullying Pack for Schools*, HMSO, London.

Elliott, M. 1997, *101 Ways to Deal with Bullying: A Guide for Parents*, Hodder & Stoughton, London.

Eron, L.D. et al. 1987, 'Childhood Aggression and its Correlates over 22 Years', in D.H. Crowell et al. (eds), *Childhood Aggression and Violence*, Plenum, New York.

Fabre-Cornali, D. 1999, 'France', in Smith et al., *The Nature of School Bullying*.

Farrington, D.P. 1993, 'Understanding and Preventing Bullying', in M. Tonry & N. Norris (eds), *Crime and Justice*, Vol. 17, University of Chicago Press, Chicago.

Fonzi, A. et al. 1999, 'Italy', in Smith et al., *The Nature of School Bullying*.

Fried, S. & P. Fried 1996, *Bullies and Victims: Helping Your Child Survive the Schoolyard Battlefield*, M. Evans & Co. Inc., New York.

Harachi, T. et al. 1999, 'United States', in Smith et al., *The Nature of School Bullying*.

Hazler, R.J. et al. 1992, 'What Kids Say About Bullying', *The Executive Educator*, pp. 20-2.

Junger-Tas, J. 1999, 'The Netherlands', in Smith et al., *The Nature of School Bullying*.

Kupersmidt, J.B. et al. 1990, 'The Role of Peer Relationships in the Development of Disorder', in S.R. Asher & J.D. Coie (eds), *Peer Rejection in Childhood*, Cambridge, Cambridge University Press.

Lagerspetz, M.J. et al. 1988, 'Is Indirect Aggression Typical of Females? Gender Differences in Aggressiveness in 11 to 12 Year-old Children', *Aggressive Behavior*, Vol. 14, pp. 403-14.

Lloyd, N. 1994, 'Girls "Hidden Bullies" in Schools', *The Advertiser*, Vol. 137, No. 42383, p. 3.

Lösel, F. & T. Bleisener 1999, 'Germany', in Smith et al., *A Cross-National Perspective*.

Maines, B. & G. Robinson 1998, *All for Alex: A Circle of Friends*, Lucky Duck Publishing, Bristol.

Maslow, A. 1970, *Motivation and Personality* (2nd ed.), Harper & Row, New York.

Maxwell, G. & J. Carroll-Lind 1997, *The Impact of Bullying on Children*, Occasional Paper No. 6, Office of the Commissioner for Children, Wellington.

Mellor, A. 1999, 'Scotland', in Smith et al., *The Nature of School Bullying*.

Moore, D. et al. 1997, *Eliminating Violence from Schools Evaluation Project Final Report— April 1997*, Auckland UniServices Ltd, University of Auckland, Auckland.

Nolin, M.J. 1996, 'Student Victimization at School', *Journal of School Health*, Vol. 66, No. 6, pp. 216-21.

Noller, P. & Callan, V. 1991, *The Adolescent in the Family*, Routledge, London & New York.

Olweus, D. 1978, *Aggression in the Schools: Bullies and Whipping Boys*, Wiley, New York.

Olweus, D. 1980, 'Familial and Temperamental Determinants of Aggressive Behaviour in Adolescent Boys: A Causal Analysis', *Developmental Psychology*, Vol. 16, pp. 644-60.

Olweus, D. 1981, 'Bullying Among School-boys', in N. Cantwell (ed.), *Children and Violence*, Akade Militteratur, Stockholm.

Olweus, D. 1984, 'Aggressors and Their Victims: Bullying at School', in N. Frude & H. Gault (eds), *Disruptive Behaviour Disorders in Schools*, Wiley, New York.

Olweus, D. 1991, 'Bully/Victim Problems Among School Children: Basic Facts and Effects of a School-Based Intervention Programme', in D. Pepler & K. Rubin (eds), *The Development and Treatment of Childhood Aggression*, Erlbaum, Hillsdale, New Jersey.

Olweus, D. 1993, *Bullying at School: What We Know And What We Can Do About It*, Blackwell, Oxford.

Olweus, D. 1999a, 'Sweden', in Smith et al., *The Nature of School Bullying*.

Olweus, D. 1999b, 'Norway', in Smith et al., *The Nature of School Bullying*.

Ortega, R. & J. Mora-Merchan, 1999, 'Spain', in Smith et al., *The Nature of School Bullying*.

Owens, L. 1996, 'Sticks and Stones and Sugar and Spice: Girls' and Boys' Aggression in Schools', *Australian Journal of Guidance and Counselling*, Vol. 6, pp. 45-57.

Owens, L. & C. MacMullin 1995, 'Gender Differences in Aggression in Children and Adolescents in South Australian Schools', *International Journal of Adolescence and Youth*, Vol. 6, pp. 21-35.

Parker, J.G. & S. Asher 1987, 'Peer Relations and Later Personal Adjustments: Are Low Accepted Children at Risk?', *Psychological Bulletin*, Vol. 102, pp. 357-89.

Pepler, D.M. & W.M. Craig 1995, 'A Peek Behind the Fence: Naturalistic Observations of Aggressive Children with Remote Audiovisual Recording', *Developmental Psychology*, Vol. 31, pp. 548-53.

Perry, D.G. et al. 1988, 'Victims of Peer Aggression', *Developmental Psychology*, Vol. 24, pp. 807-14.

Pikas, A. 1989, 'The Common Concern Method for the Treatment of Mobbing', in E. Munthe & E. Roland (eds), *Bullying: An International Perspective*, David Fulton, London.

Reinken, B. et al. 1989, 'Early Antecedents of Aggression and Passive Withdrawal in Early Elementary Schoolchildren', *Journal of Personality*, Vol. 57, pp. 257-81.

Rigby, K. 1993, 'School Children's Perceptions of Their Families and Parents as a Function of Peer Relations', *Journal of Genetic Psychology*, Vol. 154, No. 4, pp. 501-14.

Rigby, K. 1994a, 'Family Influence, Peer-Relations and Health Effects among School Children', in K. Oxenberry et al. (eds), *Children's Peer Relations: Conference Proceedings*, The Institute of Social Research, University of South Australia, Adelaide.

Rigby, K. 1994b, 'Psychosocial Functioning in Families of Australian Adolescent School-Children Involved in Bully/Victim Problems', *Journal of Family Therapy*, Vol. 16, pp. 173-87.

Rigby, K. 1996, *Bullying in Schools and What to Do About It*, ACER, Melbourne.

Rigby, K. 1998, 'Gender and Bullying in Schools', in P.T. Slee & K. Rigby (eds), *Children's Peer Relations*, Routledge, London & New York.

Rigby, K. & I.H. Cox 1996, 'The Contributions of Bullying at School and Low Self Esteem to Acts of Delinquency Among Australian Teenagers', *Personality and Individual Differences*, Vol. 21, pp. 609-12.

Rigby, K. & P. Slee 1995, *Manual for the Peer Relations Questionnaire (PRQ)*, University of South Australia, Adelaide.

Rigby, K. & P. Slee 1999, 'Australia', in Smith et al., *The Nature of School Bullying*.

Rivers, I. 1995, 'Mental Health Issues Among Young Lesbians and Gay Men Bullied in School', *Health and Social Care in the Community*, Vol. 3, pp. 380-3.

Rivers, I. 1996, 'Young, Gay and Bullied', *Young People Now*, Vol. 81, pp. 18-19.

Rubin, K.H. & R.J. Coplan 1992, 'Peer Relationships in Childhood', in M. Bornstein & M. Lamb (eds), *Developmental Psychology: An Advanced Textbook*, Erlbaum, Hillsdale, New Jersey.

Salmivalli, C. et al. 1998, 'Aggression in the Social Relations of School-aged Girls and Boys', in P.T. Slee & K. Rigby (eds), *Children's Peer Relations*, Routledge, London & New York.

Sharp, S. 1995, 'How Much Does Bullying Hurt? The Effects of Bullying on the Personal Well-Being and Educational Progress of Secondary Aged Students', *Educational and Child Psychology*, Vol. 12, pp. 81-8.

Sharp, S. 1996, 'Self Esteem, Response Style and Victimisation: Possible Ways of Preventing Victimisation through Parenting and School Based Training Programmes', *School Psychology International*, Vol. 17, pp. 347-57.

Sharp, S. & D. Thompson 1992, 'Sources of Stress: A Contrast Between Pupil Perspectives and Pastoral Teachers' Perspectives', *School Psychology International*, Vol. 13, pp. 229-42.

Slee, P. 1997, *The P.E.A.C.E. Pack: Reducing Bullying in Our Schools* (2nd ed.), School of Education, Flinders University, Adelaide.

Smith, P.K. 1999, 'England and Wales', in Smith et al., *The Nature of School Bullying*.

Smith, P.K. & Y. Morita 1999, 'Introduction', in Smith et al., *The Nature of School Bullying*.

Smith, P.K. and S. Sharp (eds) 1994, *School Bullying: Insights and Perspectives*, Routledge, London.

Smith, P.K. et al. (eds) 1999, *The Nature of School Bullying: A Cross-National Perspective*, Routledge, London & New York.

Stephenson, P. & D. Smith 1989, 'Bullying in the Junior School', in D.P. Tattum & D.A. Lane (eds), *Bullying in Schools*, Trentham Books, Stoke-on-Trent.

Sullivan, K. 1998, 'Isolated Children, Bullying and Peer Group Relations', in Slee & Rigby (eds), *Children's Peer Relations*.

Sullivan, K. 1999, 'Racist Bullying: Creating Understanding and Strategies for Teachers', in M. Leicester et al. (eds) *Values, Culture and Education, Vol. Two. Institutional Issues: Pupils, Schools and Teacher Education*, Falmer Press, London.

Troyna, B. & R. Hatcher 1992, *Racism in Children's Lives*, Routledge, London & New York.

Vettenburg, N. 1999, 'Belgium', in Smith et al., *The Nature of School Bullying*.

Whitney, I. & P.K. Smith 1993, 'A Survey of the Nature and Extent of Bullying in Junior/Middle and Secondary Schools', *Educational Research*, Vol. 35, pp. 2-25.

Whitney, I. et al. 1994, 'Bullying and Children with Special Educational Needs', in Smith & Sharp (eds), *School Bullying*.

Zeigler, S. & M. Rosenstein-Manner 1991, *Bullying at School: Toronto in an International Context*, Toronto Boards of Education, No. 196R, Toronto.

Chapter 3

Pitts, J. & P.K. Smith 1995, *Preventing School Bullying*, Home Office Police Research Group, London.

Smith, P.K. 1999, 'England and Wales', in Smith et al. (eds), *The Nature of School Bullying: A Cross-National Perspective*, Routledge, London & New York.

Chapter 4

Duncan, A. 1994, 'Resolving Group Bullying in Schools. Anatol Pikas' Shared Concern Method in Tayside's Experience 1993-94', unpub. paper, Tayside Regional Council, Dundee.

Elliott, M. 1989, 'Bullying—Harmless Fun or Murder?', in E. Munthe & E. Roland (eds), *Bullying: An International Perspective*, David Fulton, London.

Eslea, M. & P.K. Smith 1998, 'The Long-term Effectiveness of Anti-Bullying Work in Primary Schools', *Educational Research*, Vol. 40, pp. 203-18.

Laslett, R. 1980, 'Bullies: A Children's Court in a Day School for Maladjusted Children', *Journal of Special Education*, Vol. 4, pp. 391-7.

Rigby, K. 1996, *Bullying in Schools and What to Do About It*, ACER, Melbourne.

Robinson, G., pers. comm., 7 November 1995.

Smith, P.K. 1999, 'England and Wales', in Smith et al. (eds), *The Nature of School Bullying: A Cross-National Perspective*, Routledge, London & New York.

Tattum, D., pers. comm., 16 November 1995.

Tattum, D. & G. Herbert 1993, *Countering Bullying: Initiatives by Schools and Local Authorities*, Trentham Books, Stoke-on-Trent.

Tattum, D. & G. Herbert 1997, *Bullying: Home, School and Community*, David Fulton, London.

Chapter 5

For further examples of questionnaires, see:

Rigby, K. & P. Slee 1995, *Manual for the Peer Relations Questionnaire (PRQ)*, University of South Australia, Adelaide.

Smith, P.K. & S. Sharp (eds) 1994, *School Bullying: Insights and Perspectives*, Routledge, London & New York.

For a useful resource on case studies of schools' responses to bullying, see:

Tattum, D. & G. Herbert 1993, *Countering Bullying: Initiatives by Schools and Local Authorities*, Trentham Books, Stoke-on-Trent.

General reference

Thompson, A.A & A.J. Strickland 1990, *Strategic Management: Concepts and Cases*, BPI/Irwin, Howewood, Illinois.

Chapter 6

Rigby, K. 1996, *Bullying in Schools and What to Do About it*, ACER, Melbourne.

Sharp, S. & P.K. Smith (eds) 1994, *Tackling Bullying in Your School: A Practical Handbook for Teachers*, Routledge, London & New York.

Chapter 7

General reference

Bentley, K.M. & A.K. Li 1995, 'Bully and Victim Problems in Elementary Schools and Students' Beliefs About Aggression', *Canadian Journal of School Psychology*, Vol. 11, pp. 153-65.

Besag, V. 1989, *Bullies and Victims: A Guide to Understanding and Management*, Open University Press, Milton Keynes.

Cowie, H. & S. Sharp 1994, 'How to Tackle Bullying Through the Curriculum', in S. Sharp & P.K. Smith (eds), *Tackling Bullying in Your School: A Practical Handbook for Teachers*, Routledge, London & New York.

Craig, W.M. & D.J. Pepler 1995, 'Peer Processes in Bullying and Victimisation: An Observational Study', *Exceptional Education Canada*, Vol. 5, pp. 81-95.

Maines, B. & G. Robinson 1998, *All For Alex: A Circle of Friends*, Lucky Duck Publications, Bristol.

Pepler, D.J. & W.M. Craig 1995, 'A Peek Behind the Fence: Naturalistic Observations of Aggressive Children with Remote Audiovisual Recording', *Developmental Psychology*, Vol. 31, pp. 548-53.

Sullivan, K. 1998, 'Isolated Children, Bullying and Peer Group Relations', in P. Slee & K. Rigby (eds), *Children's Peer Relations*, Routledge, London & New York.

Reflective practice

Carr, W. 1989, *Quality in Teaching: Arguments for a Reflective Profession*, Falmer Press, London & New York.

Pollard, A. (ed.) 1996, *Readings for Reflective Teaching in the Primary School*, Cassell, London & New York.

Pollard, A. 1997, *Reflective Teaching in the Primary School*, Cassell, London & New York.

Schon, D.A. 1983, *The Reflective Practitioner: How Professionals Think in Action*, Basic Books, New York.

Action research

Elliott, J. 1991, *Action Research for Educational Change*, Open University Press, Milton Keynes.

Circle Time

Bliss, T. et al. 1995, *Coming Round to Circle Time*, Lucky Duck Publishing, Bristol (video and booklet).

Bliss, T. et al. 1999, *Developing Circle Time*, Lucky Duck Publishing, Bristol.

Bliss, T. & J. Tetley 1999, *Circle Time: A Resource Book For Infant, Junior and Secondary School*, Lucky Duck Publishing, Bristol.

Davies, B. (ed.) 1999, *Six Years of Circle Time*, Lucky Duck Publishing, Bristol.

Mosley, J. 1997, *Quality Circle Time in the Primary School*, LDA, Wisbech, Cambridge.

White, M. 1999, *Magic Circles: Building Self-Esteem Through Circle Time*, Lucky Duck Publishing, Bristol.

Cooperative learning

Johnson, D.W. & R.T. Johnson 1994, 'Structuring Academic Controversy', in S. Sharan, *Handbook of Cooperative Learning Methods*, Greenwood Press, Westport, Connecticut & London.

Johnson, D.W. et al. 1994, *Cooperative Learning in the Classroom*, Association for Supervision and Curriculum Development, Alexandria, Virginia.

Slavin, R.E 1983, *Cooperative Learning*, Longman, New York & London.

Sociometry

Furlong, V.J. 1984, 'Black Resistance in the Liberal Comprehensive', in S. Delamont (ed.), *Readings in Classroom Interaction*, Methuen, London.

Hargreaves, D. 1973, *Social Relations in a Secondary School*, Routledge & Kegan Paul, London.

McLean, A. 1994, *Bullyproofing Our School: Promoting Positive Relationships*, Strathclyde Regional Council, Glasgow.

Salmivalli, C. et al. 1997, 'Peer Networks and Bullying in Schools', *Scandinavian Journal of Psychology*, Vol. 38, No. 4, pp. 305-12.

Salmivalli, C. et al. 1998, 'Aggression in the Social Relations of School-aged Girls and Boys', in P.T. Slee & K. Rigby (eds), *Children's Peer Relations*, Routledge, London & New York.

Chapter 8
Role play references and web site

Adair, V. et al. 1999, '"Ask Your Mother Not to Make Yummy Sandwiches": Bullying in New Zealand Secondary Schools', *New Zealand Journal of Educational Studies* (under review).

Olweus, D. 1993, *Bullying at School: What We Know and What We Can Do About It*, Blackwell, Oxford.

Rivers, I. 1995, 'Mental Health Issues Among Young Lesbians and Gay Men Bullied in School', *Health and Social Care in the Community*, Vol. 3, pp. 380-3.

Rivers, I. 1996 'Young, Gay and Bullied', *Young People Now*, Vol. 81, pp. 18-19.

For further information on the use of role play, see, for example:

http://english.ttu.edu/courses/1302/kemp/sp96/sa1f/jcjsa1f.htm

Chapter 9

Blatchford, P. and S. Sharp 1994, *Breaktime and the School: Understanding and Changing Playground Behaviour*, Routledge, London & New York.

Boulton, M.J. 1994a, 'How to Prevent and Respond to Bullying Behaviour in the Junior/Middle School Playground', in S. Sharp & P.K. Smith, *Tackling Bullying in Your School: A Practical Handbook for Teachers*, Routledge, London & New York.

Boulton, M.J. 1994b, 'Understanding and Preventing Bullying in the Junior Playground', in P.K. Smith & S. Sharp, *School Bullying: Insights and Perspectives*, Routledge, London & New York.

Briggs, S. 1994, 'Making the Most of Your Playground', in A. McLean (ed.), *Bullyproofing Our School: Promoting Positive Behaviour*, Strathclyde Regional Council, Glasgow.

DFE 1994, *Bullying: Don't Suffer in Silence. An Anti-bullying Pack for Schools*, HMSO, London.

Higgins, C. 1994a, 'How to Improve the School Ground Environment as an Anti-Bullying Strategy', in Sharp & Smith, *Tackling Bullying in Your School*.

Higgins, C. 1994b, 'Improving the School Ground Environment as an Anti-Bullying Intervention', in Smith & Sharp, *School Bullying*.

Lichman, S. & K. Sullivan 1999, 'Harnessing Folklore and Traditional Creativity to Promote Better Understanding Between Jewish and Arab Children in Israel', in M. Leicester et al. (eds). *Values, Culture and Education—Volume Three: Political Education and Citizenship*, Falmer Press, London & Washington DC.

Opie, I. 1993, *The People in the Playground*, Oxford University Press, Oxford.

Opie, I. & P. Opie 1969, *Children's Games in Street and Playground*, Oxford University Press, London.

Opie, I. & P. Opie 1998, *Children's Games With Things*, Oxford University Press, Oxford.

Puketapu, K. 1988, *Tu Tangata: A Management Perspective*, Royal Commission on Social Policy, Wellington.

Chapter 10

Cowie, H. & S. Sharp (eds) 1996, *Peer Counselling in Schools: A Time to Listen*, David Fulton, London.

Demetriades, A. 1996, 'Children of the Storm: Peer Partnership in Action', in Cowie & Sharp (eds), *Peer Counselling in Schools*.

McIntyre, D.C. 1997, *Teacher Education Research in a New Context: The Oxford Internship Scheme*, Paul Chapman Publishing, London.

Pikas, A. 1989, 'The Common Concern Method for the Treatment of Mobbing', in E. Munthe & E. Roland (eds), *Bullying: An International Perspective*, David Fulton, London.

Chapter 11

Peer counselling contacts and references

BBC/Windfall Films Ltd, *Bullying*, available from Hopeline Videos, PO Box 515, London SW15 6LQ, England. This very useful BBC Educational Special video presents an overview of the setting up and first three months of the peer counselling scheme in Acland Burghley School in Camden, London.

Contacts and information can be found in *Peer Support Networker*, which is published four times a year and is available from PSN, School of Psychology and Counselling, Roehampton Institute London, Whitelands College, West Hill, London SW15 3SN, England.

Cowie, H. & S. Sharp (eds) 1996, *Peer Counselling in Schools: A Time to Listen*, David Fulton, London.

Paterson, H. et al. 1996, 'The Anti-Bullying Campaign (ABC) at Acland Burghley', in Cowie & Sharp (eds), *Peer Counselling*.

Peer mediation contacts, references, and web site

The address of the Foundation for Peace Studies Aotearoa/New Zealand is: 29 Princes Street/ PO Box 4110, Auckland 1, Aotearoa/New Zealand, telephone (09) 373-2379.

'Cool Schools: Towards Non-Violent Conflict Resolution', *Broadsheet*, Spring 1994.

Duncan Y., pers. comm., 5 December 1999.

Duncan, Y. 1997, *Cool Schools Peer Mediation Programme: Trainer's Training Manual*, Foundation for Peace Studies Aotearoa/New Zealand, Auckland.

Duncan, Y. & M. Stanners 1997, *Secondary Peer Mediation* (2nd ed.), Foundation for Peace Studies Aotearoa/New Zealand, Auckland.

Duncan, Y. & M. Stanners 1999, *Cool Schools Peer Mediation Programme: Training Manual* (3rd ed.), Foundation for Peace Studies Aotearoa/New Zealand, Auckland.

The Peace Foundation 1993, *The Cool Schools Peer Mediation Programme* (a video), Foundation for Peace Studies Aotearoa/New Zealand, Auckland.

The Peace Foundation 1997, *The Cool Schools Parents Mediation Programme*, Foundation for Peace Studies Aotearoa/New Zealand, Auckland.

Radford Group 1996, *The Foundation for Peace Studies: A Summary of Quantitative Research*, Auckland.

Cool Schools has a web page within the Foundation for Peace Studies Aotearoa/New Zealand web site and their address is: http//www.peace.co.nz

General reference

Rigby, K. 1996, *Bullying in Schools and What To Do About It*, ACER, Melbourne.

Chapter 12

No Blame Approach contacts, references, and web site

George Robinson and Barbara Maines have a publishing company called Lucky Duck Publishing (formerly Lame Duck Publishing) and an Internet page. The following reasonably priced resources are available from Lucky Duck Publishing, 34 Wellington Park, Clifton, Bristol BS8 2UN, England, telephone/fax 00 44 117 973 2881 or 00 44 1454 776620, or e-mail luckyduck@dial.pipex.com

Video and training packs

Maines, B. & G. Robinson 1991, *Stamp Out Bullying*, Lame Duck Publishing (video), Bristol.

Maines, B. & G. Robinson, G. 1992, *Michael's Story: The No Blame Approach*, Lame Duck Publishing (video and booklet), Bristol.

Books

Maines, B. & G. Robinson 1991, *Punishment, The Milder the Better*, Lucky Duck Publishing, Bristol.

Maines, B. & G. Robinson 1994, *If it Makes My Life Easier ... to write a Policy on Bullying*, Lucky Duck Publishing, Bristol.

Maines, B. & G. Robinson 1995, *Parent Leaflet on Bullying*, Lucky Duck Publishing, Bristol.

Robinson, G. & B. Maines 1997, *Crying for Help: The No Blame Approach to Bullying*, Lucky Duck Publishing, Bristol.

Robinson, G. et al. 1995, *No Bullying Starts Today*, Lucky Duck Publishing, Bristol.

Further information about the *No Blame Approach* and Lucky Duck Publishing can be found at their web site http://www.luckyduck.co.uk

General references

Cleary, M., pers. comm., 18 March 1999.

Rigby, K. 1996, *Bullying in Schools and What To Do About It*, ACER, Melbourne.

Smith, P.K. & S. Sharp (eds) 1994, *School Bullying: Insights and Perspectives*, Routledge, London.

Young, S. 1998, 'The Support Group Approach to Bullying in Schools', *Educational Psychology and Practice*, Vol. 14, No. 1, pp. 32-9.

Chapter 13

Circle of Friends contacts, references, and web site

Maines, B. & G. Robinson 1998, *All for Alex. A Circle of Friends*, Lucky Duck Publishing (video and booklet), Bristol.

The booklet and the video can be purchased from Lucky Duck Publishing, 34 Wellington Park, Bristol BS8 2UW, England, fax 00 44 117 9732881 or 00 44 1454 776620, e-mail publishing@luckyduck.co.uk

http://www.luckyduck.co.uk

General references

Pearpoint, J. et al. 1992, *The Inclusion Papers*, Inclusion Press, London.

Perske, R. 1988, *Circle of Friends*, Abingdon Press, London.

Snow, J. & M. Forrest 1987, 'Circles', in M. Forest (ed.), *More Education/Integration*, G. Allen Roeher Institute.

Taylor, G. 1996, 'Creating a Circle of Friends: a Case Study', in H. Cowie & S. Sharp (eds) *Peer Counselling in Schools: A Time to Listen*, David Fulton, London.

Chapter 14

The *P.E.A.C.E. Pack* contacts and references

Slee, P.T. 1997, *The P.E.A.C.E. Pack: Programme for Reducing Bullying in Our Schools*, (2nd ed.) School of Education, Flinders University of South Australia, Adelaide

e-mail address for Phillip Slee: phillip.slee@flinders.edu.au

Further details about the *P.E.A.C.E. Pack* can be found at the following Internet site: http://www.caper.com.au

Bullying in Schools **contacts**

Information about this video can be obtained by contacting either Professor Rigby or Dr Slee. Their addresses are:

Adjunct Professor Ken Rigby, c/o ARI, University of South Australia, Underdale Campus, Holbrooks Road, Adelaide, South Australia.

Dr Phillip Slee, School of Education, Flinders University, Adelaide, South Australia.

Chapter 15

***Kia Kaha* and *Stop Bullying* contacts, references, and web site**

Lee, R. 1998, *Stop Bullying: A Collection of Children's Stories*, Telecom New Zealand Ltd and New Zealand Police, Wellington.

New Zealand Police and Telecom New Zealand 1998, *Stop Bullying: Helpful Information for Caregivers and Young People from the Police and Telecom*, Communicado, Wellington.

New Zealand Police Youth Education Services 1999, *Kia Kaha: A Resource Kit about Bullying for Students*, Teachers and Parents, New Zealand Police, Wellington (includes a teaching guide, a video, and pamphlets for parents).

Sullivan, K. 1998, *An Evaluation of Kia Kaha, the New Zealand Police's Resource Kit About Bullying for Students, Teachers and Parents*, New Zealand Police, Wellington.

In New Zealand, *Kia Kaha* can be accessed by contacting any local Police Education Office. Otherwise, it can be ordered by writing to:
National Manager YES, Office of Commissioner of Police, PO Box 3017, Wellington, Telephone 04 495 1307, fax 04 474 9417.
e-mail o.sanders@xtra.co.nz
Contact: Gill Palmer, New Zealand Police Youth Education Service, Police National Headquarters, 180 Molesworth Street, PO Box 3017, Wellington, fax 04 474 9446.
http://www.nobully.org.nz/default.htm

Chapter 16

Björkqvist, K. and K. Österman 1999, 'Finland', in P.K. Smith et al. (eds), *The Nature of School Bullying: A Cross-National Perspective*, Routledge, London & New York.
Duncan, A. 1994, 'Resolving Group Bullying in Schools. Anatol Pikas' Shared Concern Method in Tayside's Experience 1993-94', unpub. paper, Tayside Regional Council, Dundee.
Fuller, A. & V. King 1995, *Stop Bullying!*, Mental Health Foundation of Victoria, Melbourne.
Pikas, A. 1989, 'The Common Concern Method for the Treatment of Mobbing', in E. Munthe & E. Roland (eds), *Bullying: An International Perspective*, David Fulton, London.
Rigby, K. 1996, *Bullying in Schools and What To Do About It*, ACER, Melbourne.
Sharp, S. & P.K. Smith (eds) 1994, *Tackling Bullying in Your Schools: A Practical Handbook for Teachers*, Routledge, London & New York.
Smith, P.K. 'England and Wales', in Smith et al., *The Nature of School Bullying*.
Smith, P.K. & S. Sharp (eds) 1994, *School Bullying: Insights and Perspectives*, Routledge, London.

Chapter 17

Assertiveness training references

Alberti, R. E. 1986, *Stand Up, Speak Out, Talk Back*, Pocketbooks, New York.
Elgin, S. 1995, *You Can't Say That to Me! Stopping the Pain of Verbal Abuse—An 8 Step Programme*, John Wiley & Sons, New York.
Pikas, A. 1989, 'The Common Concern Method for the Treatment of Mobbing', in E. Munthe & E. Roland (eds), *Bullying: An International Perspective*, David Fulton, London.
Sharp, S. et al. 1994, 'How to Respond to Bullying', in S. Sharp & P.K. Smith (eds), *Tackling Bullying in Your School: A Practical Handbook for Teachers*, Routledge, London & New York.
Smith, M.J. 1975, *When I Say No, I Feel Guilty*, Bantam Books, Toronto, London, & New York.

Anger management contacts, references, and web sites

L. Ingram, *Managing and Coping with the Angry Student*, Anger Institute of Chicago, PO Box 4505-288, Oak Park, Illinois 60302, USA.
http://www.anger.mgmt.com
Men for Non-Violence, PO Box 10 632, The Terrace, Wellington, New Zealand, telephone 04 499 6384, fax 04 499 6387.
Sydney Men's Network, PO Box 125, St Peters, NSW 2044, Australia, telephone 02 550 4053, fax 02 519 8614.
http://KidsHealth.org/kid/feeling/anger.html

http://www.peerleadership.com.au/peeraust.nsf/$About

Talk, Trust and Feel, 5398 Golder Ranch Road, Tucson, Arizona 85739, USA, or e-mail lnamka@rtd.com (for catalogues of anger management/release programs).

Martial arts references

Kauz, H. 1988, *The Martial Spirit: An Introduction to the Origin, Philosophy and Psychology of the Martial Arts*, Overlook Press, Woodstock, New York.

Lytollis, S. 1997, *Self Defence for Women*, New Women's Press, Auckland.

Mitchell, D. 1997, *The Overlook Martial Arts Handbook*, Overlook Press, Woodstock, New York.

Quinn, C. 1987, *The Budo Karate of Mas Oyama: Philosophical Foundations of Japan's Strongest Fighting Art*, Coconut Productions, Brisbane.

Select Bibliography

This bibliography draws together the best anti-bullying resources that a school may want to purchase. There are numerous other excellent books and articles, but these books together cover all the most important areas and provide a coherent and useful foundational resource.

Besag, V. 1989, *Bullies and Victims in Schools: A Guide to Understanding and Management*, Open University Press, Milton Keynes.

Blatchford, P. and S. Sharp 1994, *Breaktime and the School: Understanding and Changing Playground Behaviour*, Routledge, London & New York.

Cowie, H. & S. Sharp (eds) 1996, *Peer Counselling in Schools: A Time to Listen*, David Fulton, London.

Fried, S. & P. Fried 1996, *Bullies and Victims: Helping Your Child Survive the Schoolyard Battlefield*, M. Evans & Co. Inc., New York.

Olweus, D. 1993, *Bullying at School: What We Know And What We Can do About It*, Blackwell, Oxford.

Rigby, K. 1996, *Bullying in Schools and What To Do About It*, ACER, Melbourne.

Robinson, G. & B. Maines 1997, *Crying for Help: The No Blame Approach to Bullying*, Lucky Duck Publishing, Bristol.

Sharp, S. & P.K. Smith (eds) 1994, *Tackling Bullying in Your Schools: A Practical Handbook for Teachers*, Routledge, London & New York

Slee, P.T. & Rigby, K. (eds) 1998, *Children's Peer Relations*, Routledge, London & New York.

Smith, P.K. et al. 1999 (eds), *The Nature of School Bullying: A Cross-National Perspective*, Routledge, London & New York.

Smith, P.K. & S. Sharp (eds) 1994, *School Bullying: Insights and Perspectives*, Routledge, London & New York.

Tattum, D. & G. Herbert 1993, *Countering Bullying: Initiatives by Schools and Local Authorities*, Trentham Books, Stoke-on-Trent.

Tattum, D. & G. Herbert 1997, *Bullying: Home, School and Community*, David Fulton, London.

Index